EXPERT
SAILING SKILLS

YACHTING
MONTHLY

EXPERT
SAILING SKILLS

NO NONSENSE ADVICE THAT REALLY WORKS

Tom Cunliffe

WILEY NAUTICAL

Tom Cunliffe wishes to thank *Yachting Monthly* and its photographers Graham Snook and Lester McCarthy, and especially all the sailors who gave up their time and even their boats to be part of this project. We had a lot of fun.

This edition first published 2012
© 2012 Tom Cunliffe

Registered office
John Wiley & Sons Ltd, The Atrium, Southern Gate, Chichester, West Sussex, PO19 8SQ, United Kingdom

Editorial office
John Wiley & Sons Ltd, The Atrium, Southern Gate, Chichester, West Sussex, PO19 8SQ, United Kingdom

For details of our global editorial offices, for customer services and for information about how to apply for permission to reuse the copyright material in this book please see our website at www.wiley.com

The right of Tom Cunliffe to be identified as the author of this work has been asserted in accordance with the UK Copyright, Designs and Patents Act 1988.

Library of Congress
Cataloging-in-Publication Data

Cunliffe, Tom, 1947-
Yachting monthly's Expert sailing skills : no nonsense advice that really works / Tom Cunliffe.
p. cm.
ISBN 978-1-119-95129-2 (hardback)
1. Sailing. 2. Yachting. I. Yachting monthly. II. Title.
III. Title: Expert sailing skills.
GV811.C874 2012
797.124--dc23   2011042292

A catalogue record for this book is available from the British Library.

WILEY ✦ NAUTICAL

Front cover images: Main image © Jeanneau
Other images: Yachting Monthly/IPC Media and Tom Cunliffe

Set in 10.5/13 Minion and 9/11pt Myriad by Goldust Design
Printed in China by Toppan Leefung

Contents

Securing alongside

Walk around any marina and you'll find that no two boats are secured alike. It's a major cause of concern for many yachtsmen, but if you go back to basics and think it through logically, it's relatively straightforward

Any instructor running a Day Skipper course spends hefty chunks of time on bringing the boat into a berth. Although handling her on passage, seeing to crew and making sure there's enough water to float her are useful skills, the one that bothers people more than any other is, 'What happens when I get there?'

I'd been spending a week working on skippering skills with Simon Slade aboard a chartered Hallberg-Rassy 36. Simon was managing fine at steering into a berth, and now it was time to consider what to do with the ropes. Strolling around the marina to see how other people managed, it wasn't a surprise to find no two boats secured alike and that

all manner of ideas were used to lose the ends.

To date, Simon had been sailing with friends and his experience mirrored the sort of 'snakes' weddings' we were seeing, so we went right back to first principles. I was once mate on a coastal trading vessel. Her policy was the same as every ship I've seen since, as well as most large professionally run yachts. It works just as neatly for the rest of us.

The procedure for securing alongside

Here's how a fully crewed boat comes alongside a conventional berth.

As the dock is approached, fenders are deployed. Four lines are prepared by feeding the end that's to go ashore

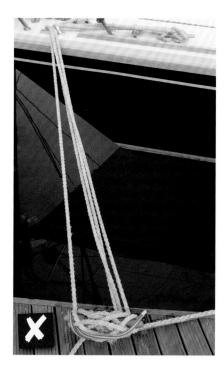

What is a bight?

The bight of a rope is the part between the two ends. Often it falls into a curve or loop and for this reason pilot books sometimes refer to a shallow bay as a 'bight of land'. Any reference to 'making fast the bight', means cleating off the middle of the line.

How do ships and big yachts secure alongside?

As simply as possible, is the answer.
> One rope, one job.
> One rope, one cleat.
> Ends on the dock.
> Slack taken up and made fast on board.
> Coils on deck.
And that's it! Even in ideal circumstances (a marina-style berth with no stream or wind), a larger vessel needs access to each line individually so that her crew can adjust them one by one. If the lines start with the end on board and are then made up on a dock cleat to be brought back as spring lines, or even to their original cleat in some form of 'doubling', the boat is immediately compromised. When the crew want to ease the bow line, for example, they can't do it without first letting off the spring. This may allow the boat to move somewhere they don't want, or fall bows-in, and so on. Using

Take a tip from the professionals

a single rope for two or more tasks turns a simple job into a nightmare.
When I put the 'one-rope-one-job' set-up to Simon, he saw the logic but asked the right question, 'How come all these boats are doing it in other ways?'
My answer is that I don't know. One thing is certain, it's far easier done like a ship, as well as being much safer. It's also a good bit quicker in the end.
Last season, I put my daughter ashore to shift a 30-footer a few feet so I could squeeze into a berth astern. It took her and her boyfriend 10 minutes to do a job that, had the boat been properly tied up, they'd have knocked off in two or three. She came back aboard breathing brimstone.

through the fairlead or guardrail, then pulling out what seems enough for the job plus an extra 50% for contingencies. There's generally no hurry about the springs. They can often wait until later. The two crew who will take bow and stern lines ashore now coil up the business ends and move to the shrouds to step off as the boat comes alongside. The end of the bow line is secured on a dockside bollard, cleat or ring –the method may depend on which it is – and the slack is pulled in aboard. The bight is made fast on its own deck cleat and that is that. The same thing happens at the stern. Run out a couple of springs in the same way, secure them to their own cleats and put the kettle on.

What if I haven't enough cleats?

This is the first fly in the smooth ointment of my ideal set-up. Simon and I found ourselves in this blighted

How not to do it: several lines on each cleat and a mess on the foredeck

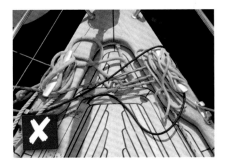

situation with our Hallberg-Rassy. I was frankly amazed at this, because the Hallberg-Rassy is a thoroughly seamanlike vessel, but life is full of little disappointments. The yacht didn't even have fairleads. Instead, she had four large cleats, one on each corner, and another pair somewhere around amidships. We had no problem with bow and stern lines, but what were we to do with the springs?

No doubt Mr H or Mr R imagined we'd use his stout midships cleat, but this would have involved piling two ropes onto it. A horror not to be countenanced, because by Sod's Law the one we wanted to ease or harden would be underneath every time. We'd get away with it in a calm marina, but never alongside a real wall. Furthermore, a spring line led from the quarter pulls the stern closer to the dock. A bow spring does the same for the sharp end, tidying up nicely. One led from amidships achieves far less. It stops her surging back and forth in a berth that's too short for the bow and stern lines to help, but that's about all.

Simon came up with the bright

idea of using the cleats themselves as fairleads, then leading the springs across to the spare cleats on the other side. This actually worked quite well. I wasn't struck on the 'lash-up' feel of it, but needs must and at least the yacht didn't look like a cat's cradle.

Spare winches can often be pressed into service for shore lines, but the lack of fairleads on our boat made it a non-starter. Sometimes a stern line can be led from the dock to the outside quarter, but the HR's transom was too padded out with kit for so delightful an answer. Never mind. We did what we could and were satisfied.

Using the cleats as fairleads was the better of two evils

Securing alongside with two crew

The 'one-line-one-job' approach is easy to operate short-handed, but it does require some modification. Here's how Simon and I did it: Simon takes the helm. I prepare the lines and fenders. I measure the bow line in the usual way, but I make the bight fast on board so I can secure her temporarily from the dock. We lead the stern line exactly as though we were fully crewed. Simon keeps charge of it and is ready to pass it to me.

1 Simon brings her in and I step off with the bow line.

2 As he takes off the last of our way with the engine, I pull in the slack on the bow line and make the bight up on the dock. The bow is now secure.

3 Next, I walk smartly aft and Simon hands me the stern line.

4 I make the end fast on the dock and he tends it from on board, taking up the slack and securing the bight. Springs are run out in the usual way.

5 Last, we sort out the bow line. Simon stays on board and I tend the dock

Securing alongside pilings

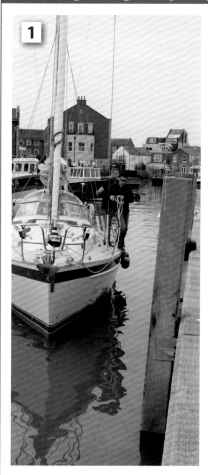

This, as you might say, is the crunch! Having practised coming into a marina berth, we all decided to refresh ourselves in a likely pub on a commercial dock wall across the harbour. The wall is tidal and beset with ugly steel pilings. We couldn't afford to get it wrong, nor did we want the boat surging around in tugboat wash while we were ashore attending to the inner man. Here's how we managed:

1 We picked our spot and came in nice and slow

2 Fenders had been secured 'fore-and-aft', with a line at both ends so they wouldn't pop out when we laid them on the pile of our choice.

3 We came in at the top of the tide and used very long bow and stern lines. These served two functions: The extra length helped check fore-and-aft movement. It also allowed the tide to fall further without our having to adjust them while partaking of the pork pies.

4 The fenders were now in the right place, but the bow was tending to blow in, making the whole affair untidy and creating the risk of damage. A stern spring was therefore rigged and the lines adjusted to a nicety in a couple of minutes, leaving the boat no possibility

of clobbering the pile.

This manoeuvre was only made possible by the 'one-rope-one-job, one-cleat-one-rope' maxim. Had we been saddled with two ropes on a cleat, or one rope doing two jobs, settling her to the inch would have taken so long the beer would have gone flat.

cleat. I let go the bight and quickly make up the end as Simon pulls it in and secures. If it were blowing hard offshore we'd rig an extra line before letting off the temporary one.

Using a bowline

Bowline – So long as the bight is made fast aboard so that it can be eased no matter what, there is no harm in securing the end ashore in such a way that it can't be let off under load. One favourite is simply to tie a bowline in the end and drop it over the cleat. In my experience, this absolutely never comes off so long as the lines remain reasonably tight. Ships do it this way (except that they have huge spliced loops) and I favour it myself because it's so easy to let go when the time comes. Slack away, lift off and you're on your way! The bowline is also good for a bollard or post, but do make sure that your crew don't use their initiative and put a bowline on each end of a loaded rope – the thought brings me out in a cold sweat!

Other methods – So long as the line can be let off when you want it (taken care of by making it up on board) and won't come undone until you're ready, I don't think it much matters how you secure the shore lines.
> Some folk like to tie a round turn and two half hitches on a cleat. Seems like a lot of trouble to me, but it certainly won't fall off! If you are stuck with a ring, this is a good option.
> Actually cleating the line makes sense, too. After all, if God gives you

ABOVE: If everyone used bowlines, sharing cleats with other yachts would be simple. BELOW: Sometimes only a round turn and two half hitches will do

LEFT: A cow-hitched bowline

a perfectly good cleat, why not use it as he may have intended?
> Cow-hitching a bowline or a spliced loop to a cleat will certainly make sure it can't fall off.

Cleating

The important thing about cleating is not how you do it. What matters is that it remains secure until you want to take it off, that it can be eased under load, and can never jam. A bad lead like this

one (Pic 1) can get caught when the load comes on, but the fair lead (Pic 2) will never snag. A round turn (or half a turn), followed by a couple of figures of eight and a further turn to tidy up will hold the Queen Mary without a locking hitch, but if you haven't enough rope, or the cleat's too small, I see no reason not to turn the last figure of eight over on itself to make sure it can't fall or be washed off – always assuming the locking hitch is made after at least one figure of eight so it can't jam up. (Pic 3)

5

Springing off

Working a boat into and out of a tricky berth doesn't have to be difficult. In fact, all you need is a length of rope and a fender and, even with big boats, tricky manoeuvres can be made simple

SUN ODYSSEY 45

In my youth I served as mate on a coastal merchant ship. She carried bulk cargo and was powered by a single screw. Working her in and out of one tricky berth after another was as much an everyday event as tucking in to the cook's world-class breakfasts, yet neither the skipper nor our pilots ever called for a tug. They moved her around using ropes. Subsequently, I've sailed on a number of large, well-run yachts, power and sail, and I've noticed that the same rules hold good. You can shove a 25-footer off a wall on a windy day most of the time, but sooner or later it blows so hard that you can't. For a 40-footer, the crunch comes more often, and so on up the scale.

Working on this book, I've met a wide variety of yacht owners and charter operators. Talking to John 'Arnie' Arnold recently, who operates a charter business, I asked him how his clients manage to handle bigger boats.

'Generally not much problem at sea,' he replied. 'In harbour, it can be a different story.'

This rang true with my own experience, so I asked him if he'd mind lending me a big Jeanneau to talk through how to use spring lines. He was all for it and, as luck would have it, we turned up on a windy day. Thirty-five knots was on the clock at times and the boat weighed in at over ten tons. So, I spat on my hands, rigged warps and fenders, and squared away for a handy pontoon.

Terminology

Terminology is always a vexed area when it comes to spring lines. Throughout my own experience – yachting and merchant – the 'stern spring' is run forward from the stern and the 'bow spring' or 'head spring' is led aft from the bow. However, some authorities equally correctly refer to a 'fore spring' and a 'back spring'. I have no quarrel with this, but for the purposes of this book we must adopt one convention or the other, so we're going for 'stern' and 'bow'.

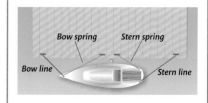

What does a spring line do?

A spring line is rigged from the bow or stern of the boat and led ashore towards amidships – aft from the bow or forward from the stern.

It has two effects. If lead at a sufficiently narrow angle, it helps stop the boat from surging ahead and astern, but perhaps more importantly, it also works as a lever. If the boat tries to move astern against the stern spring it will force her stern in and her bow out. Vice versa with a bow spring. This gives you a number of important options for manoeuvring as well as securing alongside. If you're wondering about rigging spring lines from those cleats or fairleads you find amidships on many larger yachts today, see page 9!

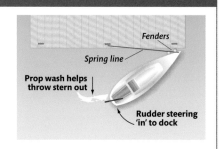

Fenders

Spring line

Prop wash helps throw stern out ↓

Rudder steering 'in' to dock

Bringing the boat close-in alongside

Think 'spring-line manoeuvres,' and ten-to-one you'll be conjuring up an image of a yacht springing herself off a tricky dock. Bigger vessels, however, often have as much difficulty getting close-in alongside as they do extricating themselves from a weather berth. Even in a smaller yacht, it can be a struggle trying to pull her in against a strong wind when you've managed to get a couple of lines ashore, but she's drifted five yards back out again in the process. The soft option is to ask someone ashore to heave you in, but this is a bit of a liberty. Pulling her in from on board is often awkward because of the guardrails. You could grind her in if one line leads to a powerful winch, but the neatest answer is to spring her in.

The first time we brought the big Jeanneau alongside, we found ourselves in exactly that situation. The yacht ended up blowing off the dock with two lines of more or less equal length at right angles between us and the wall. To bring her in, we could either engage ahead or astern, whichever was most convenient (we tried both), and apply a few revs. As we built up power, the yacht started walking in against her lines. Going ahead, the bow line now became a bow spring. Vice versa astern. She strolled in as easily as if she were one leg of a parallel ruler and the dock were the other. The connectors are, of course, the two lines. Once she was alongside, I kept the revs on just as my old skipper on the ship used to, while my crew ran out the other two lines that would keep her there. Then we shut down the power and that was the job. No grunting, no rushing around, no busted insides.

1. We've got bow and stern lines secured but the wind is blowing the yacht off and with her high topsides it would have been hard work to haul her in

2. The helmsman simply knocks the engine into reverse gear and waits for some simple physics to work its magic

3. As she moves astern she drives against the lines and swings neatly against the pontoon

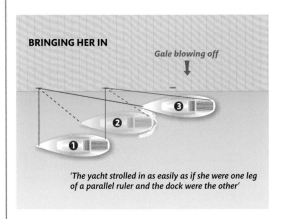

BRINGING HER IN

Gale blowing off ↓

'The yacht strolled in as easily as if she were one leg of a parallel ruler and the dock were the other'

Parbuckling

If it's blowing a gale and there's not enough room fore or aft to drive the boat in against her lines then try parbuckling. Attach a line to the dock so that when you lead it to the middle of the shore line it makes something like a right angle. Take it round the line, bring it back to where you started and heave. As you do, the dock line will take on an increasingly indented vee shape and the boat will walk smartly in alongside by the ancient principle of 'parbuckling'. Once the fenders are touching, either run out a new dock line or let go the parbuckle and have your mate snap up the slack in the dock line like lightning.

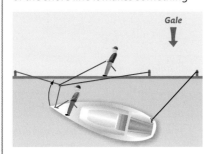

Gale

The yachtsman on the dock is parbuckling the headrope to bring the boat's bow towards the wall. When he has gained as much as he can his mate on board will snatch up the slack. The operation will be repeated for the stern line

Springing off a dock

Having brought the boat alongside our very windy berth, the next job was to demonstrate the two classic springing operations. The truth is that because the wind was blowing us off, we could have just let go our lines and let her drift, but we were on a mission. Fortunately, the Jeanneau had so much displacement that she helped us by staying put. Had it been blowing a gale onto the dock, the theory and practice would have been just the same.

Slip ropes

By their nature, spring-line manoeuvres are often chosen when things are fraught. That's the time to run the line around the cleat on shore and back on board again, so that both ends are fast on the boat. When the time comes, let off the shorter end, pull it all through and you're clear away without the danger of leaving some poor soul behind. Slip ropes can easily foul, however, and to be motoring away when a slipped bow spring nips its turn and comes tight is a sure formula for embarrassment. In sum, slip ropes should only be used if they're really necessary. If you do, take every step to ensure they run clean.

Slip ropes can be a necessary evil – only rig them if you have to as they foul easily

Springing the stern

My first thought when I'm pinned onto a dock by the wind is to try to get the bow off so I can simply 'drive out' of the berth. In a modern yacht, however, this is often not the best answer because, left to her own devices with no way on in open water, she will probably end up lying with her stern closer to the wind than the bow. Her natural tendency is to weathercock with her transom to windward. This means it often proves easier to motor out of a weather berth stern first. The favoured option is therefore generally to spring the stern off the dock.

Clambering aboard over the high bow was going to be a no-chance situation, even for my crew, who's an athletic sort of chap, so we rigged the bow spring as a slip rope. While we were at it, we also set a slip on the stern line because we were only two-handed and there wouldn't be time for my crew to let the stern off then gallop up to the bow. If the boat really were being blown on hard, he could simply have let go the stern line from the dock, stepped on board and walked forward while I was springing her off. Finally, we set up fendering immediately abaft the stem.

I slipped the stern line and put the engine into slow ahead. I also steered 'into' the dock so that the prop-wash would help throw the stern out. Away she came. When the stern was far enough out to be certain there would be a result, I went into neutral, my crew slipped the spring, and away we went.

1. Climbing onto the bow of a departing yacht is high risk so we rigged slip lines and hung fenders from the pushpit

2. The helmsman slips the stern line, steers into the dock and motors forward against the bow spring. The fenders take the strain

3. When the stern is well clear, the helm engages neutral and gives the order for the bow spring to be slipped

4. A good burst in astern puts some way on and takes the boat away from the dock

Springing the bow off

This works exactly the same as springing the stern off, except that because the engine will be running astern, there will be no prop-wash effect on the rudder, so the spring line can't be 'power-assisted'. Bear in mind that forcing the bow upwind is typically not what the boat wants to do, so if it's blowing like the clappers you'll need to screw the head well out before letting go and leaving the berth. Make sure the stern is well fendered, let go the bow, and motor astern against the stern spring line.

To work properly, a stern spring needs to be led from the extreme corner of the boat. Because the stern deck is lower and more accessible than the bow and the boat is being blown hard onto the dock, you can generally dispense with a slip rope for this manoeuvre. On my boat, the crew just stands by ashore holding the spring on the cleat with a round turn, then when the springing is done and the bow is far enough out, I go into neutral, they whip the turn off and step on board as I'm engaging ahead to drive out. On a boat with very high topsides this won't work so you've no choice but to rig a slip and make sure it doesn't foul.

1. The stern spring runs from the stern to a cleat on the dock amidships. The spring and the bow line are both rigged as slip lines

2. Tom puts the engine in astern as the bow line is slipped. If the wind is blowing off the dock it may be sufficient just to let the bow go and wait

3. Sugar scoops and bathing platforms can cause problems when springing the bow. It may be worth investing in an extra large fender

4. The helmsman takes her out of reverse, slips the stern spring and motors ahead. Always check that there are no lines near the propeller

The midships cleat or fairlead

The midships cleat or fairlead serves no purpose in the sort of manoeuvres we've described so far. It comes into its own in marinas where the finger pontoons are not long enough to set up bow and stern springs. Lines led to it from fore or aft certainly prevent the boat from surging, but they are far less effective than true springs for holding her parallel to the dock. Because the lead is so near the centre of the boat, the magic leverage of the spring line is simply not there.

Short-handed docking with the midships cleat

A modern yacht tends to be lozenge-shaped when viewed from above. It stands to reason that if she's secured alongside by a single short line from amidships she will roll forward or aft around her fenders until the line comes tight. At that point, she'll either stay where she is or rebound the other way. Sometimes, the equilibrium can be further stabilised by motoring slow ahead. Coming alongside short-handed therefore, all you need do in theory is secure this line. The boat will then remain more or less stable while you run out the permanent dock lines.

For the theory to work out in practice, the cleat or fairlead must either be dead on the boat's static pivot point or slightly abaft it. If it's forward of it, any attempt to motor ahead will throw her stern out and her bows in. Motoring astern won't help much either. If the rope is tight enough, she may lie doggo with no power on at all, but making it up that short on a bigger boat is generally impracticable. I tried it on a long-keeled yacht a few months back and the pivot point was so far aft that we had to lead it direct from a cockpit winch! Nonetheless, I've seen couples working this system to great effect, so everyone should at least give it a go. Don't be disappointed if it won't work for you, however. We gave it our best shot on the Jeanneau. We tried it with longer ropes and 'super-shorties' that could never have been rigged in anger. We motored ahead and astern, then we shut down the power, but whatever we did she wouldn't have any of it. On this particular, boat, it was a bust.

If you get only get one line ashore, consider using the midships cleat and motoring against it. It may not be pretty but it will give you time

9

Rafting up

Rafting up in harbours and marinas is an almost inevitable part of summer sailing in popular waters. And although it might look daunting, with a few simple techniques, it needn't be, as long as you keep your neighbours happy

With more boats on the water than ever before and town quays no longer growing in size, the envitable result is more and more rafting up in harbours and marinas.

You've only to glance at a Victorian photograph of 'The herring fleet in harbour' to see that walking from wall to wall on the packed-in luggers is nothing new. Those fishermen had unwritten agreements about conduct. They had to, because they managed the whole affair without engines. It's all comparatively easy for us but, like all situations where many are gathered together in strict confines, without a generally accepted structure of conduct we'd soon descend into anarchy and chaos.

There's nothing in the Colregs about how to raft up, yet few experienced sailors would argue about what's acceptable and what won't do at all. Some of this lore is about the practicalities of ropework and fenders, but much is about how to behave. To quantify the conventions as best I could, I borrowed three yachts and, with two friends as crew, took them to a local marina to test out the theory.

Read on if you're nervous about rafting up. If you're an old hand, why not dip in and see if I've missed anything…

When can you raft up?

Arriving in a strange harbour, you see boats nose-to-tail along the town quay. Not a foot of dock is to be had. Your only chance is to start rafting up, but it takes confidence – some would say, a brass neck – to be the first. Can you or can't you? Here are your main sources of authority:

〉 The harbourmaster tells you to: Lovely. Nobody can argue with that!

〉 Your pilot book recommends rafting: Pretty good. The pilot is more than likely to be correct.

〉 Your own authority based on common sense and no alternative: Fair enough. Pick a boat similar to your own with someone on board and see how you get on. It's not an unreasonable request.

Who do you raft up to?

Take your time approaching a raft so you can relax and eyeball the options. If a number of rafts are building up, opting for one with fewer boats will keep things tidy. Thereafter, the initial selection is generally made on grounds of size and topside shape.

〉 Small on big: On the face of things, this is ideal. If you lie outside a bigger yacht you are unlikely to stress her cleats too much, or crush her should an onshore gale develop. Her crew understands this too, so you're more likely to be received by smiling faces.

〉 Big on small: Large discrepancies should be avoided if possible. People with little boats don't like to see monsters shaping up with a crew of ten hanging over the side waiting to clump across their decks at closing time just as the baby is finally nodding off to sleep. If needs must, however, it's OK to ask politely.

〉 Incompatible bedfellows: A sailing boat with skinny fenders is going to have an expensive time of it lying alongside a motoryacht with a flaring, high freeboard. You're likely to end up with bent stanchions and an insurance claim for damage to the neighbour's topsides. However, with courtesy, care and proper fenders, such issues can often be overcome. I've made friends with many a jolly motorboater on a raft.

Take extra care if rafting to a motor boat

Ask before rafting up

There you are, settling in below for a nice cup of tea when the dreaded call comes from outside in the rain, 'Mind if we lie alongside you?' This is the question we all must ask and

Always ask before rafting up

it pays to remember what the other party may be thinking. If it's you that's arriving and you have chosen a sensible boat as your victim, here's how to maximise your chances of a happy response:

> Ideally, find a boat with someone on deck so you can make immediate contact. Failing that, choose one where you can see activity down below. If you have to call out to someone who isn't aware of you, use their boat's name. 'Ahoy, Jack the Ripper!' is all that's required until the hatch slides open. If it stays obstinately shut and there's nowhere else to go, come in quietly, tiptoe aboard and knock on the coachroof with the same call. If this doesn't generate a reaction, call an ambulance in case they're dead! A 'bare' boat has its attractions because if there's nobody to ask, nobody's going to say 'No' either. Unfortunately, empty yachts have a nasty habit of filling up when all hands come back at midnight

bent on putting to sea.

> Once you've established contact, the next question is simple, but be ready with clarification. 'OK to lie alongside?' is no more than an opening gambit. Assuming the insider isn't a total curmudgeon or he knows something that you may not (perhaps the harbourmaster specifically forbids rafting), the main issue is usually, 'who's leaving when?' If you're greeted by a typical, 'You're welcome but we're leaving at 0500,' it's absolutely OK to respond with a cheery, 'No worries, then. We'll get up and let you out.' It may be easier to do this than to hang off a difficult-looking raft next door.

> If rafting is clearly acceptable and someone generally makes it clear you're not wanted, the person who's refusing you has no moral rights at all unless your boat is obviously unsuitable for the proposed raft-up. What you do about this, if anything, is up to you.

Securing to a raft

Basic line discipline

Initially, coming alongside the outside boat on a raft is no different to berthing on a pontoon. However, it's even more important than usual to stick to basic line discipline. The rule of 'one rope one job, one rope one cleat', may not be possible as far as the cleats are concerned but, because of the potential for mix-ups and unexpected loadings, it is even more important

than usual not to ask a rope to fulfil more than a single function. I once had to hacksaw a spring line off when I used it to double as a shoreline.

Who supplies what?

The boat arriving supplies all her own lines and fenders. She might then choose to leave a couple over the 'offside' in case anyone else decides to lie outside her,

The new arrival provides all lines and fenders

but there is no need to do this unless you want to encourage visitors. The deal is that the next guy looks after himself, just as you have.

Setting the lines

1 Arrive with fenders rigged and breast lines ready for bow and stern. Step off on to the inside boat with these, or hand them across if her crew are showing willing. Whatever you do, secure the ends of the breasts to the inside boat and make up the bight on board your own yacht. Don't toss over a great mass of line and expect the other crew to pull you in. After all, why should they? It's also better not to pass the bight round their cleat and take the end back, unless you're in Holland or Scandinavia. Here, for some reason, it's universal practice. It makes sense in locks but in a raft-up the ropes clutter up already over-subscribed cleats and can easily jam. It also demands twice the cleat space on your own boat, since an end as well as the bight needs making fast.

2 Once the breasts are on, rig springs in the same way. You may have to use winch barrels and anything else strong you can find, because cleats are going to be in short supply, but do what you can to avoid securing one line on top of another. You can be sure it'll be the bottom one you need to adjust.

3 Next, take long lines ashore from bow and stern. Make the ends fast ashore and take up on board so that your breast lines go slack. This means you're taking your own weight rather than lying to the

neighbour's lines. A courtesy and a sensible safety precaution. Shore lines are usually led around each boat in turn, outside everything, but a good line-thrower can save a lot of messing about.

4 Once the shorelines are secure, it's often possible to remove the breast lines altogether and lie to 'shores' and springs. The springs stop fore-and-aft surging and, if properly set up, the shorelines keep bow and stern tucked in sweetly.

RIGHT: Adjusting the shorelines on a three-boat raft. LEFT: Use winches as substitute cleats if needed

Exceptions to the norm

All raft-ups are subject to oddities caused by different sizes and types of boat. The two main exceptions to the norm are these:

Small boat outside a big one

A two-tonner outside a ten-tonner isn't going to trouble the host's cleats or lines a bit. What's more, it's often

impossible to lead a shoreline around the big boat. The new arrival can propose running out shorelines and hope for a sensible response. If you're the big fellow inside, offer to take the load without being asked and save the hassle of shore lines. They'd end up draped in the water, taking no strain, anyway.

Check spreaders won't clash

Large boat outside a small one

In these cases, at least one breast line will probably serve instead of the relevant spring. If so, it won't require replacing at all when the shoreline goes on.

Leaving the raft

Outside boat
No problem. Quietly gather in your shorelines then potter away. Try not to run slip lines around other yachts' cleats at unsocial hours. They wake the dead down below as they graunch around.

Inside boats
Let's assume there's a single boat outside you. Ideally, her skipper will say, 'No worries. I'll just let go and stand off until you've gone, then reattach myself.' This is the easiest way of dealing with the situation. If there's nobody on board, or they don't fancy this simple option, you'll have to slip out. Whatever you do, be sure to move away down-tide:
> All shorelines are taken off the boat that's leaving (your boat).
> Remove the down-tide shoreline on the outside boat. Lead it around your up-tide extremity, carry it ashore or on to a boat further in on the raft.
> Take off all ropes on both sides of your boat, double-check they've all gone, then go for it! Don't hang around staring at the woodwork, because for the few seconds it takes

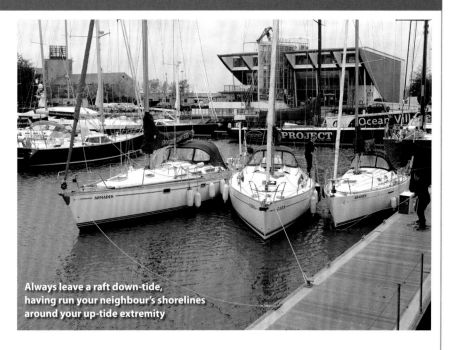

Always leave a raft down-tide, having run your neighbour's shorelines around your up-tide extremity

for you to slip clear, the outside boat or boats are at your mercy.
> The moment you are clear, the outside boat is hove back into the gap using both shorelines. Whether the heaving is done from ashore or on board is a matter of convenience. Springs can then be run out.

> All this can take as long as half an hour if you aren't used to it. Don't be rushed. When a mid-raft boat gives her engine the gun only to find she still has an outside spring attached, it doesn't half make your eyes water…

In-raft etiquette

You can make good friends in rafts, or you can drive the neighbours to distraction. A few guidelines have developed over the years that have kept homicides to a minimum.

Communicate
Always try to ask the first time you cross someone's boat. Just a questioning look followed by a nod is fine, but a sailor's yacht is his castle and we venture over another chap's guardrails at our peril.

Cross forward
Always cross forward of the mast if possible, and resist any temptation to peer down companionways and forehatches.

Keep it quiet
It goes without saying that boozy parties in the cockpit should pipe down by bedtime if you have a family alongside. Crossing another yacht silently is an art form, and jumping on to someone else's deck should be punishable by public

execution. Apart from the inevitable displacement shift that accompanies my 16 stone, I pride myself on folks not knowing I'm there. Walk on the outside edge of the shoe for a quiet footfall. The real killer, after you've tried so hard to be quiet, is to 'ping' a shroud or trip over a booming-out pole. Watch out for these booby-traps, especially creeping home at 0130 after a convivial evening spent up to no good. Or you can always ask the neighbours to join you!

RIGHT: The skipper should be untroubled while you raft up alongside. BELOW: Step on the outside edge of your shoes

LEFT: No peeking down hatches.
ABOVE: Courtesy works wonders

13

Mooring stern-to

Mooring stern-to is a great way to squeeze into small, awkward spaces – and it's a must in many foreign ports, including most in the Med – but few of us know the best way to do it

The author picks up some tips from sailing instructor Dave Chambers

You never know when you might need to secure to a quay stern-to. It makes more sense than alongside berthing wherever there's a rough old quay and a chance of some swell. But many harbours are dominated by marina pontoons and swinging moorings, so it's a skill we rarely get the chance to practice. More and more of us are sailing to distant shores where 'Med-style' mooring is the norm, and many of us take short breaks chartering in warmer climes, where even the most experienced skipper can find himself sadly lacking in berthing expertise.

When I skippered my first charge I once took David Niven's lines as he arrived for drinks with the heiress on the next-door motor-yacht in his Riva speedboat. Marinas were literally unheard-of then, and so were bow thrusters. Backing the owner's long-keeled pride and joy onto a stone quay in a howling crosswind while my wife second-guessed my intentions from the windlass far away at the sharp end was a lottery.

I've berthed end-on many times since those days, but not in circumstances that have encouraged analysis. To produce this piece I needed a mentor. Like me, Dave Chambers grew up miles from the sea, yet he now runs a sailing school and charter operation in Majorca. We couldn't have found a better instructor. He lent us a boat, spent an hour talking us through how he teaches mooring here, then left us to discover how well his brief had worked.

Getting started

End-on moorings in non-tidal waters divide into two categories, each offering a couple of options. If the berth is equipped with a permanently rigged haul-off line, as many are in the Western Med, your anchor can stay put on the bow roller. It only remains to decide whether to come in bow or stern-to.

Where there is no pick-up line – many Greek and Turkish harbours don't have them, and if you're cruising off the beaten track you'll be lucky to find one – it's a case of deploying the anchor to hold yourself off, either from bow or stern, depending on your fancy and local convention.

However you intend to moor, it will pay to spend 10 minutes in open water manoeuvring the boat so she can confess her habits and preferences. Don't wait until you are committed to a berth to find out how she steers astern.

Mooring with a haul-off line

The best approach?

This system relies on a series of moorings set well out from the quay which arriving yachts access by a pick-up line secured to the dock. Grab the line, work your way along it and sooner or later you come to the big mooring rope that will hold you off.

I'd always imagined that hooking up to this arrangement involves a scramble to grab the mooring with the boathook while trying to send a stern line ashore. Not so. Dave showed us that all our efforts should concentrate on securing the stern to the dock. Once the windward stern line is on, driving the yacht against it allows her to sit there in equilibrium while we pick up the mooring at our leisure. Equally contrary to expectations was his remark that berthing stern-to is far less fraught with potential problems than bows-to. Take your time, relax, and be happy was his clear message.

LEFT: Pick up the shore end of the mooring line. RIGHT: Then tie off your bow line at leisure

Berthing stern-to

Assuming no other boats are on the dock, here's how the set-piece goes:
› Start well out and manoeuvre so you're ready to back in.
› Decide which haul-off line you fancy. Steer in so that it's on your weather side if the wind is strong enough to affect the manoeuvre.
› Back up to the berth and get the windward stern line on. Ideally, hand it to a passing marinero. Alternatively, either lasso the bollard or step ashore off the stern and make it fast. Don't jump. There's no need.
› On board, the cleats are usually immediately forward of the rudder. This enables you to motor ahead against this line and maintain a reasonable level of control while you set everything else up. Essentially, you're now 'in'. All the rest is tidying up.
› Before picking up the haul-off line, ease off the stern line a short way. Now grab the light line from the water between you and the dock with the boathook. Do not allow it to get near the propeller. Take the bight forward and hang it over a midships cleat if possible to make sure it doesn't get chewed up by the prop.
› Now heave in on the pick-up line until you have the heavy mooring line in hand. Pull this hard in with the stern line eased and secure it at the bow.

Take a very long run-up to overcome propwalk and adjust to any crosswind

Get the windward stern line secured before worrying about the mooring line

› Motor gently astern, step off with the second stern line and adjust all three until you're satisfied.
› Finally, run the engine at half astern to

Motor against the stern line to steady the boat while the mooring line is run forward

The leeward stern line can then be made fast ashore

satisfy yourself you can't be driven back onto the dock by an unexpected squall, then pour yourself a large gin.

Leaving a stern-to mooring

Let the helm know that it's all clear ahead

Finally slip the windward stern line

This is a re-run of the arrival process, but there are one or two issues that can cause embarrassment if they are not attended to.

> Let go the lee stern line and make sure your weather stern line is ready to slip. Rigging it double is generally worth while, unless a marinero or some other willing hand is waiting on the dock to assist.

> Station a hand at the bow. He or she will slip the mooring on the word, but first they need to check that the way out is clear. The order for getting to this stage is, 'Stand by forward.'

> Start motoring against the remaining stern line to get full control of the boat.

> Next, order the foredeck to 'Let go.' Their job is to take a final glance around, to make sure you're clear to go. If not, they hold up a hand. If it's all systems go, you get a thumbs-up and they can slip the mooring.

> Making certain the ropework isn't heading for your propeller, sit tight going ahead against the stern line until the mooring and its pick-up have fallen down well out of the way.

> Throttle back, let go aft, and drive out.

Pinched in with a cross-wind

> Don't be afraid to take a slip rope across to a windward boat. Have the crew handle this as you motor ahead between the yachts so as to keep your head up as she starts to come out from the shelter of the raft, then slip it when you've enough way on to counteract the wind.

> The secret is to get way on as soon as you can. If you can't do this for lack of space ahead, just let the head blow off and motor out astern. Most modern yachts are more than happy to oblige if you ask them to do this.

Berthing bows-to, with a mooring line

Oddly enough, this is trickier than coming in stern-to in a yacht that steers astern, as most charter boats do. The reason is that once the bow line is on you can only motor astern against it, which offers no way of diverting propeller wash across the rudder so as to 'steer' her at a standstill. Although

Things get busy at the bow as one crew lassoes the bollard while another picks up the mooring line

you can hang back going astern for a while, in the end, any wind will take you away. It is therefore critical to grab the mooring and clap it on as soon as possible after the bow is attached to the dock.

Joining an existing raft is a real bonus, because as soon as you are snuggled in between two others, you're safe in the warm embrace of their fenders. It's important to accept that bows-to mooring is not ideal. Often, it can be an unseemly grab and shuffle. You just have to do the best you can. Here are a couple of useful tips :

> As soon as the bow is on, grab the pick-up line promptly.

> Always go for the windward mooring line if you can.

> If you can't, watch your prop, and lead it round to the weather side once you have it in hand up forward.

> Bows-to mooring has the advantage of doing wonders for your on-board privacy and security. It is, however, less easy to get ashore over the pulpit. Don't despair, however. In areas where bows-to is favoured, many boats have cutaway

pulpits to help out.

> If your preference is for stern-to and you come across a raft of boats lying bows-to, go with the flow. There may be a good reason for their choice, such as a nasty shelf sticking out that will smash your rudder but which won't trouble your bow one bit.

The mooring line needs to be led quickly to the stern and hauled in

Mooring with an anchor

Keep it simple

The difference between backing up to a berth in a 40ft Jeanneau with a modern windlass and plenty of space to manoeuvre, and trying the same trick in my boss's old, long-keeled 20-tonner in a tiny harbour was remarkable. I backed Dave's yacht onto a visitor's berth at Alcudia and was astounded at my own expertise. Anyone who can steer astern and communicate with the foredeck can do this. No problem. Be assured. Bows-to is similarly simple, although one or two tricks of the trade may help.

Stern-to with anchor

> Start well out to give yourself room to go astern in a straight line when it counts.

> Size up the berth, place the yacht, and come in with plenty of way on.

> As far out as you dare (assess the boat's available length of cable), drop the pick and make sure it runs cleanly. If the foredeck snub you off early, stop their rum ration because they will certainly make you look stupid.

> Surging cable all the way, drive in astern laying it in a straight line until your crew can step off onto the dock with the windward stern line. Secure this, motor against it, then back it off a couple of metres to let the boat come away from the wall.

> Heave in on the anchor, by windlass if you have one, until the cable indicates the hook has taken. Now motor astern to dig it in.

> Drop back, send the second stern line ashore, even up, and broach the gin again.

ABOVE: Keep surging cable until someone can step ashore and make a stern line fast. The helmsman can then drive against this line. LEFT: The helm can communicate with the crew at the bow by using hand signals. A raised, clenched fist means 'Stop'

Bows-to with anchor

Bows-to berths are often steep-to. If you have a length of chain before the anchor rope, hang it all over the stern in a big loop before you let go the pick. This is an old trick from a Greek charter skipper of my acquaintance who assures us that it does away with the chain snagging as it tries to run. If you don't fancy this, at least flake it into a bucket for easy management. If you're lucky enough to be a Scandinavian, your stern anchor will be on a length of tape wound onto a neat reel. Strong, easy to use and entirely problem-free.

Once you've mastered the technicalities, bow-to anchoring is simple. As before, drop the hook as far out as you dare, and if you're convinced the breeze will blow from one direction, give it a windward bias to keep you straight when it pipes up.

ABOVE: These yachts have anchored from the stern and led long lines ashore

Extra mooring tips

1 Slip safely in

It's tempting to rig every fender you've got when entering a raft, but this may not be the best bet. As you squeeze in you can almost guarantee yours will hang up on the neighbours'. At worst, they'll snag badly and ruin your manoeuvre. Rig them ready, don't be in a hurry to kick them over, and keep a roving fender ready for all eventualities. It's absolutely OK to lie gently against neighbouring boats for support as you enter a raft. Using them as well-fendered cushions on either side makes the job even easier. Just squeeze in politely, then rig your lines.

2 Keep way on

Shaping up for a gap in a tight raft, it takes nerve to keep plenty of way on, but if you chicken out the keel will stall and the boat will start going sideways. That's the beginning of the end, so hang in there and give her enough gas to maintain control.

The most effective way to keep control of a boat going astern is to

Mind your fenders don't get tangled

Drive her like a car!

Keep your sliplines as simple as possible – cobbling up extra ropes often leads to snagging

Use your thruster positively, in long bursts

Don't let marina crew bully you into an unsuitable berth

face the way she is going. Sit alongside the console if she has one and drive her like a car.

3 Fairleads and sliplines

Fairleads are often sited awkwardly for handling stern lines. Even if they started life well intentioned, it's a pound to a penny that by the time you arrive on the scene they will be shrouded with safety gear and GPS aerials. Leave them out of the equation when running your lines. You can always jam the bight in later if need be.

Always keep sliplines simple! In fact, keep everything as simple as you possibly can. These manoeuvres are not complex and trying to cobble up extra ropes often leads to snagging and resultant nastiness.

4 Bow Thrusters

These are a revelation on boats with shallow bows that blow around like paper bags at slow speed. If you have one, use it positively in long bursts. The mark of the tyro is to jab at it like a button on a video game console. And watch out for pick-up

lines being drawn into thrusters. It can happen all too easily.

5 Judge the berths for yourself

If the marinero or some self-appointed assistant on the dock starts telling you to go into one you don't like the look of, give him your straight opinion. After all, it's you who is going to mess it up. Some end-on berths are impossible in a big crosswind or an onshore blow. Don't go there, even if the 'experts' are shouting at you. Sort something else out, or cruise away and anchor behind a headland.

Conclusion

Dave Chambers' overriding watchwords were, 'Take it easy and keep it simple.' With these maxims in mind, I discovered that today's Mediterranean mooring in a moderate sized modern yacht is not nearly the nightmare I remember from the days of long keels and small harbours. I'm looking forward to astounding my family and friends with my expertise next time I'm down in the sun.

Going astern

Arriving stern-first into an unfamiliar marina or berth can be a daunting prospect, particularly as different types of yachts – bilge-keeled, long-keeled and fin-keeled – demand different tactics, and some are trickier to handle than others

B ack in the 1920s, W O Bentley told his colleague Ettore Bugatti that his racing cars had lousy brakes. Quick as a flash, Bugatti responded, 'I make my cars to go, not to stop!'

I'll bet if you'd complained to any of the great designers of the past about their boats being unpredictable backing out of a berth, they'd have retorted with, 'Who on Earth wants to go astern? My boats are meant to sail sharp end first…'

Times have changed. These days, many of us are stuck with marina pontoons that demand some degree of manoeuvrability astern, and Mediterranean sailors can find themselves backing up to the quay on a daily basis. Arriving stern-first can be a daunting experience, and numerous long-keel yacht owners have said to me in the past, 'My boat has a mind of her own.' So, determined to do something about it I climbed into my boat-handling boots and jumped aboard three very different yachts.

The tiller is an extension of the rudder, imagine the two in a rigid straight line

The theory

Steering when going astern

The secret of remembering which way to turn the helm going astern is to imagine you can see the rudder, then point it the way you want the stern to swing. So long as you're looking astern, this makes the process logical.

Doing the job with a wheel is exactly the same as if you were driving a car. Forget about port and starboard. If you want the stern to go to your left as you are looking, wind the wheel left and you can't do more.

Ideally, the trick is to site yourself forward of the helm so it's between you and where you are going. If you can't manage this, at least sit or stand abeam of the wheel. That way, you can't get your trousers in a twist. With a tiller, just remember that it is an extension of the rudder. Imagine the two in a rigid straight line, pivoting in the middle. To move the rudder so that it points left and takes the stern that way, you'll have to shove the tiller to the right.

Whatever you're steering with, there is often a serious time-lag between pointing the rudder and getting the response you're after.

Indeed, the boat may continue to go the wrong way for quite some time. Don't panic. Hang in and wait. If it's going to happen, it will in the end. If it isn't, you're done for and you'll have to think again. Wiggling the rudder will not help.

Propwalk

Most propellers come with an inbuilt tendency to take the stern one way or the other, especially with the engine running astern. The majority are said to be 'right-handed', which

means that, looking from behind, they are revolving clockwise when going ahead. The important thing is what happens when the engine is thrown into astern. A right-handed prop will cartwheel the stern to port, a left-handed vice versa. Before you can expect to steer a yacht astern, it's vital to know which you have.

Underwater profiles

One reason why traditional long-keeled yachts steer so sweetly on passage is because they have a lot of draught aft and less near the bow. Going astern, the situation is reversed and it does them no favours. The position is often similar, though less destructive, in yachts with a long fin keel and a rudder hung from a skeg. Boats that are essentially flat-floored with a bolted-on keel and an unsupported spade rudder don't suffer from these draw-backs. They often steer almost as well going astern as ahead. The situation is even easier if they have a vertical trailing edge to the rudder, which many do. Their only failing is that, with little or no appreciable draught at the bow, they can be subject to blowing around uncontrollably at speeds too low for the rudder to bite. The only sure way to combat this is with a bow thruster.

It's vital to know which way your prop kicks

21

The test

The weather, the boats

Westerly Centaur 26
Tormentor

Twister 28
Indigo

Bénéteau Océanis 43
Sailfin

I joined the boats on a cold November day with the wind blowing straight down the river at Force 6. A local sea school had kindly fixed

us up with its 26ft Westerly Centaur, *Tormentor*. This classic Morris Minor of the sea has bilge keels. So far as I was concerned, her performance

astern was a blank slate. Next, we had a 28ft Twister, *Indigo*, designed in 1963 and owned by Ken Munn, who gave us a couple of hours en route to his

winter haul-out so we could get a feel for handling a long-keeled yacht. Last, a sailing club had loaned us a brand-new 43ft Bénéteau Océanis, *Sailfin*.

There seemed little point in trying to thread all these boats into awkward berths. In the real world, every pontoon is different, so an infinite shading of technique is required. I've found that so long as I keep my head and remember the essentials, I can usually see what's needed for a specific situation. To fish out these basics, we analysed the performance of all the boats with three tests.

The natural tendency of most sailing craft left to free-float in open water is to settle with the wind abaft

the beam. From here, it doesn't take much to pull the stern up towards the breeze and keep it there, so almost any boat will motor astern upwind. Try going astern downwind, however, and the bow will attempt to blow off to where it really wants to be. It takes a manoeuvrable yacht to overcome this at low speeds.

So here's test one: motor downwind astern and see how fast we need to go in order to beat the propwalk and the wind.

Tests two and three relate to manoeuvring across the breeze, and

the same principles hold good. One way, the propwalk will be taking the stern upwind, the other, downwind. The bow is trying to blow downwind in both cases so, if the propwalk is exaggerating this, the rudder has a lot of work to do. If the prop is fighting the bow's natural desire to blow off, you're in with a good chance of quick control. The exercises, then, are to motor astern across the wind, first with the propwalk trying to keep her in line, before sampling the effects the other way, 'against the prop', as it were.

The Westerly Centaur performed beautifully going astern upwind

The Centaur

Finding the propwalk

The 26ft Centaur had the original 25hp Volvo. In her day back in 1968, this was a huge engine and it still pulls her along powerfully. To discover the propeller effects, we secured her alongside then ran the engine astern. Immediately, we could see a lot of prop-wash welling up on the port side, and much less coming out to starboard. Given a chance, the stern will tend to shy away from the net turblence, so this boat kicked her stern to starboard, not to port as is more usual. She had a left-handed propeller. Just to make sure, we took her out into the river. Moving slow ahead, we threw the engine hard astern and noted which way her bow swung. Sure enough, it cartwheeled away to port with her stern swivelling to starboard.

Upwind and downwind

With her stern pointing upwind, the Centaur kicked it a little to starboard as we put her into gear, but she soon accelerated to around 2 knots, which was plenty for her rudder to take charge, and away we went, steering at will. The story was not dissimilar with the stern facing downwind. She had enough grip on the water to hold her position as we lost headway, but her bow swung off positively as we started going astern. However, I'd given her a sheer to starboard so we'd a bit of slack in the system, so to speak. By the time her propeller had dragged her back to wind, we were steering sweetly at that magic 2-and-a-bit knots.

Going cross-wind without enough power the Centaur tried to swivel her head downwind to port while her stern went to starboard. The 'left-handed' propeller added to the effect

Cross-wind

With the breeze on the starboard bow, the boat was trying to swivel her head downwind to port. As the other half of the equation, her stern would be tending to swivel to starboard. This, of course, is also where the propeller will try to take Centaur's transom. I expected trouble, but didn't really get it. As I put the power on, she swung around until her stern lay about 50 degrees toward the wind as she accelerated steadily. Once up to 2.5 knots, the rudder had taken charge and she pulled back into line. Pretty good! Crossing the river with the wind on the port side, the propeller levered against the bow as it tried to fall away. In no time the little boat was steering beautifully.

Setting up a sheer

When a boat has notable propwalk to one side, try giving her a tweak in the opposite direction before you start going astern. The first kick of the prop will then be used up pulling her back into line, giving you a better chance of 'catching her'. If you're port-side-to with a right-handed prop and you must leave astern, you know that when you start off the propwalk will graunch the quarter into the dock. The answer is to give the blunt end a kick out to starboard against a bow spring before you let go. With luck, by the time you have enough stern-way on to steer, she will have just pulled herself back into line.

The Twister

I had been fearing that Ken Munn's lovely Twister, *Indigo*, would be trouble, but shrewdly he said very little as I started trying her out.

Finding the propwalk

Secure alongside, we slipped the Twister's engine into astern and waited for what seemed an age while the small one-lunger engine overcame the inertia of a serious flywheel. There was some evidence of a right-hand propeller, but not a lot. The real significance was that this boat was going to take quite a while to gather way, which could leave her a victim of whatever wind was blowing.

Upwind and downwind

I began with the stern upwind – the easy one – and was confounded when the Twister wandered all over the river. To be generous, she remained under what might pass for some sort of control at a drunk's wedding.

'Bow upwind, forget it,' I thought, and I wasn't disappointed.

Cross-wind

Beam-on with the wind on the port side was the washout that was now predictable. With the starboard side onto the breeze, I couldn't believe that I wouldn't be able to control this delightful yacht with her right-handed propeller pulling her into line against the wind on the bow, but the Twister would have none of it. By the time she'd gathered enough way to be in with a chance, it was far, far too late. In a lull, we contrived a sort of compromise at revs low enough to generate only minimal propeller effect, and when we popped her out of gear altogether and let her way carry her, she did improve, but only a little.

'Time to come clean!' I thought, and asked Ken if he had a secret.

Dealing with a difficult boat

'There isn't a secret really,' Ken said laconically. 'I've tried it all.'

Beam-on with the wind on the port side, Kenn Munn's Twister, *Indigo*, was uncontrollable. Even with a large sheer it was impossible to get the boat moving in the desired direction cross-wind

With its heavy flywheel and small capacity, Ken's engine takes so long to rev up that he's more or less given up hope of a result in any strong wind. Fortunately, this potentially world-girdling cruiser is only 28ft long and she's very handy. Ken can usually either warp her in and out of an impossible berth, or somehow contrive to wind ship so she's pointing where she should be. If all else fails, he knows that the breeze is king and will take her bow where it wills. So long as he doesn't fight the inevitable, he enjoys a surprisingly quiet life.

The lesson we learn from Ken's prudent seamanship is that if a boat is unwilling, don't try to force her against her natural tendencies. Accept her for what she is, be grateful for her other fine qualities, and find ways of living with it.

Keep control

Once a boat is moving fast enough to steer astern, her rudder can take charge very easily – the Centaur, for example, took me by surprise. If you let it, it'll ram across right to the bump stops, and woe betide any poor soul stuck between tiller and coaming! At speed, keep the tiller firmly near the centre. Getting under way, make sure it doesn't take charge. Wheels are less dramatic, but the same applies. It isn't hard to break a wrist between the spokes when five tonnes of yacht spins the helm hard over!

The Bénéteau

Finding the propwalk

This beamy modern yacht had so much body aft that it wasn't as easy to observe the prop-wash in the berth as on the other two boats. It did suggest a kick to port in astern and experience told me she would almost certainly have a right-hand propeller. We checked this out on the river by throwing her half astern at low speed and watching the bow. Sure enough, it slid off to starboard as the stern swivelled to port.

Upwind and downwind

After the classic small cruisers, our Bénéteau seemed seriously big. In theory, however, she had all the hull and engine characteristics to make her a good performer astern, and so she proved. Upwind and down, she accelerated so rapidly that her barn-door rudder took charge of the propeller at the usual two knots, but so little time elapsed in getting there that her bow had not blown away appreciably.

Cross-wind

Across the wind against the prop, the Frenchman fell off like the two smaller yachts, but when I gave her

The Bénéteau put in an exemplary performance across the wind as the bow blew away, with the propeller working hard to pull the stern into line

the gun she gathered enough way to sort herself out in what seemed like no time and I didn't feel any temptation to feed in the power tentatively in fear of massive propwalk. She overcame what there was in short order. That said, in tight waters such as a narrow marina corridor and an awkward berth, I'd have wanted

a bow thruster to control so hefty a boat in any weight of wind.

Across the wind with the prop working to pull the stern into line as the bow blew away, the Bénéteau put in an exemplary demonstration.

Conclusion

Without doubt, the secret of controlling a boat astern under power is to know her habits, to consider how these will be affected by conditions, then set up any manoeuvre to give her the best chance. If our knowledge of her suggests she's going to sulk instead of doing what we want, we must either think again and find a different way, or at least have the crew standing by with fenders at any likely crunch points. Working in harmony with their natural tendencies, most yachts will do what they're told in the end, given enough space and a determined hand on the helm, but there are one or two that just won't come into line. They are often found among the classic passage makers of our day; to balance the equation, it must be said that some modern yachts that steer perfectly astern are skittish in a seaway. As Mr Bugatti might have observed had he been a yachtsman, it pays to remember what the boat is really for.

Negotiating locks

Locks are infamous for causing a great deal of stress to skippers and damage to their boats' topsides. Yet they needn't be, and if you follow the protocol, passing through them should be reasonably straightforward

1. Traffic lights

Like the entrance lights to any other harbour, these tell you when it's safe to proceed. If you're unsure what they mean, consult your almanac. Some locks don't have them, and rely on VHF radio communications instead.

Hythe

2. Lock master

Looking down from his lofty control tower, the lock master controls the sluices and gates. Call him on the VHF radio if you're unsure of anything.

3. Look out for signs

Most locks have a sill. Look out for signs or markings, especially when going down.

4. Tide guage

If you're unsure about the depth in the lock, you might have to use binoculars to read the gauge before you enter the lock chamber. It's often easier to call the lock master on your VHF radio.

The lock-keepers at my local marina have produced a DVD of clips from their CCTV cameras, built up from a seemingly endless procession of 'cock-ups'. Boat after boat is seen arriving full of hope, only to end up sideways-on, bouncing from wall to wall, or hung up by her cleats as the water level falls inexorably. Any old hand who watches starts out by laughing fit to bust, but ends up with a sneaking feeling of guilt at all the near misses he or she may have got away with.

The marina has a well-ordered lock generally patronised by responsible mariners. It's a very different story piling into a lock on the French coast at the top of a Spring tide with what feels like 100 other vessels, all queue-jumping, half of them without fenders, less with a rope handy and few indeed with any discernible plan of action. Small wonder that we treat locks with respect. Anyone who has yet to have the experience is bound to be wary.

What's the protocol? How do we secure, if at all? What's going to happen in there when the water starts dropping like a brick? These are all sensible questions, and there are many others. To answer them I went to my local marina and asked my friend Rex Woodgate, who deals with a lock every time he goes for a sail in his Hallberg-Rassy 36, to walk me through the essentials. There's no such thing as a typical lock, but many lessons learned here hold good for all.

5. Lock gates

Make sure you're clear of the gates when you tie up, but remember that other boats will probably want to come in astern of you. As the lock fills there may be some turbulence.

Tidal gates, such as this sill, require no special skills. You simply go through if it's open, or wait if it's not

How a lock works

Locks and tidal gates

It's important to understand the difference between a lock and a tide gate. A gate closes the entrance of what would otherwise be a drying harbour, usually at some pre-set time in the top half of the tide, to trap the water in and maintain a work-able depth inside. Entry hours are restricted, but depths are guaranteed.

A tide gate, be it an automatic 'flap' on a sill, or a full-on gate with hinges, requires no special skills from us. It is either open or shut, and nothing we can do will alter the status quo.

The gated lock

A lock with gates at each end allows the keeper to maintain the depth inside a harbour while letting boats enter and leave at all states of tide. Some locks with shallow approaches from seaward only open at set times

either side of High Water, but many are available 24 hours a day, seven days a week. If a boat arrives when the tide is lower than the level inside, the outer gate is opened and the lock is drained down to let her in. Once inside, both gates are closed and water is allowed to sluice into the lock from inside the harbour. When the levels have synchronised, the inner gate opens so that the boat, now floating at harbour level, can cruise in.

Sluices

Water isn't generally let in or out of a lock by opening the gates. Often, the pressure on them won't allow it, and even if it did, the resulting waterfall could render life untenable. Instead, the lock-keeper opens a door in the depths. This may be in the lock gate itself, or it might be a tunnel in the stonework. In some modern locks, the doors themselves rotate and, while still maintaining a tight seal, reveal open waterways at their edges

which serve as sluices.

With the sluices open, the boat experiences a degree of turbulence. This can be very noticeable, or, in some huge Dutch locks, where rises and falls are typically small, barely perceptible. When the levels are almost equal, the doors are often 'cracked' before being fully opened to speed up the equalisation.

Traffic lights and depth gauge at the entrance to a marina's sill gate

A gated lock. The lock has been filled up by the sluices and the inner pair of gates are opening

Water from the sluices (left and right) equalises the levels before the lock gates open

At this French lock, you slip your lines on bollards in the 65m-long basin. There's a friendly lockmaster to take your lines

PHOTO: TOM CUNLIFFE

How do you secure in a lock?

If you're lucky, the lock gates will already be open as you approach, offering a clear view of the arrangements inside via binoculars. A more typical scenario is for them to open at the last minute, with the set-up obscured by boats milling out. The object is to secure bow and stern alongside in such a way that you can control your lines. The walls may well be 20ft high or more, with slime thrown in free of charge. Rig fenders on both sides and be ready for any of these options:

Floating pontoons

This is the Rolls-Royce answer. A narrow floating pontoon, complete with cleats, rises and falls up one or both sides of the lock. Step off and get two lines on it.

Risers

Chains or heavy ropes – often plastic coated – are stretched vertically down the wall, secured at top and bottom. Pass your lines round the back of these and bring them back on board as slips. They should slide up and down with the rising water.

Flights

Where vessels must be raised considerable heights, several locks are run in series. Boats literally step up through them, lock by lock. Such flights of locks are rare for seagoing craft, but the Caledonian Canal is a notable exception. A skipper peeping for the first time over the parapet at the top of Neptune's Staircase (below) in the Western Highlands can only rub his eyes in disbelief. And yet, with gentle applications of power and a humble submission to the physics of gravity, it isn't long before he's safely down, ordering a morale-stiffening pint in the pub at the bottom.

This marina lock has both ready-rigged lines and risers

Ready-rigged free lines

Another convenient option is lines ready rigged for you and made fast at the top of the lock. Grab a couple and make up.

Dockside mateys

The huge lock at St Malo appears to have no means of securing at all, until a small figure appears halfway between you and the sun, tossing a line down. Be ready in big locks where nothing appears possible.

A dockside matey may well be just finishing his cigarette.

Ladders

Not a pleasing option for the elderly or infirm, some locks feature only ladders set into the wall, up which the most athletic crew member must swarm with a couple of lines to make fast on the quayside above.

Dutch bollards

In Holland, a truly professional country, locks often have bollards mounted in recesses in the wall. British yachtsmen generally scrabble their bow and stern lines onto these – lines are invariably rigged as slips in Holland – while the efficient Dutch carry special boathooks that drop the bight over and lead it back.

Free flow

Many locks stay open when levels inside and outside are close enough to knock out any serious currents around the gates. This 'free flow' period is the lock-bound sailor's delight because, while it lasts, the lock is effectively an open tide gate. Waiting a little while for free flow can save considerable hassle.

Rush hour fun in a big French lock during the summer holidays.

10 Steps to safe locking

Coming up to the marina lock from seaward, Rex took charge. I crewed while he walked me through the various factors to be considered, observing wryly that when he was a motor racing engineer he always used the smallest possible hammer, because it hurt less if he hit his thumb. 'Boat manoeuvring is just the same,' he said, 'keep it slow and use minimal revs – especially in locks!'

1 Call the lock

The first job was to call the lock-keeper on the VHF when we were close to the entry channel, not when still half an hour away. This allows a check on availability, and can also clear up any depth issues that may arise near Low Water. Check with the pilot book or almanac for the VHF channel used by the lock-keeper if you can't spot any signs. If the lock isn't busy, the response is likely to be, 'Come in when you see the green light.' If traffic is heavy, you may be asked to wait until called. Rex was very specific that if this happens, you must do as directed. Queue-jumping is generally considered un-British. In other countries, I have noticed that different conventions sometimes apply. Watch the locals and be ready to reveal the iron fist if need be.

If there is no sign of a VHF presence, motor up to the lock and hang around. Leaving harbour, call when you're ready to slip your berth.

2 Wind and current

Water often dribbles out of an open lock if the inner level is higher than in the approaches. With things the other way around, you can find yourself running in with a flowing tide, as it were. It therefore pays to opt to lay your favoured side onto the dock if there is any choice. If the lock is open to a broad fetch and the wind is onshore, this is doubly important. Wherever you are, watch out. The only bonus is that cross-sets are self-evident as usual, and where a strong breeze is blowing across a drained-down lock, you'll be delighted by how things quieten down once inside.

3 Positioning the boat

We didn't need to be told to take the Hallberg-Rassy right up to the end of the lock near the inbound gates. If traffic had been heavy and we'd parked in the middle, the keeper would certainly have leaned out and instructed us to move up. It's common courtesy and it makes sense.

4 Line handling
Rex kept a midships line handy for all eventualities, but pointed out that this particular lock has lines permanently rigged for crews to grab. As sole deckhand, I was directed forward with a boathook to hitch up a bow line, then walked aft to the stern, where I handed the second line to Rex to control. In our case, we knew which side we would be lying because the lock wasn't busy, but if things had been more hectic and we'd been using our own lines, we'd have rigged them on both sides to prepare for all eventualities.

5 No locking hitches
We now had one line each, secured out of reach up on the dock wall. We both knew the dire dangers of these locking up on our cleats if the lock level was due to drop. Indeed, if turbulence isn't excessive and the boat is not unduly heavy, there is much to be said for keeping them in hand. If a line locks on a cleat with the water level falling, the results speak for themselves. If your rope-work isn't above suspicion, at least make sure you have a sharp knife in your pocket.

6 Keep a bit of slack
Whether taking in slack as we rose, or letting it out as we fell on leaving, Rex was keen on keeping a bit of slack in the lines. Just enough to let her swim freely and not be pinned against the wall was the ticket, he said.

7 Risers and the midships cleat
Some locks also feature risers along the lock wall, and Rex showed me how, when singlehanded, he can slip his midships line round one of these and

Leave the lock as you would wish to find it. Ropes left dangling in the water can easily foul another boat's propeller.

take it back again, securing it very short indeed. As the boat rises or falls, the rope slides up and down without fouling, but he is doubly careful about how he makes it up on the cleat, just in case!

8 Fenders
Even though we knew which side we were going, Rex rigged fenders to port and starboard. This would protect our topsides should things not go as we'd hoped and we ended up coming into contact with the wrong side of the lock. If another boat rafted up at the last minute, we were ready

for her as well. My own experience in crowded locks calls for a roving fender and, where crew aren't in short supply, a crewman is instructed to watch for crunching bow rollers and other horrors that my insurers would rather I avoided.

9 Engine and radar off
A lock soon fills up with diesel fumes, so we turned off our engine once secure. Rex noted that it was a kindness to shut down the radar as well. Nobody wants to be zapped as well as suffocated. My own boat displaces over 20 tons and if turbulence is heavy I can't always control her manually as the lines go slack. If things look like getting out of hand, I start my engine and manoeuvre on the lines as gently as possible, but I only indulge myself like this if it's really necessary.

10 Leave in good order
When the gate finally opens, leave promptly. If it's crowded, have a chat with the other skippers and decide who's going first so that there's no confusion.

Passing the line around the cleat like this stops it jamming

Have fenders ready on both port and starboard sides

Easy anchoring

Concerns about dragged anchors cause some sailors to deny themselves the delights of a night spent in a beautiful and secluded spot. Get the basics right, however, and there's no need to worry

LEFT TO RIGHT: Martin, Tom and Jim choose a spot to drop the hook

Have you ever noticed that folk who don't actually go to sea are fascinated by those of us that do? The fact that we can sail over the horizon as masters and mistresses of our own destiny boggles the mind of the landlubber, which is why they tend to corner us at parties and ask: 'What do you do on passage at night? Do you anchor?'

Before wondering what planet these good folk come from, I have to remind myself of the numerous marina-based sailors who've come up with an almost equally daft query about lying in a sheltered bay.

'Do you set an anchor watch overnight?'

The answer is simple. 'No.'

I've spent well over a thousand nights lying to anchor and setting a watch is an extreme rarity, yet – always touching a large lump of teak – dragging anchor is not something I've made a habit of. Any ocean cruising sailor will say the same. Our anchors simply do not drag unless we've dropped them on to something stupid.

I recently met Jim McGuinness and Martin Lewis. The two friends sail together on Jim's Bavaria 36 and have been cruising the Channel for a few years now, but they've been a bit leery about turning in with the anchor down. I joined them to see if I could help them get a good night's sleep.

There was very little breeze as we set off to find somewhere to anchor. The light weather mattered not a jot, because our objective was to get right back to basics. Most people use their engine when anchoring and we wanted a realistic, helpful situation. It's simpler to produce a set-piece under power, too, so the conditions suited us well.

Shelter

Our choice was easy. The lower reaches of the harbour offered two obvious anchorages, and because there was no weather, either would do. Had it been blowing, we'd have selected the one that gave us shelter to windward. We were anticipating a sea breeze from the south or south-west, so we sounded in an area where shoal water extended west, as this would dampen wind-driven waves if it blew in from seawards.

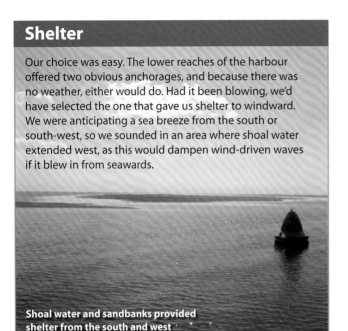

Shoal water and sandbanks provided shelter from the south and west

Open and shut anchorages

Our anchorage was exposed to the north so it was not a perfect all-weather spot. My wife never sleeps easily if she can see the sea, and there's a lot of sense in her position. It's not usually the wind that makes an anchorage untenable, it's the waves. All-round shelter offers peace of mind by killing these stone dead. On the other hand, so long as the wind is blowing offshore, a wide bay open to leeward will do equally well. A little swell may hook in, but the boat will be as safe as the owner's house.

Our spot was open to the north – no problem unless the wind swung round

Depth

If the water's going to be flat, you can theoretically anchor with an inch under your keel. However, two or three times your draught gives the cable more chance of damping the boat's surging around. Thereafter, you can anchor in any depth you like, so long as you've enough chain or rope for adequate scope.

Tidal height

As an examiner I've seen some convoluted ways of working out a safe depth to anchor on a rising or falling tide. In fact, this bogey-man is the easiest tidal calculation of them all.

Here it is:
> Grab yourself a tidal height curve, either from your chart plotter or the one you've worked out in your almanac.
> Note the time, and see how much the tide will fall between now and Low Water.
> Add this value to your draught, plus a clearance figure for safety at the bottom of the tide.
> Sound in until you find this depth, then go for it. Remember that the wind may swing through 180 degrees. Work out whether you'll have enough water if the breeze changes.
> If the tide's rising, peer over the top

of your graph to the next Low Water. Carry on as before.
> The only function served by soundings on the chart is to give you an overview of the shape of the bottom. The depth you need in real life is the actual one on your sounder.

Trust your sounder, not your chart

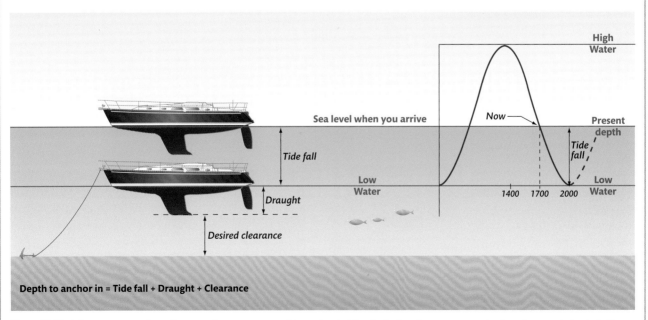

Depth to anchor in = Tide fall + Draught + Clearance

Use a tidal height curve to work out how much water you need to anchor in. They're in the almanacs or can be found on most chart plotters

33

Holding ground

The chart promised fine sand and mud out in the channel. The nearby beach looked lovely, and sand was what we got. Reasonable holding and clean chain when we weighed after lunch. The only times I've dragged my own anchors are when I've been obliged to lay them on hard substrates such as rock or coral. You can hear them rumbling over the ground down below, and you've only yourself to blame. The nature of the bottom is generally stated on Admiralty charts (though not on all electronic ones), so get to know what those tiny letters mean;

> M = mud – a safe, dirty option
> S = sand – more friendly, and clean
> St = stones – not a favourite
> And so on…

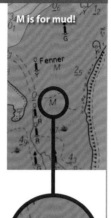

M is for mud!

Contingency plans

There's no doubt that if an anchorage has an open side, Sod's Law will prevail and the breeze will come blasting merrily in. Unless your anchorage is of the type favoured by Mrs Cunliffe (no sea in view and shelter all around), it pays to consider what you'll do if the wind takes a turn for the worse.

Had we been staying in this anchorage with a possibility of the wind blowing in northerly, I'd have worked out a pilotage plan to get me up to my alternative anchorage. I know for a fact – because I had to do exactly this a couple of years back – that the half-tide shoals up there would give me all the shelter I need. It's important that the plan can be executed in darkness and that the deck is left ready for weighing anchor when you'd prefer to be in your bunk.

Work out where to go if the wind direction changes

Ground tackle and scope

In chain we trust

I was encouraged to see that Jim's Bavaria featured a sensible-sized hook and enough chain to be serious about anchoring. The deep waters in many parts of the world make nonsense out of Mickey Mouse ground tackle. Typically, anyone cruising the English Channel, especially on the French side with its huge tides, really needs at least 45m of chain cable. This allows a 3:1 scope with a bit to spare at the top of an 11m tide in a charted depth of 3m. In such depths, 3:1 is generally adequate, although in shallower water, 4:1 may be preferred. Personally, I carry 55m. Even if you plan only to anchor in 10m, on a filthy night you'll be craving a 5:1 scope of cable. Less than this and you won't deserve any sleep! If you're using rope, 7:1 is a good rule of thumb when it's blowing hard.

Other anchored craft

It was no surprise to find a dozen yachts in this anchorage. I was pleased to see them because it laid the responsibility on us to find a deep enough spot out of the main channel, with enough clearance not to cause our neighbours any anxiety. If the yachts are all wind-rode, the trick is generally to nudge up halfway between two likely boats and let go on the imaginary line joining their sterns. Where tidal stream is an issue, allow more space to take account of what may befall when the tide turns. Pick yachts as similar to your own as you can and, if you're using chain, beware of the yacht on rope. Her scope may exceed yours by a substantial factor.

We dropped the hook between the two yachts

Cleating chain

If you're pre-planning a length of cable, always make the bight fast so that you can ease more out if need be. It's not uncommon for a loose cable to be secured to the cleat 'upside down' before anchoring. When the weight comes on, it then pulls on the top of the belay and you're well and truly stuck. Basic seamanship, but chain can munch fingers if you get it wrong.

Will you be able to take the chain off the cleat?

The bitter end

Secure the bitter end of the chain tied off

Make sure the inboard bitter end of the chain is tied off securely. If the the worst happens and all the chain goes over you won't want to lose the lot. Tie off the end with webbing or strong line so that you can cut it clear if you need to buoy the anchor and leave in a hurry.

Laying the anchor

This is the crunch of the whole operation. Dig a decent-sized anchor well in, on enough cable, and your troubles are over. Allow it to do what it likes, and a disturbed and expensive night may be your portion.

❯ Decide on scope and prepare the cable. If, like Jim and Martin, you've no windlass, lay out the chosen length of cable along the sidedeck. I had a measured length of deck on one of my boats: 'a fathom from the forward window to the cleat.'

❯ Prepare the anchor so it's ready to go 'on the word'.

❯ Bring the boat to the spot you've chosen and take off all way.

❯ Let go the anchor and lower it under the tightest control the crew can muster. If this is impracticable because of weight or depth, have them do their best.

❯ When it hits the seabed, motor steadily away astern (or let the tide/wind take you) as the foredeck crew pays out cable in a line along the bottom. When the required length has passed over the windlass or the cleated bight is reached, take off power and let the boat's way carry her on astern.

❯ Soon, she'll be brought up, either by the anchor beginning to 'take' or by a bight of chain dragging on the seabed. At this point, go slow astern

A post and the trees behind were a useful transit

once more. You'll note the boat begin to gather way, then falter again. At this point, she's digging in the pick.

❯ Keep slow astern and watch transits abeam: this can be any two objects lined up behind one another. I was looking to see how a channel marker lined up with the edge of a copse of trees behind. Wait for the point when she actually loses all way with the engine still engaged. The hook is now almost certainly into the bottom.

❯ Increase revs to around half astern, watching your transits. They may move a little, but if the anchor's OK they'll stabilise again very soon. At this point,

you are literally working the anchor flukes deep into the seabed. The crew should be watching the cable for any 'jumping' (bad news). If the hook holds with this amount of power on, it's going to take more than a gust of wind to pull it out.

❯ Once you're satisfied, take the revs off slowly so that the boat doesn't bounce back over the anchor.

❯ Hang up your anchor ball. Set the riding light at sunset and settle in for a stress-free night. Your worries are over.

Check the chain doesn't jump as the anchor is dug in

Lay chain out along the sidedeck

Checking for drag

As we went below for lunch, Jim suggested activating the GPS anchor alarm to let us know if we moved out of an area that he could set with a couple of button presses. Here's my response: The first premise is that the pick has been properly dug in. The second is that if you're on deck you generally know when a boat's dragging because when her bow falls off the wind it doesn't come back up again. You shouldn't be going below until you're happy all is well, but there are times when further reference is required.

Compass bearing – The

traditional method is to take a bearing on a fixed object and make sure it doesn't move. This is sound, but cumbersome, and it's far less accurate than a transit. Its main use for yachts is on a dark night where the only reference point is the odd light ashore that can't be lined up.

GPS – The best practical value I can think of for these alarms is in a wide bay with a lot of sea behind you. If you dragged in the night, its call would save the disappointment of waking in the morning to find yourself 30 miles out to sea. In a

tight anchorage, you're obliged to set the alarm's limits very tight to alert you to the possibility of hitting other craft. It would then wake you up every time you swung. Who needs that? Better to dig the hook well in, turn the thing off and save power.

Transit – The seaman's answer. Line up any two objects ashore that come at right-angles to the direction you're concerned about dragging. If they move, wait for them to come back in line. If they don't, haul up and start over – get cracking at the windlass!

Conclusion

When it comes to successful anchoring, it pays to cut right back to basics. The Bavaria had an excellent anchor and plenty of chain. I'd have been happy lying to them in a gale of wind so long as we were in the right place. Peace of mind comes down to five factors: Good tackle (as much of it and as heavy as you can stow), a sound choice of anchorage for the conditions, a workable contingency plan for a nasty turn in the weather, a well-dug-in hook and a good set of transits.

Mooring under sail

Boat handling in close quarters under sail can be a satisfying experience, and a useful skill, too. It is one that is rarely practised today, however, as we become ever more reliant on our engines

I always think that boat handling under sail in close quarters is one of the most satisfying aspects of yachting. Steve Osgood gave me the perfect opportunity to tackle some of these skills head-on when he invited me aboard his Contessa 28, *Cicada*. Steve is semi-retired and enjoys a challenge in his well-sorted boat. He and I had planned to cover a good deal of ground during our day on the water, and, in particular, look at the issues that arose while working in the vicinity of his swinging mooring.

Like all Contessas, *Cicada* showed herself to be remarkably well mannered. During the day, I experimented with all sorts of nasty, underhand tactics to make her lose her cool and I failed delightfully. For anyone who just wants to cruise the coast, she'd be a hard boat to beat.

The Force 4 that was forecast never materialised, but we still turned up enough breeze to make the points we needed, and everything described here would hold true in stronger conditions. When it comes to tide, the harbour we were sailing in has a tiny range (1m on the day), but a tight entrance and a huge surface area make for strong streams whose timing is hard to predict, especially around High Water.

Steve is an experienced sailor who has served his apprenticeship on dinghies, so he understood the theory of what we were about to take on. Like many of us, however, the transition to larger boats with reliable engines has left him less willing to sail into tight situations than his history might suggest. This is quite common, and I suspect it results from skippers not making the time to analyse the intuitive skills that they may well possess, so we began by discussing the nitty gritty of boat control.

Sailing slowly

Taking off way in a standard fore-and-aft-rigged yacht depends on removing power from the rig. This can be tackled by three actions: spilling wind, shortening sail, or a combination of the two.

Spilling wind – headsail

This is easy because a headsail can ditch air on any point of sailing. Just ease the sheet until the sail starts to collapse and the boat slows down.

Spilling wind – mainsail

Not quite so simple. If you try to spill the main with the wind on or abaft the beam, the sail fetches up hard against the shrouds and remains full of wind. On a close reach or close-hauled, however, the main can tip out the breeze at will. If a beamy sort of wind is leaving the leech hung up on the shrouds and full, letting the kicker off ('dumping' it) can some-times make the difference.

Shortening the mainsail

This is easy on a gaff-rigged yacht because by dropping the peak you can lose up to a third of your area in an instant. 'Tricing up your tack' has a similar result. Bermudan rigs have to be reefed in advance unless the kicker can be eased right off and the

Steve Osgood gets set to sail

topping lift hauled in to scandalise the sail.

Shortening the headsail

Today's roller headsails are highly flexible in this respect. Rolling away all or part of a genoa is often more effective than spilling wind from it, as proved the case with us on more than one occasion.

Stalling the keel

A yacht's keel only really prevents her tendency to slide sideways when she is moving comfortably ahead. When her speed falls below a critical point, the keel stalls and she will begin to slip to leeward. The symptom is 'lee helm' (having to

shove the tiller to leeward – wheel to weather – to keep her going straight). It is vital to understand and recognise this effect, because a controlled stall is a powerful tool. Once the boat is travelling at sub-stalling speeds the only way to steer her is usually with the sails as well as the rudder.

Steering with the sails

When a boat has almost stopped she can be persuaded to luff up (come closer to the wind) by heaving in the mainsheet and letting fly the jib. Similarly, if the jib is hardened and the mainsheet eased compre-hensively, she will be more willing to bear away from the breeze. A boat moving at normal speed is still governed by these factors to some extent, but once the keel is working properly they are less pronounced. The exception is when an ill-balanced boat takes a gust of wind and rounds up to weather. Dumping power from the mainsail is the only way to correct this.

1. Leaving the mooring

Steve's mooring lies among a clutch of others, all of which are occupied. When we first left, the last of the flood tide was running with a gentle wind. Under these circumstances, any boat will lie head to wind on her mooring, so the main can be hoisted. The question, however, was whether *Cicada* would manage to bear away before she slid into one of her neighbours close abeam. If she could gather way quickly enough to beat the stall, the answer would be 'yes'. If not, we needed another means of being sure of making the turn. We didn't know the answer so we opted to steer with the sails, grabbing what help we could from the rudder as we accelerated.

Because bearing away was the keyword, we

overhauled (pulled out) the mainsheet until it was fully slack. This meant that as the bow swung to leeward, the main would not be able to draw and try to make the boat luff. Next, we unrolled about half the genoa and, as Steve let slip the buoy, I sheeted it hard aback to starboard. The wind caught it and forced the head away to port, the main could not fill, so the boat kept right on bearing away until the wind was abaft the beam. Now the main drew, but by this time we were safely pointing astern of the boat abeam of us and away we went.

Conclusion

Always give plenty of thought to what the sails will do to the steering if space is tight.

Wind

Tide

Get set to unfurl the genoa after first letting the mainsheet right off so that the mainsail will not fill

Backed genoa

Mainsail not drawing

With the main loose and the genoa backed to starboard, Steve lets slip the buoy

The bow is blown off the wind, the boat heads astern her neighbour and the main can now be sheeted in

2. Picking up the mooring, wind against tide

After sailing off, we toddled around the moorings for a few minutes sorting out our gear, then went back to pick it up again. It had seemed reasonable that this would be a straightforward wind-with-tide pick-up, but no. As we both would normally have done for such a scenario, we rolled away most of the genoa and approached largely under main through a likely gap in the boats. It didn't take long to see that we had boobed. Although the other craft hadn't yet really swung, the tide had in fact turned and we were in a wind-against-tide situation. As I luffed up to stop the boat on the

buoy, she kept right on going and Steve could only watch as the buoy went by. He could have grabbed it, but if he'd been successful, the boat would have lurched round head to tide and filled her main, an ugly situation that can lead to big trouble in a hard wind. So we let it go and tried again.

The second time around, we dropped our main on a close reach, away from the moorings, and approached up-tide and downwind, under genoa only. Letting this fly as we got closer it was clear that the windage of the flapping sail would carry us past, so we rolled it away altogether and picked up our buoy under bare poles.

Conclusion – This is the sort of classic that a Yachtmaster examiner dreams of. Any attempt to pick up a buoy 'wind-against-tide' with the mainsail up is doomed to failure or, at best, a messy cobble-up. The only answer is to drop it. If the wind is going to be across the boat when she is head to tide, the same rules apply so, if in doubt, always drop the main. Finally, in a modern boat with a roller headsail, there is no harm in floating around the harbour with no sail set at all. You can always unfurl some if you need it, and the best way of taking off way downwind is to divest yourself of the sail altogether, as we did.

The main is dropped in preparation for another approach upwind and down tide under genoa alone

The genoa sheet is adjusted to control the speed of approach

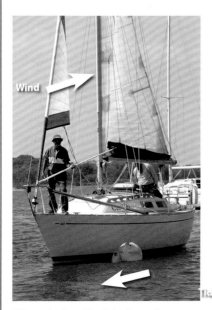

If Steve had grabbed the buoy the boat would have lurched round head to tide and filled her main

The last of genoa is wound in as *Cicada* approaches her mooring downwind and against the tide

3. Slipping the buoy, wind against tide

Leaving again after a cup of tea was far easier than the first time. We now had wind against tide, which, in most situations, is actually the easiest combination for a Bermudan sloop with a roller headsail.

Hoisting the main was an obvious non-starter with the wind abaft the beam, so we considered unrolling some jib before slipping.

We ditched this idea on the grounds that the flapping sail would inconvenience Steve on the foredeck. Instead, he simply let go the mooring and I

used the fact that the boat was already making way through the water (her speed when moored stationary in the flowing tide) to steer her while he came aft. We then quietly unrolled the genoa, sailed clear of the moorings, luffed up to a close reach and hoisted the main at our leisure. Easy as pie.

It's a common misconception to think that the boat must be head to wind to hoist the main. Any point of sailing where the main can flap is OK; the close reach is favoured as it maintains full control throughout.

4. Picking up a mooring with a strong tide

Tide

The yachts are lying to the tide with the wind on their starboard bow as Tom approaches the mooring from abeam. He plays the mainsail to control *Cicada*'s speed

The final pick-up was with a light breeze and a strong tide, and it was tailor-made for an enjoyable piece of boat handling. The trick here was to slide sideways, or ferry-glide, though the moorings, rather than try to power up from leeward, where the tide might have the last word. We approached from beam-on between two boats, then literally slid sideways over the bottom, under mainsail only, powering up or spilling wind to trickle back or drive forward.

We approach abeam the mooring, sliding between two neighbours, spilling wind so as not to fore-reach on our destination.

Now we have a challenge. The mooring is abaft the beam. Should we bear away,

inevitably filling the main and accelerating, ought we to spill, or even come almost head to wind to lose way? Answer: the second option – keeping just enough speed up to be able to steer. The boat drops back sweetly. If we'd borne away we would have blown the manoeuvre by powering up too much.

We're almost ready to pick up now, but we've lost so much way that we're falling back, so we pull in the mainsheet and bear off just enough to fill the sail and get going again.

Conclusion – Ferry-gliding is a skill worth practising. It's useful with the engine, too, but under sail, the confidence to carry it out makes all the difference in a tideway.

He's overdone it and needs to drop down. He pushes the helm over, luffs up the boat and with the mainsail flapping the tide carries her down

Now Tom can sheet the main in again and allow *Cicada* to ferry-glide onto the buoy

Tom gives the mainsheet a final tweak to keep the Contessa 28 driving forward so that there's some slack on the mooring line as Steve makes it fast

**LEFT: The tide running against the rudder gives *Cicada* enough steerage for the helmsman to steer away from the buoy.
ABOVE: The genoa is unfurled once Steve is clear of the foredeck**

ABOVE: After finding some open water, *Cicada* is luffed up onto a close reach and the mainsail hoisted

Anchoring under sail and power

Anchoring opens up endless possibilites to explore new places, but is all too often rejected in favour of marinas. However, it is an important aspect of boat handling that should not be forgotten

Before there were marinas, anchoring was a routine matter that nobody thought anything about. The same is true today in the ocean cruising world, yet there is a widespread and growing mistrust of it among those who have the choice not to do it.

Recently, my wife and I were totting up how many nights we have spent lying to our own ground tackle. We stopped counting when the total ran into four figures. I can add up on one hand the number of times we have dragged, and still have a finger or two to spare. We very rarely lay out more than one anchor, and we haven't kept all-night watch on more than half a dozen occasions.

Anchoring opens up endless possibilities for exploring new places. And it's a shame to miss out because of unwarranted doubts. Given good gear and a seamanlike approach, it's often safer than picking up a mooring of unknown quality, while a snug berth swinging behind a solid lee is far preferable to lying alongside with a gale blowing you on. Anchoring under sail and power is an important area of boat handling that causes increasing uncertainty as marinas proliferate. Following our success at picking up a mooring under sail (see above), Steve Osgood was keen to brush up on his anchoring skills, too, on board his Contessa 28, *Cicada*, and I was only too willing to help.

Good ground tackle

I've seen yachts with such pathetic equipment issued as standard by the builder that they may as well have shipped a cod hook with toilet chain as cable.

As a rule of thumb, my experience has been that for medium-range work, a heavy 32-footer needs a 35 lb CQR (or equivalent) and a minimum of 50m of 3/8in chain. You can scale this to suit your boat, but if a different authority suggests a lighter specification, treat it with suspicion. I have never taken part in a test operation, nor applied science to the issue, but I have watched many a yacht drag, and I know for sure that my spec will deliver peaceful nights while the gales roar overhead.

Where light-displacement yachts are compromised by such a weight of cable, they will be obliged to use a much longer rope with a length of chain at the business end to keep the anchor down and deal with chafe. On the subject of weight, it's been an axiom of yacht design for well over a century that this is to be kept out of the ends of the boat. However, modern manufacturers often leave owners with little choice but to stow chain right in the eyes of the ship. This leads to a lack of stomach for carrying enough cable. I'll say no more…

Types of seabed

Given good ground tackle and sensible shelter, the third factor in successful anchoring is the right sort of seabed. Some anchors are better than others in varying substrates, but one or two universal truths hold good.

No anchor will take on rock and coral, unless your flukes somehow grab a lucky bite in a hole, in which case you'll probably never get it up again. Weed in general, and kelp in particular, are also bad news. Very few yachts use big fisherman anchors, but these are the only things that can penetrate kelp reliably. The toy fishermen sold as 'kedges' are for pub walls only.

Regardless of your choice of hook, you are looking for something reasonably firm for it to dig into. Clean sand, mud (not too soft) or, ideally, clay are favourites. The info is usually on the chart.

The chart should tell you what the bottom's like

Types of anchor

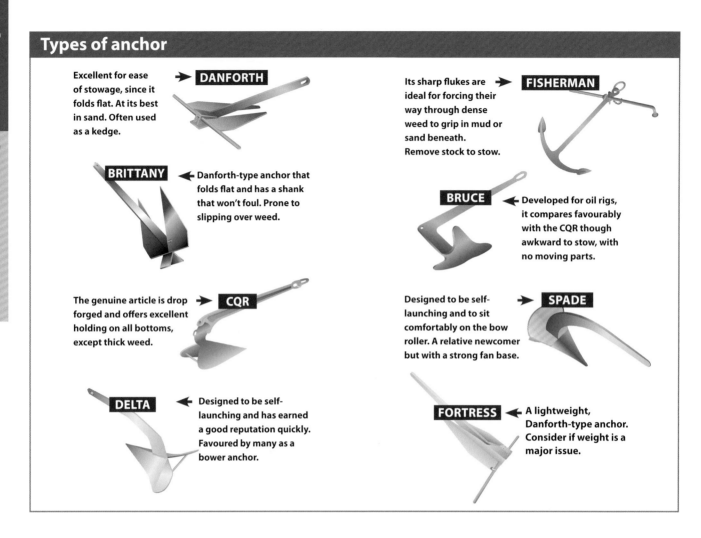

DANFORTH Excellent for ease of stowage, since it folds flat. At its best in sand. Often used as a kedge.

BRITTANY Danforth-type anchor that folds flat and has a shank that won't foul. Prone to slipping over weed.

CQR The genuine article is drop forged and offers excellent holding on all bottoms, except thick weed.

DELTA Designed to be self-launching and has earned a good reputation quickly. Favoured by many as a bower anchor.

FISHERMAN Its sharp flukes are ideal for forcing their way through dense weed to grip in mud or sand beneath. Remove stock to stow.

BRUCE Developed for oil rigs, it compares favourably with the CQR though awkward to stow, with no moving parts.

SPADE Designed to be self-launching and to sit comfortably on the bow roller. A relative newcomer but with a strong fan base.

FORTRESS A lightweight, Danforth-type anchor. Consider if weight is a major issue.

Scope

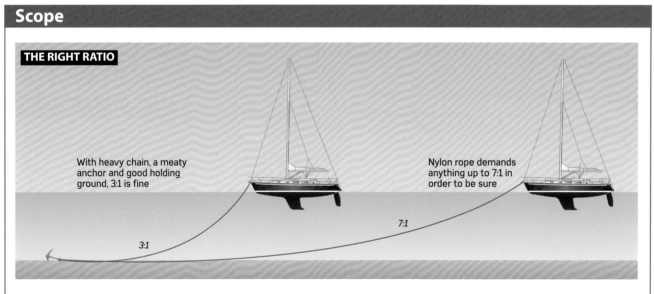

THE RIGHT RATIO

With heavy chain, a meaty anchor and good holding ground, 3:1 is fine

3:1

Nylon rope demands anything up to 7:1 in order to be sure

7:1

Endless discussion surrounds the issue of how much cable to lay. In practice, this depends on circumstances, but with heavy chain, a meaty anchor and good holding ground, 3:1 is fine – always assuming it is adjusted for tidal rise! A figure of 4:1 is quoted by many authorities. This certainly makes sense in stronger winds, but I have found that three is usually sufficient. It isn't enough if the gear is too light, however, and if you expect a blow, the more scope you lay the merrier you will be. Nylon rope demands anything up to 7:1 in order to be sure. Of course, it doesn't matter what you use if it all goes down in a heap.

Digging in the anchor under power

The same basic rules apply to anchoring under power as to mooring. Come in up-tide or up-wind, at the same angle as you expect to lie when the manoeuvre is finished.

Cicada is kitted up with excellent ground tackle and, in the absence of a windlass, Steve flaked out enough chain for a 3:1 scope of cable (three times the depth of water). When I had taken off all way, Steve lowered the hook, signalling as he felt it hit the bottom in 5m. I went slowly astern as he laid the rest of the cable in a straight line along the seabed, then I popped the engine out of gear and let the boat's weight give the anchor its initial bite.

As soon as her head swung a touch to the cable, I put her slow astern and Steve monitored the chain as it rose steadily out of the water. It dipped once as the pick took a better hold, then we stopped moving again. At this point, I increased revs to 'half astern'. My shipmate watched to see if the cable faltered while I checked a transit I had found abeam. The transit stayed put and the foredeck reported all well, so I throttled back a bit and let the boat creep ahead as the cable took up its natural catenary.

Only when the boat was stable did I shut down the engine, so as to prevent her from 'bouncing' back over the anchor and dragging our carefully laid chain into a heap in the process. We could safely have spent the night here with no worries at all.

Take a transit abeam when the hook's dug in to make sure it's not jumping

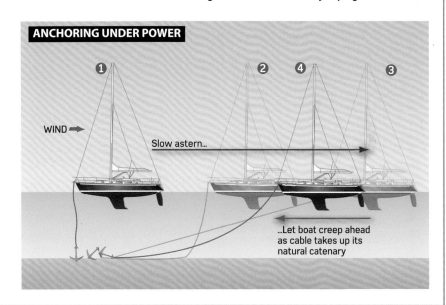

Breaking out the anchor under power

Rather than 'busting a gut' to pull out the anchor, which was well dug-in, we shortened the scope as far as we could, then motored hard astern. This flipped it clear with no nasty side effects. If we'd motored ahead over it, the anchor would have broken out all right, but we'd have crunched the cable along our topsides and even risked it interfering with the propeller. Much tidier to go astern.

Pushing the throttle to hard astern was enough to break out the anchor

Anchoring under sail

Wind with tide or no tide: As we had no tide, once the breeze returned, the easy option for anchoring under sail was to approach under main only, keeping the foredeck clear for Steve to work. The problem with this in practice is always that as soon as way comes off and you let go the anchor, the yacht's head falls to leeward. In extreme cases, the sail fills and chaos results. One answer is to drop the main as you let go the anchor. This is fine on a windy day because the boat's weight falling back will be enough to dig it in. In light weather, this doesn't happen. To be certain it has taken hold, the best answer is to sail astern.

A crew of three is ideal for this, but we had to manage with the two of us. As Steve let go the hook head-to-wind, I hopped up and backed the main by shoving the boom hard out. Had I been able to reach the helm, I could have steered her astern to keep the sail aback. As it was, I had to do an untidy jack-in-the-box act between boom and tiller. In the end we did have to change tack, as it were, but we made it and Steve reported a good solid 'clunk' from the cable as it took up. The transits stayed on and we boiled up the kettle.

Wind against tide: Sadly, we didn't get the option to do this. If we had, we'd have dropped the main and come in up-tide under headsail, spilling wind to control our way over the ground. If we'd not been able to stop, we'd have rolled away the headsail and done it under bare poles. Once stationary over the bottom we'd let go the anchor and pay out cable as the tide carried us away. Digging in can be dodgy with wind against tide, so care is needed to watch the transits until the tide turns and everything settles down.

ABOVE: Steve lets the anchor go as the helmsman releases the mainsheet and prepares to push the boom out. BELOW: Tom holds out the boom until *Cicada* gathers some way astern

Backed mainsail

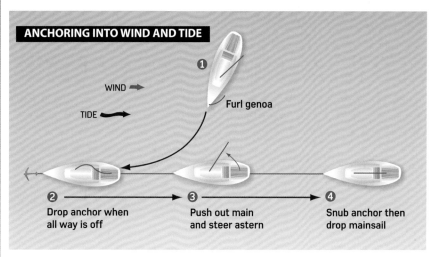

ANCHORING INTO WIND AND TIDE

WIND

TIDE

① Furl genoa

② Drop anchor when all way is off

③ Push out main and steer astern

④ Snub anchor then drop mainsail

A hand for the boom and a foot for the tiller as *Cicada* is steered astern

Weighing anchor under sail

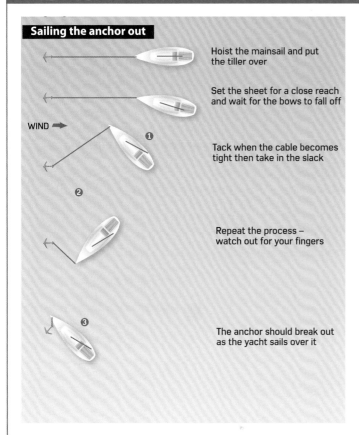

Sailing the anchor out

WIND ➡

Hoist the mainsail and put the tiller over

Set the sheet for a close reach and wait for the bows to fall off

① Tack when the cable becomes tight then take in the slack

②

Repeat the process – watch out for your fingers

③ The anchor should break out as the yacht sails over it

Steve gets set to haul in the cable as the boat starts to sail

Tom pushes the tiller over as Steve snubs the cable

Steve holds tight as *Cicada* sails over her anchor, breaking it free

In our tide-free conditions, we were lying head-to-wind. We therefore had no difficulty hoisting the main before we started weighing. Nothing was likely to happen to bring the wind abaft the beam and embarrass us, so this was the sensible thing to do. *Cicada* is not fitted with a windlass so we didn't have the option of simply cranking ourselves up to the hook, breaking it out and sailing away. The wind was theoretically light enough for Steve to heave us up to the hook, but we were digesting an excellent lunch, so we opted to sail it out instead.

The main was sheeted for a close reach and we waited until the head paid off far enough to fill the sail. I then hove the helm up to weather and *Cicada* gathered way out to one side of the anchor. After a few seconds, the cable came tight, Steve caught a turn and I encouraged her to come about using the helm. As she picked up on the new tack, Steve gathered the slack in the cable. As soon as it looked like taking charge, he snubbed it again and we repeated the process. Three tacks was enough to see *Cicada* sail across her anchor and pluck it clean out of the bottom. The technique works just as well in a hard wind, but watch your fingers on the foredeck!

With wind against tide, it may be necessary to pull up the anchor with no sail set at all, then unroll some genoa once it's free.

Conclusion

Anchoring under power or sail should present no problems for a well-found cruiser. With good kit, the right place, and due care in setting the anchor, there is no reason why a crew should not be able to enjoy 'all night in' with total confidence.

Taming your ropes

We all like to think we 'know the ropes' – but mediocre ropework is the Achilles' heel of many a seasoned sailor. Tangled lines are so often the root cause of stress, panic and accidents aboard...

Rope is our primary tool. It has been the seaman's friend and joy since someone first laid up a few lengths of horsehair to hoist a reindeer skin on his log. It converts the power of sails into forward motion, it secures boats to the dock, it hoists us aloft and, in many cases, it provides the vital link between ship and anchor. To perform to its full potential, it deserves a bit of care.

You can always gauge the true measure of a sailor by looking at the lines on his deck. The ropes are stowed with pride. They're neat and ready for action, and they may even look decorative into the bargain. At the other end of the scale is a cockpit like a snake's wedding. To high-light the difference, I haven't gone sailing on a specific yacht as I have done for most of this book. There's no need. These are basic truths that apply to every boat, whether she's light, heavy, old, or fresh out of the builder's yard.

The RYA Yachtmaster syllabus reflects the times we live in, and changes introduced over the years have generally kept in line with developments on the water. Not all the modifications are winners, however. The ageless skill of whipping a loose end has disappeared somewhere, and the requirement to execute even a simple eye splice has also vanished. The next few pages are about stowing cordage, not sorting out the ends, but the implication is clear: The sailor of today apparently has more important things to do than fiddle about with rope. I beg to differ, and I'll bet plenty would agree with me.

Rope must be treated with respect. It is more than just stuff that ties things together, and you need special expertise to handle it effectively.

Coil clockwise

Three-strand rope

My first coiling instructor was my mother, who taught me to stow the clothes line long before I'd achieved school age. Her technique was to catch one end between her thumb and forefinger, then force the coils around her elbow. The technique worked, more or less, but the coil took on a sort of cross-over look in the middle. Her method will never be any good, because it forces the rope to go where it may not wish to follow, and it takes no account of which way it is being turned.

Any three-strand rope you're likely to find today is laid up 'clockwise', or right-handed. It has an in-built 'memory' that encourages it to turn in this direction – to the right, following the hands of a clock or, as northern hemisphere sailors said before clock faces were invented, turning with the sun. Try to force it against this and it will fight all the way. Even if you subdue it, it will come off the coil in a series of kinks just to spite you, so always coil three-strand clockwise.

Three-strand rope is laid up clockwise

Braidline

Much of a modern yacht's running rigging is braidline, with a thin, braided cover that protects and holds together a core of strong but loosely woven fibres. Unlike three-strand, it has no directional 'memory' and can be coiled either way. However, a real sailor would have to think twice before trying to coil anti-clockwise, so why not just coil everything right-handed? If ever you find yourself on a traditional boat with long, three-strand halyards, you'll be glad you bought into the ancient system of the sea.

MAIN PICS: You can tell a lot about a skipper from his ropes INSET: Every sailor should be able to execute a neat gasket coil

Stowing ropes in general

Most people's favourite stow for cordage such as sheets and modest shorelines is the square-rigged seaman's 'gasket coil hitch'. I've seen all sorts of methods for more or less achieving this, but only three really succeed. The good techniques leave the rope ready for use, they look great and they never come unravelled. The dodgy coils come unravelled easily, whether they're in the rope locker or on the foredeck.

The cornerstone of rope stowage

Stand-alone gasket coil hitch

1 Make up the clockwise coil, then take the whole thing in your left hand and squeeze it together into a sausage shape. Whether you can physically do this or not determines whether the hitch is appropriate for the rope in question and your hand size. If it's too big, go straight to the page opposite and use Captain Avellar's method! With your right hand, take hold of the last coil (or maybe the last two) as it comes up from the bottom of the sausage.

2 Lead its end clean around the sausage a bit more than halfway up and start frapping (wrapping) round and round towards the top. Nip the first turn in with the second, nice and tight, to hold it together. In fact, keep all the turns tight.

3 When you're a few ropes' widths from the top, there should be a foot or so of line left to play with. If there isn't, start again until you find the right proportions. This takes a bit of practice, but it's well worth the trouble. Even experts occasionally have to go back to the beginning.

4 Now comes the clever bit. Lead a bight (a loop) of what's left through the hole in the top of the sausage, Fold it back across the upper end, snug it down, then pull it tight with the very end. You've actually formed a cow hitch, but there's no need to worry about that. The important thing is that the coil will hold together no matter how it is kicked around.

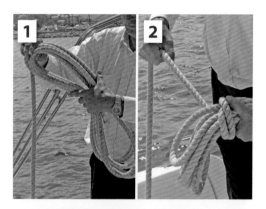

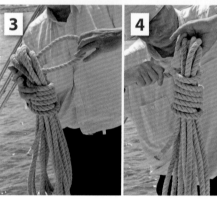

Neat, secure and ready in a flash

Gasket coil for a working rope

This is the trickiest of the three gasket coil hitches, but it is guaranteed to hold together even on a wave-swept foredeck, and with practice it comes as naturally as breathing. It serves for anything led aft if there is no more convenient way of stowing it, and for anything forward that's not a halyard requiring instant release. Classic examples are a reefing pennant coming out of the boom at the gooseneck or a semi-permanent roller genoa halyard at the mast.

❯ Take the line in your hand a few feet from where it is made fast or jammed off. Coil it towards the bitter end in the usual way.

❯ Now, hold the coil in your left hand and do the usual sausage trick, but don't wrap the bitter end around it as you'd assume. Instead, use the part that lies between the coil and the jammer, and wrap that around the coil instead. You'll be lucky to get more than a single turn on and nipped before what's left starts to kink horribly, so if more than a couple of wraps are required you'll have to 'wind' the whole coil in towards the jammer.

❯ When you're nearly there, shove a bight of what's left between the coil and the jammer or cleat through the last of the coil and bring it all the way over the top, as in the basic hitch. Pull it tight by heaving the coil away from the jammer and you've cracked it.

Hanging gasket coil

This is the same in principle as the basic gasket coil hitch. The last bit is different, however, and leaves a clear rope's end on which to hang up the coil – very pretty and seamanlike, too.

1 Start and continue as before with the sausage-shaped coil, passing the bight through the gap at the top of the turns.

2 Instead of looping the bight back all the way over the top then pulling tight, only bring it halfway, so that it stops at 'top dead centre'.

3 Now pass the end you've been working with through the bight and pull this tight instead. The end is now free to hang the coil up. Great for mainsheets!

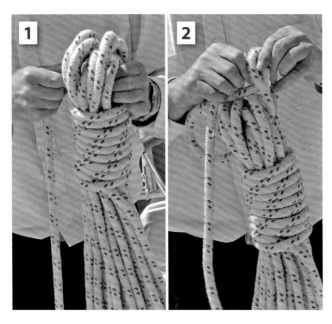

Hanging coil keeps your cockpit tidy and lets sheets drip-dry

If it's too thick to coil in hand, turn to Captain Avellar

Captain Avellar's method for larger ropes

I learned much of my deck seamanship in America from my first skipper, an ex-Grand Banks fisherman of Portuguese extraction who knew more about the sea than most of us. His name was Justin Avellar. Here's how he coiled our schooner's shorelines. I use the same method today for any rope that's too big to coil readily into my hand.

❯ Coil the rope clockwise onto the deck. This is a modest skill well worth acquiring, especially for those with smaller hands.

❯ When the coil is made, take one end and pass it under and around a single 'leg' of the coil. Don't try to bring the coil together into a sausage.

❯ As the end comes up from behind the parts of the coil, pass it under itself to form the first part of a clove hitch.

❯ Now pass it around one more time in the same direction, nip this turn on itself just as you did the first, and you've completed a simple clove hitch around the leg of the coil, as shown.

Captain Avellar's hitch is so easy to execute that it is very popular with my crews, but it's hard to describe in words. Look carefully at the pictures, especially the one above. The end result and the obvious clove hitch says it all.

Flaking ropes

A coil is without doubt the best way to stow a rope, whether it be a shoreline or a halyard. When the rope is required, a good coil is in with a fair chance of running cleanly right to the end, but in reality it's hard to guarantee this. We don't all have the skills of a 19th-century Nantucket whaler stowing his harpoon line into a basket, and not all rope runs as sweetly as we'd like. The answer is flaking, or 'faking' as it was sometimes traditionally known. The technique is simple and invariably effective.

Basic flake

Before letting go a halyard, for example, if a clear run is demanded, dump the coil on deck with the bitter end on top.

Grab hold of this and lay it on deck in front of you. Now run the rope through your hands, dropping it into a casual pile without forcing it to go in any direction. The part made fast, from which the rope will have to run first, thus ends up on top. The only refinement is to make sure the bitter end is left a short distance clear of the general pile of line so that it cannot be caught up and swept through a running loop.

Formal flake

While the 'useful heap' of the basic flake serves in most circumstances, if there's any doubt that it might not, or the system offends your standards of tidiness, a formal flake is achieved by laying the line onto its bitter end in a series of figures-of-eight. The opposing turns negate any lay or memory the rope may have and ensure a straight run. The method is favoured for long lengths of braidline, and I've sailed aboard one classic schooner that always kept her mainsheet like this at sea. There was even a teak framework to hold it in place that the designer had specified in 1935. It still worked perfectly and I never saw the sheet snag.

Locking hitches

In the days of Nelson, when men were men and rope was made of natural fibre, locking hitches were rightly abhorred. Laid on in good faith in the sunshine, they could lock up solid after the rain had shrunk and stiffened the rope. Sailors avoided them like the press gang. Today's rope is synthetic. It no longer alters significantly with weather, so locking hitches have found their place. However, it's important to use them only to hold a belay onto the cleat rather than to take the direct pull. A loaded-up locking hitch can jam as surely in the third millennium as a wet one might have done at Trafalgar. The answer is to make sure there's at least one completed figure of eight before any locking hitch. Use them when there's no room for a full belay, or if the rope is just too slippery to trust without one. A seaman's locking hitch always follows the natural line of the figure-of-eight underneath it. If they end up against the lie of the rope they look scruffy and are less secure.

A useful belay begins with a half-turn...

...followed by at least one figure of eight...

...and ends with a locking hitch. It's secure and, with modern synthetic fibres, easy to release

Lines at the mast

Many yachts today lead halyards aft to the cockpit, but plenty keep them forward where nature intended. At the mast, the halyard for a permanently rigged roller genoa will be made up with the gasket coil hitch for a working rope, described earlier, but for a main, spinnaker or changeable headsail halyard, one you're likely to use more often, first belay then stow the halyard like this:

Belaying

The way a halyard is belayed, turned up, secured, or whatever other term you prefer, depends on the nature of the rope and the size of the cleat. The requirements are that the rope will remain secure until it's released, and that it can then be eased under load and never jam. The ideal way is to take a half turn around the cleat, then lay on a couple of figures-of-eight, finishing with a round turn. In practice, this is rarely achievable on a modern yacht because the rope is too big or the cleat too small. A compromise must be found which will very likely involve finishing with a locking hitch, or 'back hitch', to hold things together.

With the rope snugged up taut, take a half turn around the cleat

Lay on at least one figure of eight, leave some space on the top horn

Finish with a locking hitch to make sure everything stays secure

Stowing the halyard

Like any rope, line or warp, the fall of a halyard is always coiled from the belay towards the bitter end so that the kinks can fall off the end. Try it from the bitter end inwards, and well-deserved confusion will result.

1 Once it's done, take the coil in your left hand close up to the cleat, reach through it and grab the halyard where it comes off the top of the cleat.

2 Lead it through the coil, giving it half a turn as you do, then bring it up over the top of the coil.

Loop it over the cleat, and that's the job.

The trick that I can't describe in words is to get the lengths right. This can only be achieved after some trial and error. The halyard has to be led through the coil so that it's fairly tight. Ideally, it must almost be forced onto the cleat to hang the whole thing up. If it's too slack, the first wave will carry it away.

When it's time to lower the sail, unhook the halyard, drop the coil on deck right way up and just let it run.

Halyard bags

Boats with halyards run aft to clutches on the coachroof can end up with a cockpit swamped with tangled lines if you don't keep your ropes neatly stowed. Race boats flake their halyards down the companionway, but on a cruising boat these will get tangled round things and wick any water down the hatch. For a boat with halyard bags, a figure-of-eight formal flake, stuffed into the bag, works best – especially if you lift the whole bundle out of the bag before you drop the sail. The same principle applies if you've got reefing hooks to hang your coils on. Use a winch and your forearm to wind the rope in a loose figure-of-eight pattern.

Sailing among shipping

The amount of commercial shipping on our waterways has increased significantly in recent years and, even for experienced sailors, sailing among it can prove testing. Knowing how to steer clear of confusion or collision at sea is vital

Elaine and John Budgen are experienced sailors

The question of how we in small yachts should handle ourselves in the vicinity of shipping has come to the forefront in recent years, with several well-reported incidents involving small yachts and big ships. Much has been written about the subject, but it is worth considering the hands-on practicalities of sailing among commercial craft. The world hasn't many busier waterways than the central and eastern Solent, so I set off on a morning sail where I

expected to encounter *Liberty of the Seas*, the biggest cruise liner on the planet at 1,112ft LOA. To be honest, this was a scene-setter, because it was in nobody's interests to engineer a close encounter with her.

Talking things through with me and making sure I didn't get carried away were lifelong sailors John and Elaine Budgen, 67, first in their native Scotland and more recently on the South Coast. Their sons are a Volvo 70 helmsman and a Sigma 38

racing skipper. John still competes – in Southampton Water as it happens – and he immediately made the point that on board his race boat one crewman is detailed off for a 'take' on shipping movements.

As we enjoyed our day out on a Hanse 315, we discussed the many questions that arise in seas both wide and narrow. We stuck to 'ships in sight of one another', and here are some of our comments.

Collision course or safe heading?

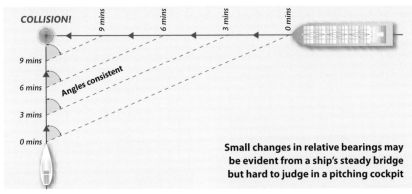

COLLISION! 9 mins 6 mins 3 mins 0 mins

9 mins
6 mins
3 mins
0 mins

Angles consistent

Small changes in relative bearings may
be evident from a ship's steady bridge
but hard to judge in a pitching cockpit

Ship transit
❯ At long and
medium ranges,
a preliminary
judgement can
often be made
by keeping your
head still and
lining the ship
up with a stanchion, winch or
anything else handy. If she stays
'on' with this as she closes, it's
decision time.

Create a transit
using a winch or
stanchion

If a ship is on a steady bearing relative to
your own heading, she will collide with
you in due course if no action is taken.
If she isn't, she won't. Electronics aside,
there are three ways of determining
whether this is happening.

Compass
❯ Use the compass.
If a distant ship's
bearing stays the
same over a period
of minutes, the
situation needs
addressing.

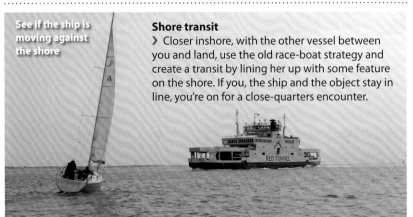

See if the ship is
moving against
the shore

Shore transit
❯ Closer inshore, with the other vessel between
you and land, use the old race-boat strategy and
create a transit by lining her up with some feature
on the shore. If you, the ship and the object stay in
line, you're on for a close-quarters encounter.

Points of view

Stay clear of
ships' blind
spots

Night and day
The collision regulations make
no differentiation between night
and day. Many experienced sailors
actually prefer watchkeeping after
dark, because ships' lights permit
no ambiguity about their aspect.
Modern ships have superstructure
in unconventional places, which
can make their aspect confusing
at a distance. Use binoculars if in
any doubt.

**Coming or going? Unambiguous
by night, tricky by day**

The ship's viewpoint
It's well known that a loaded container
ship may not be able to see a yacht at all
if she's less than a quarter-mile under the
bow. Watch officers start to feel uneasy
when yachts look like disappearing
up front. Pilots have major last-minute
manoeuvring problems which makes
them edgy if a yacht approaches blithely
on a collision course. The yacht's skipper
may intend soon to tack out of the way,
but unless VHF contact is established,
the ship's people have no means of
knowing this. It's important to try to
stand in their shoes.

Liberty of the Seas can cruise at 20 knots
with a minimal bow wave

Deceptive bow waves
John made the valuable
point that we mustn't be
fooled by a modest bow
wave. Today's bulbous
bows and the extremely
long waterlines of
large ships can mean
minimal disturbance
at comparatively high
speed. Check a well-
designed ship like the
old QEII making ten
knots. You can hardly tell
where she's been.

53

Open water tactics

Single ships with sea room

The classic set-piece comes when a yacht under sail finds herself on a steady bearing with a distant ship in open water with no other vessels involved. If the ship is really enormous it may be a courtesy to make a small alteration of course when she is still five miles off. This will avoid any further decisions by either party. There's a lot to be said for this policy, but John and I felt that with vessels of less than Goliath status a case could be made for standing on until the ship was perhaps three miles off – two at the very least – to give her the opportunity to comply with her duty. If no sign of alteration is forthcoming, we'd then execute a major course alteration and give way unambiguously.

Play it safe and act early, even in open waters

Good manners

This motorboat was on a collision course with us. He could have stood on and nipped behind us at the last minute – however the skipper was obviously a proper seaman and made his intentions clear, reacting early and making a major change of course to pass us astern

The motorboat is heading for us...

so makes a clear course change...

and passes astern. A wave of thanks is always appreciated

Judging distance

Many stand-on/give way decisions depend on distance. The best way to learn to judge this is to compare what you see with the known factor of a radar display. Constant application trains the eye. If you've no radar, AIS (see

'Electronic aids to collision avoidance') can give you the same data. Failing either piece of kit, get into the habit of looking at ships whose distance off is known. Perhaps near your local port entrance, or across a loch. It's all about familiarity.

Collision or all clear? It can be hard to judge

Crossing shipping lanes

Anyone traversing the Channel, or other major stretch of water, has to cross shipping lanes. If these are a formal TSS (Traffic Separation Scheme) our duties are laid down in the Collision Regulations. We must cross with our course, not our track, at right angles. It's common sense to do so as smartly as possible and endeavour to keep out of everyone's way in the process. If no TSS is in operation, ships using a 'main road' generally have no special rights or duties. However, in the central Channel, a note on the Admiralty chart missed by many users indicates that the lane defined by a dotted line should be treated 'as nearly as practicable' as if it were a TSS. The legality of this has not been tested, but the coastguard advises that yachts would do well to comply where they sensibly can.

When it comes to ships in a lane, it's easy to say, 'Play safe and give way to them all.' The trouble is that giving way to one may put you in a compromised position with the next and the one after that as well. You might end up miles off course when you were the stand-on vessel in the first place. Standing on boldly with the three-mile (two at least) criteria firmly in mind can often deal with such situations. A ship's watchkeeper may well have to make only a minor alteration that won't cost his owners a penny. As always, if it looks as if this isn't going to happen, make an obvious course alteration and go round his stern.

The three cases of crossing a non-tss shipping lane

1 Ships coming from your starboard side – you under power. However you

look at it, you're give-way vessel. Keep well clear of everyone.

2 Ships coming from your port side – you under power. You're showing them your red light so you are technically stand-on vessel. Apply common sense in good time.

3 Ships from either side – you under sail. Once again, you're stand-on vessel. If you're compromised by being closehauled or on a dead run, carry on with caution to 3 miles or so, but be ready to alter quickly. Tacking is an unmistakable signal of intention to give way, even to a merchant seaman who has never sailed. Put your crew on standby before the time for action comes. Too often, a yacht holds on for longer than she should because her watch puts off turning out the sleepers. If in doubt, call the ship on VHF.

Give way!
1

2
Stand-on!

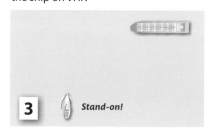
3
Stand-on!

Ships in tight waters

Special situations

While we were sailing on the Hanse, we watched as a supertanker steamed in from the east. Our chart pointed out that while she was in a clearly defined area, she operates within a 'moving prohibited zone'. The notes state that vessels under 20 metres in length are prohibited from entering an area 1,000 metres ahead of her and 100 metres to either side. I know from personal experience that failure to comply results, if you're lucky, in a short sharp reprimand from the Harbourmaster's launch.

Another such area has a precautionary zone – again defined by a chart note – which tells us to give due consideration to large vessels transferring pilots who may be constrained by draught.

It's easy to be cavalier about these places, or even not to notice that they're there. Once again, I can testify to the fact that ships in areas such as this don't always appear to behave rationally to uninformed observers. In areas of heavy commercial activity, it's vital to read the notes on the chart!

Get to know the local rules

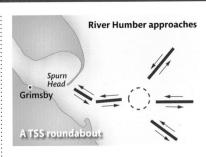

River Humber approaches

Spurn Head
Grimsby

A TSS roundabout

TSS Roundabout

Those of us who sail the North Sea are well acquainted with the tricky issue of the TSS Roundabout. These are literally what they say they are, and to find yourself in a big one in dense traffic can be harrowing. They are best avoided if your route can be modified without sending you home via the North Cape.

Dodging the shipping channels

Where ships are navigating narrow or twisting channels, it behoves us to stay well out of their way. We can often do this by nipping out of the channel as they approach or at least staying at its extremities. Local VTS (Vessel Traffic Services) broadcasts on VHF radio can help keep you in the picture.

Don't assume that local ferries will necessarily keep inside a main shipping channel. These skippers know exactly where the water is and they often make full use of it.

Keep to the edge of the channel

Ferries use local knowledge to go beyond buoyed channels

Electronic aids to collision avoidance

Calling ships up

Today's accurate fixing systems mean that you can identify a ship more easily to call her up for clarification. For example, 'Large red tanker in approximately 51 degrees, 57.2N, 1 degree 43.1E. This is the yacht *Saucy Sue* on your starboard bow. What are your intentions?' There is absolutely nothing wrong with making such a call if you're considering standing on – or even if you aren't. Make it in good time, though. Remember, it takes a long while for a ship to react.

If you're operating AIS, you can call the ship by name. No excuse for ignoring you then! If you have a DSC VHF radio you can enter the ship's MMSI number, displayed on your AIS, to call up the ship directly.

Radar and MARPA

The benefits of radar for collision avoidance are huge. A set enhanced with MARPA (Mini Automatic Radar Plotting Aid) allows you in theory to select a contact and be shown its course, speed and CPA, but the yawing of a small sailing yacht renders such information dubious, even when fine-tuned with gyros. AIS is far more solid, but only ships over 300 tons are obliged to broadcast the data. Anything smaller may be identified by MARPA. In the end, however, it's hard to beat putting the radar's electronic bearing line (EBL) on the contact and seeing if it stays there as the ship approaches. If it does, it's on a steady bearing, and we all know what that means!

AIS

AIS (Automatic Identification System) is a means whereby large ships broadcast their position, course and speed to anyone with the gear to receive it. You can install this relatively cheaply, and benefit from a graphic display that tells you not only this, but also a ship's name and her closest point of approach (CPA). AIS takes much of the doubt out of a potential collision situation.

Conclusion

John and I had a productive sail while talking through these issues. We were both emphatic about the need to avoid close-quarters situations by all available means. Bright flashlights and white flares were considered essential after dark in cases where all else failed and we feared we had not been seen. In the daytime, we'll be taking early avoiding action when a ship leaves us in any doubt at all. We'll call her if need be, and we'll be thinking about what's in the other guy's mind. The bottom line is that we'll both be steering well clear of trouble before it can get close enough to strike.

LEFT: Call another ship directly via DSC VHF

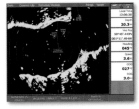

Troubleshooting a diesel engine

When an engine stops or won't start, many yachtsmen treat it as a crisis. Yet with a bit of basic knowledge, a decent tool kit and few spares, a crisis can be turned into an inconvenience

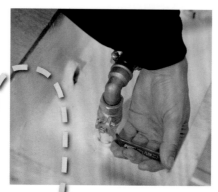

The plan was to head out to sea with photographer Graham Snook to take some images of sailing a Jeanneau Sun Odyssey 35 short-handed in heavy weather. The masts in the marina sounded like all the banshees in Hell, but Snook's a Falmouth man and a capful of breeze doesn't bother him, so we stowed our gear, psyched ourselves up and started the Yanmar engine. It kicked into life as a brand-new unit should, but it didn't sound right. Instead of that reassuring gush of water from the exhaust, we were served up a hollow noise more like a motor car. I peered over the stern at the outlet. Sure enough, rather than the inter-

mittent whoosh you'd expect, only a wretched trickle met my gaze. We'd forgotten to open the inlet stopcock!

As I tended to the Yanmar, the gale hit 45 knots, the clouds exploded, the rain came down like scrap rod rigging, so we agreed to bottle out and look at the sort of things that go wrong with engines instead. Graham put the kettle on while I pulled my cap hard down and battled through the tempest to the car for my tool box.

The three necessities
A typical modern marine diesel asks only three things: electricity to start it, clean fuel to keep it running,

and a supply of seawater to stop it over-heating. It's rare for today's units to fail so badly that a properly equipped, modestly competent skipper can't get them going again. We can do little about mechanical catastrophe, but for the sort of common stoppages considered here, a 'can-do' attitude, a few spares and a decent tool kit will transform a crisis into an inconvenience.

Spares: the essentials

• Oil filter	• Alternator belt
• Fuel filters	• Engine oil
• Impeller kits	• Hose clamps

Problem 1: Engine spins over but fails to fire

The 'stop system'

Failure to fire might indicate a fuel supply problem, but more likely the 'stop' arrangements are misbehaving. In spite of the fact that some diesels are now shut down with the ignition key, they don't switch off like petrol engines by cutting the supply of power to a spark plug. They don't need electrics to run, so the only way to stop them is to shut down the injector pump that squirts fuel into the cylinders to make it all happen.

On many engines this is achieved mechanically by pulling a toggle on a cable. The toggle activates a small lever on the pump, situated on the side of the engine. If the motor won't fire up and you have such a system, ten to one somebody didn't shove the toggle back properly last time it was used. Do the necessary and it will burst into life.

Engines that are turned off with the ignition key have exactly the same arrangement, but instead of the toggle and cable, they cut out the pump by

means of an electric solenoid operated by the starter switch. I've known these clever pieces of kit fail, and some at least won't let you start the poor old motor until you've sorted the issue. If I'm to be shipmates with one, I make it my business to find the activating mechanism on the pump and watch it work. Then if one day it doesn't, I can see what needs to be done to deal with it manually. It may be impossible, but often it's just a matter of disconnecting a clevis pin and pushing the lever.

Flat battery

You need at least 12v across the terminals of a battery to start a healthy engine. If you've a dedicated starting battery and your charging system is doing its stuff, finding this should never be a problem unless the battery is shot and no longer holds its charge. If, on the other hand, you have two identical batteries and a multi-choice switch offering '1', '2', or 'both', try to keep '1' specifically for engine starts for a cruise, then use '2' next time

A reading of around 12.5v indicates that a battery is healthy and happy.

around, to ring the changes and stop the accumulators getting into a rut.

If you've been burning lights, fridge and heater all night long and your domestic supply is down to 11v, don't switch to 'both' to start up in the morning. Turn to the good battery that has been resting. It's volts that will start the motor, not a joint effort where a fit young battery is dragging a flabby old loser along as well as trying to boot the diesel into life. Once the engine is running, switch to 'both', of course, and keep it turning for at least half an hour.

The terminal case

If your dedicated start battery has somehow contrived to flatten itself, you'll have to use the domestic supply to boost it. Switch them together if this is an option ('both' on the multi-switch). If not, dig out those high-quality jump leads you always carry on board against the day when the unthinkable comes to pass.

Volt meters

If you have a volt meter in your instrument panel, check the voltage of the resting batteries before starting the engine and make sure the one you choose for today's 'start' unit is up to the job. If both are reading over 12, you're in good shape. Once charging, the reading may rise to 14, but it won't stay there long after the engine stops. Both batteries should settle around 12.5.

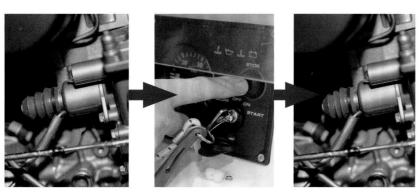

ABOVE: The red plastic cover hides the engine shut-off mechanism on this Yanmar. Press the STOP button in the cockpit and it contracts, cutting off the fuel

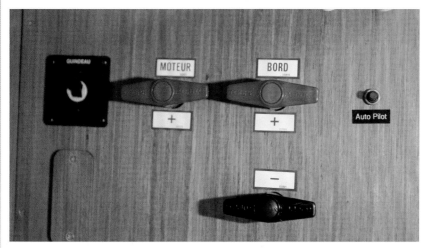

This French system has separate batteries for engine and domestic use. Always start the engine using its dedicated battery

Problem 2: Engine stops under way

The silence that follows the cough and splutter of a dying diesel is a terrible thing – but don't panic. Try and find some sea room or chuck out the anchor while you investigate. The odds are that there's a problem with the fuel.

Diesels need a plentiful supply of uncontaminated fuel. Serve this up, keep the engine cool, and, once running, it will plug on for ever. If anything interrupts the flow of fuel, the pumps will suck in vain, creating air bubbles which, to all intents and purposes, means 'lights out!' There are two main ways of starving the engine of fuel – running out and clogged filters.

Running out of diesel

To do this doesn't necessarily brand you as a pariah. I've suffered from a failed sight-glass fuel gauge myself.

Others have equally honest reasons, but if there's no fuel in the tank, it makes no matter whose fault it is. As a good skipper, you'll have a few gallons squirrelled away in jerry-cans, but it's not enough just to tip this into the tank through a useful funnel or via that siphoning device bought years ago from your friendly local chandler. There will be fuel and to spare, but the rogue parcel of air that actually stopped the motor will still be lurking.

Unless your engine is a miracle of science, you can crank away until the batteries are flatter than Aunt Jemima's pancakes. Knowing the trick of how to bleed out those bubbles will make the difference between a happy return and a night at sea waiting for the wind.

Bleeding a diesel systematically

You don't have to be an expert on a specific

engine to get rid of the air that stopped it. All that's required is a linear approach.

> **Tank** – start here. You know there's diesel there because you just dumped some in.

> **Fuel cock** – This is usually at the tank itself, but may be remote. Make sure it's on.

> **Pre-filter** – Follow the fuel line towards the engine and you'll probably come to a filter unit like the one illustrated below. At the top will be a bleed screw, but you may not have to use it. If all else has failed, proceed with this as for the fine filter described below.

> **Lift pump and fine filter** – Keep following the fuel pipe and you'll come next to a unit attached to the engine, usually shaped like a small, flat cylinder. This delivers fuel to the injector pump itself which serves the engine. It also lifts diesel to the fine filter which is generally

Bleeding a diesel engine

1 FUEL COCK

Make sure the fuel cock is turned on and that there's fuel in the tank. It makes sense to carry a spare can just in case, and top up the tank sooner rather than later so any dirt in the bottom of the tank is not sucked into the engine

2 Pre-filter

Only bleed the pre-filter if bleeding the main filter doesn't sort the problem

3 If required, loosen the nut on top of the filter and pump the bubbles out

4 Locate the manual overide lever next to the fuel pump

Lift pump

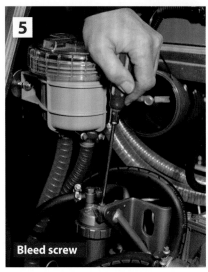

5 Bleed screw

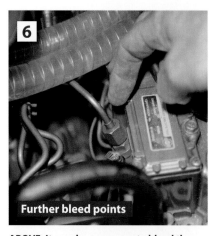

6 Further bleed points

ABOVE: It may be necessary to bleed the engine at the injector. Some injectors will have a bleed screw on the side – this Yanmar did not

mounted on the engine at the highest point of the system. It is at this filter that most modern systems are best bled. Find the bleed screw at the top of the unit. Usually this is a hexagon, but it may be a screw. Our Yanmar had both, a hexagon with a cross-headed screw slot in the top.
> **The bleeding process** – Undo the bleed nut a turn or two, then find the manual override lever on the lift pump as shown. Work this up and down to push fuel. Soon you'll find a bubbly mix coming out of the bleed nut. Keep pumping until all the air has gone and clear fuel is running out. Now tighten up the bleed nut and crank the engine. You'll have to turn it over for a good few seconds to push any air out of the injectors and into the engine, but keep faith and it should start.

Dirty fuel and clogged filters
If you take on a dirty fuel or your tanks could do with a clean, your filters will prevent the rubbish arriving at the delicate injectors whose tiny nozzles squirt diesel into the engine. If there's enough junk floating around, it will clog the filters and cause the pump to suck air. The effect is the same as if you'd run out of fuel – the engine slows down and dies. Most engines today use disposable filter units and all boats should carry a supply.

Changing filters and bleeding
> **Pre-filter** – This is the likeliest candidate for blockage. Shut down the fuel cock at the tank, open the bleed screw in the filter and see if it has a water trap at the bottom. Many do. These can be emptied without removing the filter unit by opening a small integral tap.

Water will stop an engine as surely as lack of fuel. If water isn't the problem, unscrew the filter element and replace it with a new one from on-board stock. Bleed the system as described opposite and away you go.
> **Fine filter** – If necessary, these are changed the same way as pre-filters. Some installations do not have a pre-filter. If so, the fine filter is your first and last bastion against muck. Treat it like a well-loved baby and change it frequently whether it needs it or not. Always carry spares.
> **Further bleed points** – Some engines need further bleeding, typically at the injector pump. This is found by following the fuel pipe from the fine filter onwards. If it needs a bleed screw – ours did not – it will have one or more on the side. Check the manual for location.

Filters

Fuel filter

LEFT: Fuel filters should be inspected regularly and changed every 200 hours

Pre-filter tap

LEFT: This filter has a drain tap

Are you seeing black?
Black smoke issuing from the exhaust is usually a sign of a blocked air filter. If you don't have a spare paper filter try tapping it lightly to clear the dirt.

LEFT: This Racor fuel filter has a glass chamber so that any dirt and water can be observed. Contaminants can then be drained into the collecting bowl beneath

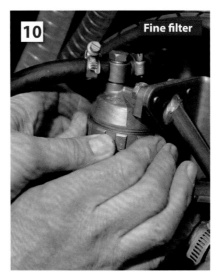

Fine filter

LEFT: The base of this fine filter is removed by twisting. Clean fuel is essential and the fine filter can be the only barrier between contaminated fuel and the fine nozzles of the injection system. Change it regularly

Problem 3: Engine overheats

An overheated engine may cause itself terminal damage. You can tell it's happening by listening to the exhaust, as we did, by looking at the water coming out, or when you're awakened from your watch below by the overheat alarm screaming in your ear.

The cooling system
Most engines are cooled like a car, with an antifreeze/water mix that circulates around the block. However, while the automotive unit keeps this cool by means of a radiator and fan, a boat uses a heat exchanger cooled by seawater. This is drawn in through a seacock in the boat's bottom, passed through a filter or strainer unit, then pumped around the exchanger itself before being ejected by way of the exhaust pipe which it cools and silences as a bonus on the deal. Two things can go wrong: a blocked filter or a failure to turn on the seacock (as we did). Any failure to allow circulation can result in damage to the pump impeller.

What to do:
> **Seacock** – Shut the seacock.
> **Locating the strainer** – Follow the inlet pipe until you reach the strainer. This may be a small metal unit on the cock itself or, more likely, something like the one pictured below.
> **Clearing the filter** – Open the strainer, remove the filter element and clear it if necessary. Reassemble and turn on the water. If it doesn't fill, detach the pipe from the seacock and see if water flows when it's opened. If not, the through-hull is blocked, probably with a plastic bag or a misguided and now doomed jellyfish. Poke it clear fearlessly with that useful wire coat hanger without which no boat should go to sea. Water will gush into the bilge. Shut the cock, re-connect the pipe, open up and flash up the power.
> **All clear but no water at the exhaust** – You've probably damaged your water pump impeller by running it dry. No worries. Locate the pump by following the pipe from the strainer towards the engine.

> **Changing the pump impeller** – Shut the seacock and unscrew the front plate of the pump, making sure not to lose the screws. Note how the water seal is achieved. It may be an 'O' ring, or a gasket of some sort. Using two screwdrivers, one either side, prise out the rubber impeller. Note which way the blades are bending. Replace it with your spare, making sure the blades are bending the same way as its predecessor. If in doubt, use the manual to decide. Replace the end plate, taking special care to locate any O-rings or gaskets. New ones may be supplied with the impeller kit and no self-respecting yachtsman should set sail without at least one of these lurking away among the spares.
> **Last ditch** – If none of this cures the issue, there isn't much more you can do for now. Sail the boat and save that 10 minutes of motoring you may have 'from cold' to squeeze into your berth and call an engineer.

Seacock

Always re-open the seacock after repairs

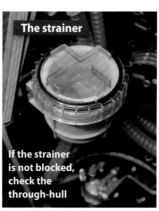
The strainer
If the strainer is not blocked, check the through-hull

The impeller kit

Changing the impeller is a job we should all be capable of. Check which direction the blades bend as you remove it – and if in doubt, refer to the engine manual

The pump impeller
Problems with the cooling system will often require the impeller to be replaced

Conclusion

'Forewarned and prepared' is 'forearmed and sorted'. All boats must carry spare filters and impellers, as well as a workable tool kit that has been tried on all the nuts and bolts that may be needed in these minor engine emergencies. Oh yes, and don't forget the coat hanger. It would be a shame to lose the ship for want of one of these. You can even use it for your blazer while it awaits its moment of true glory...

Pre-engine checks

Before you start your engine, it's worth carrying out a few
basic checks to make sure all is running smoothly and prevent
any potential problems before they happen

Raw water filter
Shut the cooling water
seacock, remove the filter
element and clean it if
necessary. Replace the
element, screw the lid back
onto the filter body and
open the seacock.

Battery switch
Turn the battery
on before starting.
Do not switch it off
while the engine is
running.

Bilge blower
If you have a bilge
blower or engine
room extractor
fan, run it for a few
minutes before
starting the engine.

Fresh water level
Some engines have fresh water
cooling systems as well as raw
water. Carefully remove the
header tank cap and top up
with water/antifreeze mixture
if necessary to bring the level
within about 50mm of the top.
Carefully replace the cap.

Visual check
Check belts and
hoses for cuts,
splits or fraying and
look out for oil or
coolant leaks.

Fuel filter
Some boats have a
transparent water
separator/filter in the fuel
line. Inspect the bowl for
water or dirt and drain off
any visible contamination.
This filter has a screw
underneath, allowing a
sample to be drained and
inspected for water

Gearbox oil level
Check the gearbox oil
level with the dipstick.
Some gearbox oil levels
can only be checked
with the engine running.
Many gearboxes need
special oil: engine oil will
not do!

Fuel
Make sure you have
enough fuel for your
intended trip, plus a
reserve of about 20%
of the tank's capacity.
The fuel tap on a
diesel system should
normally be left open.

Stern gland greaser
Boats with traditional
transmission systems
often have stern gland
greasers. Give the cap or
handle one full turn.

Engine oil level
Check the engine oil
level with the dipstick
and top up if necessary
to keep the level
between the 'max' and
'min' marks.

Sailing in fog

No yachtsman enjoys sailing in fog, but it is something that we're all caught out in from time to time. Knowing how to cope with the disorientation of low visibility, however, can help ease your fears

Martin and Joanne Ross get to grips with fog

I recently met Martin and Joanne Ross aboard their MG335 club-racer to help them with boatspeed. We had a cracking morning putting the boat through her paces, then over lunch we discovered an unexpected area of interest. As we sat around the cockpit table enjoying the victuals, we began discussing fog. I was expounding my views about why we find the inevitable disorientation so alarming, when Martin made a shrewd observation.

As an ex-serviceman, he had served his time as a diver. During his training he'd been required to free-dive to 20ft in near-zero visibility, then bring up a handful of mud. He remarked that, weighted to neutral buoyancy and with only one breath to sustain you, it's easy to lose track of which way is up and which way is down. Very like the emotions we feel in fog, except that a diver has to cope with three dimensions instead of our comparatively easy two.

'So what do you do?' I asked.

'You get a grip on yourself and fall back on your training,' he said. As a wry afterthought, he added, 'Actually, you breathe out a little bit and see which way the bubbles go. Unless someone switched off gravity, that way has got to be up!'

What began as a general chat now led us to focus on practical steps to take when robbed of visibility at sea. We set up an exercise with Joanne as volunteer 'blind navigator' and she ordered courses from a darkened chart table with us throwing snippets of information down from the cockpit. Next we considered a classic scenario that can develop in those uneasy waters at the cusp of the English Channel and the North Sea. Working it through made us all better prepared for the next time the fog rolls in.

The scenario

The three of us are on passage from Dover up into the North Sea. We've decided to pass inside the Goodwin Sands. The wind is a light westerly and visibility is forecast as moderate or poor with fog patches. Being typical optimists, we sail anyway and hope for the best, but we haven't gone far before fog descends on us in a big way. In fact, we've just passed

Goodwin Fork South Cardinal when visibility closes in drastically. We carry on steering NNE towards West Goodwin but our circle of vision soon shuts down to 150ft and all we can see is a seagull flapping off into the murk. It's decision time, on various fronts. We're going to need a navigation strategy pretty quickly, but first, we must secure our immediate safety.

Actions to take when the fog comes down

Make sure your lifejacket is adjusted to fit

❯ Lifejackets If, like me, you don't wear one of these all the time, it makes sense for all hands to do so now. The worst and most likely calamity is that you'll be run down. The boat may then sink in short order and you don't want to be all fighting for the only available lifejacket! Even if you know where they are and have one with your name on it that is pre-adjusted, there may not be time to grab it. If your crew haven't gone to this trouble, don't let them imagine that 'one size fits all'. Check and see whose is a bit on the small size... You have to wonder what sort of world the lifejacket manufacturers live in. Size is not just about 'buoyancy Newtons' or whatever they're called this week – or it shouldn't be. At least I've adjusted the straps so it'll go around me.

❯ Radar reflector It's probably more important to be seen in fog than to see for yourself. You must generate a solid radar echo. Unless your boat is huge and steel, you need a radar reflector. Lots of boats have one permanently rigged and much has been written about the best sort to use, but I like the modern 'narrow-gauge' items like Martin and Joanne's. I appreciate its low weight and windage, and I hate to see a beautiful mast disfigured by a dustbin. If the reflector is not permanently mounted, it should be hoisted high up at all times after dark and in any daytime visibility that's less than moderate.

Don't forget to switch on nav lights

❯ Lights Switching on the relevant running lights increases the chance of being seen.

❯ Sails Even if there's no wind, hoist the main. Not only does it steady the boat, it's a lot more conspicuous in thick visibility than a low-lying hull.

❯ Fog signal Big-ship watchkeepers are unlikely to hear your fog signal, but sounding every two minutes as per the collision regulations helps a lot with small-craft traffic. Don't forget, under power it's one long blast – 'Here I come, sounding one'. Sailing, it's 'Dah-dit-dit' which is also the Morse code for 'D' – 'I am manoeuvring with difficulty'. Always carry a back-up 'lung-powered' foghorn.

Pressurised foghorns will eventually run out

❯ Lookout In fog, the compass is king. The helmsman is going to be concentrating on it, so an extra lookout is more than worth any inconvenience. A crew member on the foredeck is 20 or 30ft closer to any vessel approaching in the danger sector, so put someone up there if you've enough hands. If you're motoring, he'll also be more likely to hear fog signals or bow waves. Then there's the folks playing with their dogs on a beach that's too close for comfort. Stop the engine every so often for a listen-out.

❯ Fix the position Although this presents no problems these days with GPS, taking a last fix used to be the crowning priority as visibility shut down. It remains high on the list because that plotted fix is the rock on which you'll build a survival strategy.

Fog strategy

Given a good idea of her position, a yacht has four options when confronted by fog:

Go out to sea

Although rarely popular with crews, this is often the easiest and safest choice, especially if you don't expect the fog to last long and shipping is light. In our case, it was a non-starter. We had the Goodwins directly to seaward of us; to the southward lay the Dover Strait, a veritable shipping spectacular. Northeastwards lay a narrow channel that we could probably negotiate with GPS, but which is frequented by many a medium-tonnage vessel on passage, including coasters.

Consider heading away from land

Anchor in the shallows

Safety can be found close to shore

This takes a yacht into water that's not deep enough for any serious commercial vessel. It's also often unchallenging as a navigation exercise, so if GPS is down, it could well prove the best answer. It might have been a sound decision for us, but Joanne mentioned she'd be happier finding a safe haven and popping ashore for a meal than anchoring out and waiting for the thud of fishing boat engines. A good point, you'll agree. Far worse arguments have prevailed against this option before now.

Carry on regardless of the fog

In these days of reasonable navigational certainty, this is often a sensible selection, but it scored 'nul points' with us. Our official passage plan led straight up through the Gull Stream, a busy shipping lane with danger on either hand – a very bad place to be when you can't see more than 250ft beyond your pulpit.

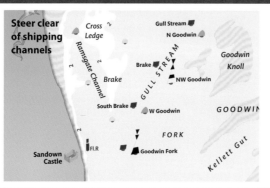

Steer clear of shipping channels

Find a safe haven

There's nowhere safer than a marina berth

If fog looks like persisting, this is everyone's favourite. It was certainly going to be ours. The tide stood fair for Ramsgate, a mere 5 miles away. In any case, Dover would have been highly unattractive because of the ferries. The question was, how to find the chosen refuge safely and surely.

Piloting tactics

1. Using GPS alone

Leave the shoals to port and work northwards, avoiding the Gull Stream with its shipping. We could use GPS to keep the South Brake and Brake red can buoys to starboard. Next, we'd steer north to a waypoint at the buoyed channel into Ramsgate, turning west towards the entrance along the southern edge of the channel itself to keep clear of shipping. We'd call the

2: Using depth and GPS

Leave the shoals to starboard by initially steering west to a waypoint on the flashing red beacon off Sandown Castle, then work northwards along the 2m contour (currently with 4m of water on it), past various other waypoints as checkpoints, until we fetch up close enough to the South Breakwater to be able to see it. Thereafter, it would be a matter of radioing the harbourmaster for a slot to enter safely. The contour left something to be desired for straightness, but it would serve.

We liked this scheme because it left plenty of slack for things to go wrong. Without GPS at all it would have been by far the safest option. Our policy on the day was to navigate as we would have done with no GPS, then use it to maintain a constant update on how things were progressing.

One reason why we could have executed this plan with no GPS was that we wouldn't even have to know precisely where we were when the fog came in. Rather than waste time with an accurate GPS fix, therefore, Joanne just drew a circle of likely position and gave us a course for the shore, making

Conclusion

Our plan worked well in practice. With Joanne running the contour on the well-tried '15 - 25' method, we steered along the correct depth on the echo sounder as best we could. If the water deepened, we swung in 15°. When it shoaled below what we wanted, we swung a reassuring

We were bound for Ramsgate but would have to work around the drying Brake banks and the Cross Ledge shoal. This left two options:

harbourmaster on the VHF radio to report our intentions and to be advised of any shipping movements.

There was much to be said for this plan, but it had an overriding weakness. It relied on a continuously updated GPS fix. Had this failed we'd have been compromised. We'd reason to believe our GPS set-up was not rock solid, so we went for the second choice.

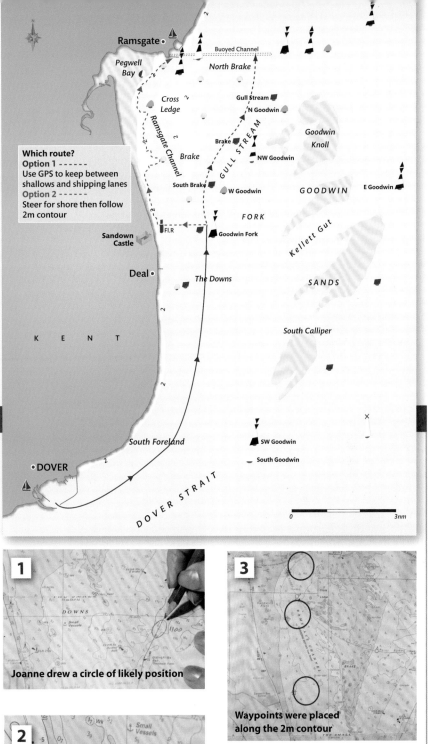

Which route?
Option 1 - - - - - -
Use GPS to keep between shallows and shipping lanes
Option 2 - - - - - -
Steer for shore then follow 2m contour

better use of her time by plotting the 'red beacon waypoint' from where she would commence running the contour. With no GPS, we could safely have missed the beacon altogether because we were well clear of the shoals and would surely find the 2m contour as we ran in. We'd know which way to turn, then we'd just keep going until we found what we were ultimately looking for.

Back in the real world with GPS, Joanne and I plotted a series of likely waypoints then asked Martin what he thought of them. He was happy, except that he didn't trust the one we'd placed right at the root of the breakwater, arguing that it was 'too close for comfort'. He had a point, so we shifted it to a nearby yellow buoy they both knew. We'd only have to steer north-east from here and we couldn't miss the breakwater. We agreed it was better to find the final waypoint shortly before making landfall, then have all hands on deck looking out, especially as the South Breakwater is a pile of boulders that could have the odd danger tumbling off to seaward.

1 Joanne drew a circle of likely position

2 She made a GPS waypoint on a flashing red beacon

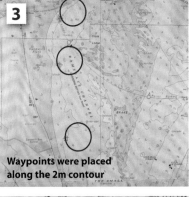

3 Waypoints were placed along the 2m contour

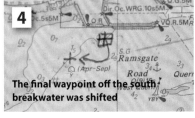

4 The final waypoint off the south breakwater was shifted

40° to seaward. This left us running out at around 25° to our contour until it deepened once more. We checked off the waypoints one by one, which gave us a huge lift in morale over pre-GPS navigators but, most importantly, we had a contingency plan up our sleeves for GPS

failure. The scheme would also serve if we blew it altogether. We knew more or less where we were, and the water was too shallow for ships. If our nerve had failed, we could always anchor under the lee of Kent, as sailors have done for millennia.

All navigation in this topic refers to IALA System Region A

Climbing a mast

Being able to climb your mast swiftly and efficiently is essential – not least so you can carry out regular checks or running repairs. With the right gear and techniques, it's not hard either

When I was a nipper, I worked on a big gaff schooner. She had full ratlines, so going aloft was a breeze for a fit young man. I soon overcame my fear of heights and the view was great at sea or in harbour. The wind seemed sweeter, too, and I felt like a real sailor. These days, rather than regularly scampering aloft, I seem to find myself having somehow to scale the masts of various modern yachts a few times a year. I still have no terror of heights, but the physical business of cranking 16 stone of Cunliffe 40 or 50ft upwards against the honest efforts of gravity has provided a challenge more than once.

Recently, I was working in a Majorca marina. On the next-door yacht, local riggers Peter and Alex were zipping up and down the mast like spidermen. I wandered across to find out how they did it, and ended up a good deal wiser, but because we didn't have their kit on board, what I'd learned didn't help us to get up and change our defective deck-light bulb. For that, we had to resort to old-fashioned seamanship. The comparison in methods was not far short of a joke, so as soon as I got home I ordered the gear they used.

The Ascender

Although the riggers were both fit and young, their athleticism up the mast was as much the result of carefully chosen kit as well-honed muscle.

Somehow, Peter was climbing under his own power, while Alex was leaning back against a halyard and taking up slack round a winch. The secret was the 'ascender'.

The ascender grips and slides

This simple item can be bought at any climbing shop, or via the Internet. It can grab the bight of any rope between 8 and 13mm in diameter, and when offered up to a rope running from deck to masthead, winched tight, it can be slid up when the weight is off it. Once the weight comes back on, it grips like a vice. It also features a handle and a suitable hole for attaching further lines.

The full monty: ascender, foot loop and harness

Rig your own bosun's chair
It's an ancient tradition of the sea that anyone about to go aloft rigs their own chair or harness. The reasons for this are obvious!

The climbing harness

You could perform this operation using an old-style bosun's chair, but you wouldn't be as safe as you are in one of these remarkable items. Unlike a bosun's chair, they allow full use of arms and legs without the remotest possibility of falling out. The downside is that they're far less comfortable to sit in for long periods.

Safety aloft

Professional riggers attach a fixed line between the ascender and the climbing harness, as one would if going up single-handed. This line looks after itself as the climber goes progressively aloft. The spare halyard is then attached to a modern bosun's chair, in which the climber 'sits' as he goes up. The deck hand takes up the slack as before, and the climber is doubly safe – if the spare halyard or its gear should fail, he has his own weight on the line joining the ascender to the harness. Once aloft, the bosun's chair is more comfortable than the harness for a lengthy stay. I strongly recommend this refinement.

Climbing a mast with ascenders

You can climb the mast singlehanded with a pair of ascenders, but for perfect safety and no ruptures, make it a two-person job. This technique is a winner on any boat, no matter how feeble her winches.

A line is set up between deck and masthead. Typically, this might be a rope sent aloft on the main halyard and then winched up tight. Note that when going aloft, professional riggers nearly always choose a rope, rather than a wire halyard, because the latter is more likely to fail without warning.

The climber settles into the harness and attaches a spare halyard to it. Ideally, this would be a spinnaker or cruising chute halyard. Failing all else, a topping lift might do. Never use a snap shackle, nor even a screw shackle – it's best to knot the halyard to the harness. It's critical that the spare halyard – and its blocks – are above suspicion.

Attach a loop of rope to the eye on the lower end of the ascender. Try about 4ft long to begin with, but the length varies very much with the individual. Adjust it until you're happy.

The deck hand takes his end of the spare halyard and wraps a few turns around a halyard winch, either at the mast or by the cockpit. He won't be needing a winch handle.

The climber stands by the mast, grabs the masthead line with the ascender and shoves the tool up to a height that allows him to get his foot into the loop well above the deck.

The climber then hooks his foot into the loop and literally steps up by straightening his leg. Some people like to put two feet in the loop. Others manage with just one.

continues overleaf ❯

Climbing a mast with ascenders (continued)

The spare halyard is now slack because the climber has all his weight on his straight leg. The deck hand rattles up the slack (no effort required at all) so when the climber relaxes his leg all his weight comes onto the climbing harness. He knows it's safe to do this because he's heard the winch spin and he trusts his mate to hold the turns. The climber can now slide the ascender up the rope and take another step up. As soon as the spare halyard goes slack, the deck hand whacks it in and the process is repeated, literally step by step, until the climber is as far up as he needs to be.

When the required height is achieved, the climber calls out, 'Belay!' The deck hand secures the spare halyard and that's that.

To come down, the deck hand eases out the spare halyard while the climber guides himself past the shrouds and other obstacles.

That, in a nutshell, is the best way to do it on a yacht whose winches aren't up to hoisting someone. If you're on a charter boat, as I was, or perhaps if you haven't yet got around to kitting up, you'll have to improvise.

1 The climber settles into the harness and attaches the halyard

2 Never use a snap shackle!

3 Adjust the ascender until you're happy with it

4 The deck hand wraps a few turns around the winch

5 The climber slides the ascender up and hooks his foot in the loop

6 He then hauls himself up...

7 ...and straightens his legs. The deck hand takes up the slack

8 With his weight supported by the harness, the climber slides the ascender up again...

9 ...and they repeat the process until he's as high as he wants to be

10 The deck hand cleats the halyard securely while the climber is working, and stands clear

11 To ease the line for a smooth descent, two turns on the winch are about right

12 On the way down use the lower shrouds to steady yourself

'Stand from under!' was the call on J-Class yachts when a man at the masthead dropped his marline spike. On deck, hands had just enough time to react. You wouldn't on a 30-footer, so clear all hands away from the mast.

Using a bosun's chair

The bosun's chair

All yachts, even charter boats, should be equipped with a bosun's chair. If yours isn't, she's not fit for purpose. This old favourite isn't quite as safe as a climbing harness – it is possible to fall out of one, if things go very badly wrong – but they are much more comfortable to sit in for extended periods, so if you're faced with a long, difficult job at the masthead, you may well choose the chair, even if you have a harness on board.

Primary winch or windlass?

An ex-racing boat with huge, self-tailing primary sheet winches may have enough grunt in them for a strong person to grind a light crew member aloft. If so, it's just a matter of finding a lead to get a halyard onto the sheet winch. A bit of ingenuity and perhaps a spare block or two generally does it. If the halyard is too short, make sure it's long enough next time you replace it.

On a typical cruiser, however, there won't be a sheet or halyard winch on board powerful enough to tackle this job without risking cardiac arrest for the grinder. There's also the unthinkable contingency of a pawl letting go. Don't attempt it unless you're confident the winch has been well serviced.

The windlass

Many a yacht carries an electric anchor windlass nowadays. If yours has one with a warping drum, then it's the obvious choice. Even if it has no motor and is driven only by 'Armstrong's Patent', it may still be the best bet. The challenge is always to lead the halyard to it, so that it sits sweetly on the drum.

The lead

On our charter boat, the spares kit contained few shackles and no snatch blocks – indeed, there were no extra blocks of any description. Our halyards came out the bottom of the mast and it was obviously 'a windlass job' to get any of us aloft to fix our deck-light bulb. There was nothing for it but to cannibalise, so we set to with spanner and shackle key. Half an hour later, we'd no workable kicker and only half a mainsheet, but a stout halyard was led more or less cleanly onto the windlass and I was up at my work, 20ft above the deck.

For some reason, when leading to a windlass it is difficult to get the final angle as low down as the winch barrel really wants it. As a result, the line tends to create riding turns, especially when you're easing it away. Only some smart work with a size 12 deck shoe holding the bight down kept me from being stuck swinging around while the hands sloped off for their sundowners.

Powered winches

If you've managed to side-step the recession and have a yacht with electric winches, your problems are over. No need for any ascenders. Just hook up a bosun's chair of your choice or, better still, a climbing harness, and up you go. If the climber is heavy and the winch none too huge, he or she should take as much weight as possible by hanging onto anything convenient as it passes and heaving up. Regardless of this, give the winch a rest to cool off every 20ft or so, otherwise the circuit breaker may trip and leave you stranded. If you're the skipper and you've opted to climb, make sure that the deck hand knows where this breaker is and how to operate it, or you may have a long spell aloft.

continues overleaf ❯

Be prepared

After my 101st trip aloft, I finally learned to be prepared for all eventualities. The last thing you want is to have to come down again for a spanner. The answer is to take all you need in a bucket tied so that it can't invert. For backup, also chuck in a mast-long length of twine that you can dangle down for your mate to attach the shackle you've forgotten.

Safety lines?

In theory, you should never send someone aloft on a single halyard. The reasons are obvious and the answer is to rig a second halyard to the chair or harness as backup. Unfortunately, this can sometimes be so cumbersome as to defeat its own object. The answer lies between the skipper, his conscience and perhaps his Maker. We must do all we can to be seamanlike, then decide for ourselves.

Who goes up?

For short-handed crews, this is often a vexed question. Typically, the skipper wants to see what's happening up there. The trouble is that if he's a chap in his prime, he's very likely also the strongest person on board as well as the heaviest. Should the boat have powered winches or an ascender, none of this matters. Up he goes, so long as he's trained his deck crew well. Otherwise, a compromise may be required, with a less qualified but lighter person clearly briefed as to what's required. If decisions are going to be made that aren't yet known, how about taking the mobile phone aloft instead of hollering across half the harbour in a stiff breeze?

A head for heights

Some people don't mind heights at all. Others hate them. Usually, this causes no problems because the person who volunteers will be the best man, or woman, for the job. If nobody on board fancies the view from 40ft up, try taking a pragmatic approach. Rig a safety line, concentrate on the job and enjoy the view, but try not to look directly downwards. You may find, as I did, that after a trip or two up to the halyard sheaves you start to enjoy it.

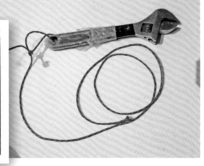

Using a bosun's chair (continued)

In the absence of spare blocks, we 'cannibalised' the kicking strap

Blocks on the spinnaker pole track and the toerail gave a good lead to the electric anchor windlass

Tom sits back in his harness and braces his foot against the mast as the deck crew starts the windlass

Tom uses the lower shrouds to guide himself up...

...and 'walks' his feet up the mast

Take care getting past the spreaders

The windlass operator should keep a close watch on the person aloft

Tom uses a pre-arranged signal to tell the winch man to stop and belay the halyard

ABOVE: A foot was needed to prevent riding turns on the windlass
RIGHT: A gentle touch down

Alternative ways to climb a mast

Flexible ladder
Favoured by the SAS! Very compact and ultra-light, but tiring to climb and swings about when in use

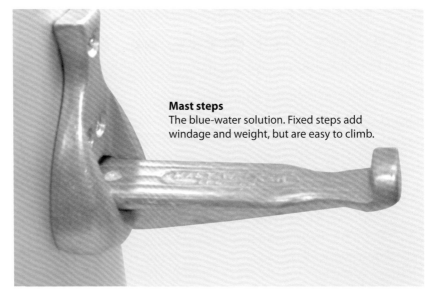

Mast steps
The blue-water solution. Fixed steps add windage and weight, but are easy to climb.

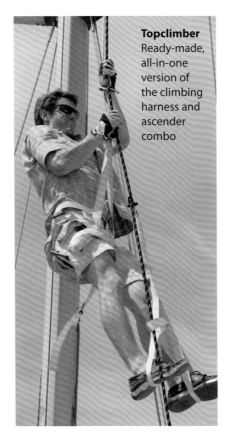

Topclimber
Ready-made, all-in-one version of the climbing harness and ascender combo

Mast track ladder
Less effort to climb than a flexible ladder, but more cumbersome to stow and still awkward to use

Mastlift
The 'armchair solution': almost as easy as hoisting a flag. Impressive but expensive

Conclusion

Watching the professionals at work convinced me that we live in a new era for mast climbing. If you don't have electric winches or a suitable windlass, you need to buy some climbing gear, but the modest investment will be richly rewarded, especially for a two-person crew. Because either can now climb the mast with equal ease, the one most suited to the job can go up, regardless of who is the stronger and who the lighter.

Eye-splicing braidline

Splicing an eye into braidline looks far more difficult than splicing one in three-strand rope, yet with the right tools, and a bit of skill, the job isn't nearly as hard as it seems

Show me a modern sailor and I'll show you a person familiar with braidline. We can knot it, jam it and coil it, but few of us can splice it. Splicing the ship's working ropes was once a given skill of any sailor. Three-strand rope used to be the standard issue, and many of us can splice this with one hand tied behind our backs. After all, the whole thing is out in the fresh air. We can see the parts of the rope, so we can tell what's going on and if we get it wrong, it's obvious straight away. Braidline is seen as a different animal altogether. But the job isn't nearly so hard as it seems. It's also highly satisfying and so long as you're not too ambitious about finesse, with a little practice it can be a piece of cake. The splice we show here is not the most sophisticated one under the heavens, but all of us can do it on our own boats, with no special kit other than a set of splicing fids.

Anatomy of braidline

Braidline can come in various guises, but the most common is double braid, or braid-on-braid. Variants with different types of core require alternative techniques. If I'm specifying braidline for my boat, I always go for this, because the choice means I don't need the services of a rigger.

Tools of the trade: (from top) sharp knife, set of fids, mallet, scissors – all available from your local hardware store and chandler's

A mallet is ued to help the rope's core run smooth as an eye is spliced into a length of braidline

Braid-on-braid has a braided core as well as a cover. The core is much more softly laid than the outer sheath

72

The braidline eye splice

1 First, sharpen your knife. If it's blunt, it will rip up the rope and make life a misery. Cut a fresh end carefully on a chopping board. The rope will try to unlay as soon as you lay the knife on it, so guard against this as best you can throughout the job.

2 Find the right size fid for the diameter of your rope - there should be a number on the fid to guide you – and measure one fid length from the end. Make a small dot on the rope with a marker pen (Mark A).

3 Take the rope around your thimble (or if you're not using a thimble, just decide how big you want the loop), and mark again as shown (Mark B).

4 a,b,c The splicing will disturb the rope's core and you need to tie a knot in the rope to stop it unravelling. Tie the knot about 6ft from Mark B. Set the knot up on a hook, if you have one, or contrive a substitute. The knot I used is shown to the right.

The braidline eye splice (continued)

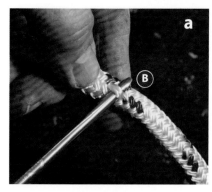

5 a,b,c Carefully open the coat at Mark B so that you can tease out the bight of the core. I use the smallest fid for this, but any reasonably blunt prodder will do. Part enough strands to get a good grip on the core. If the core doesn't come easily once you have hold of it, you've trapped a bit of the coat. Look carefully and sort it out.

6 When the core is clear and in hand, pull it right out from the bitter end so that you have the two parts lying next to one another. Finally, smooth out the coat with a 'milking' action towards the end to make sure any distortion is knocked out of it.

7 Lay the fid alongside the coat as shown. Then, holding the end of the fid and the core together between finger and thumb, pull out one fid length of core. It will come easily.

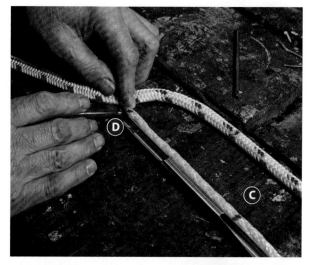

8 Put Mark C on the core at the point it is now exiting the coat.

9 Now pull out a further length of core. Lay the fid alongside it and place another mark two-thirds of a fid length from C. This is Mark D.

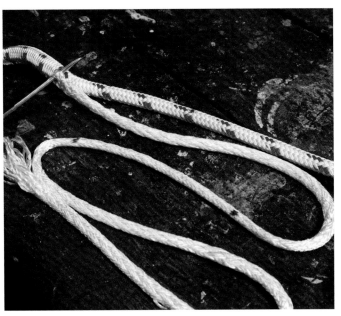

10 Pull out as much core as you can comfortably persuade to cooperate and pin it temporarily with your smallest fid. This serves no real purpose other than to make life easier.

11 Load the coat into the fid by pushing the end into the hollow towards the sharp tip of the fid. When it's inside, lay the rest into the blunt end, where a built-in hook will grab it.

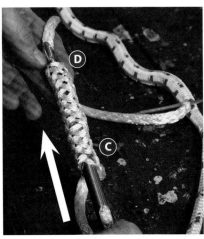

12 Open up the core at Mark C (the mark nearest the core's end), insert the fid.

13 Work it along the inside of the core to Mark D.

14 Poke it out there and pull the fid and the coat all the way through.

15 Disengage the fid.

16 Next, very carefully, milk the core so that it closes neatly around the coat.

17 Then gingerly pull the coat back so that its end just disappears inside the core.

The braidline eye splice (continued)

18 Take the tiny fid away from where it's been pinning the core and push it through the core/coat assembly. If you don't pin this, there's a real danger that the coat will slide out of the core while you are attending to the next stage.

19 Load the end of the core into a fid. Select the biggest fid you can conveniently pass through the inside of the coat. The core end will be breaking up by now, so wet it and stuff it into the fid as best you can.

20 Insert this fid at the point where the core that is surrounding the coat ends. This is also approximately Mark A. Work the fid towards Mark B where the core is exiting the coat. The fid will actually disappear inside the coat during this stage. This is the trickiest part of the splice.

21 Weasel the fid a little way past Mark B, at least one circumference of the rope. It is vital that once you are past Mark B, you don't snag the core in the undisturbed rope with the fid. If you do, the whole thing goes to rats. The way to be sure it isn't snagged, is to work the bight of the core where it's exiting the coat as you manoeuvre the fid. So long as it moves freely, all is well.

22 Do not be dismayed if you're struggling. You can tease it along quite nicely, but you need some perseverance to persuade it to exit neatly.

23 Free the core from the fid, then pull the core through until the loop, pictured here to the right, just disappears.

24 Remove the pin and carefully smooth everything down, paying particular attention to the section of coat which is now part of the eye. This may have been distorted. Sort it out so that it looks natural.

25 Now, at last, it's fun time! Holding the loop in both hands, pull the splice away from the knot on the hook. You'll see the bare core part of the loop swallowed up rapidly into the coat.

26 As the core/coat combo arrives at the splice, things will not go so easily. If it looks like sticking, don't force it. Instead, milk some slack out of the coat, away from the knot and towards the loop. Literally hold it tight and run your hands along it. You'll see the slack moving towards the splice. Keep the tension on and, as you milk, the splice will swallow it up. As one friend of mine observed, it's closely akin to threading knicker elastic.

27 When the combo has disappeared and all you've got left is a diminishing loop that looks like complete rope, introduce the thimble and carry on with the good work of milking.

28 As the thimble pulls up tight, slip some sort of stout tommy bar into it and heave hard, still milking if necessary. I use the long extension from an old socket set.

29 As soon as you think you're nearly there, cut off that untidy length of core that's hanging out below the splice. Now take the tommy bar in both hands, lean back, count to three, and jerk it hard a couple of times. What's left of the core will vanish inside and the thimble should be tight as a nut. If it doesn't look perfectly smooth, give it a whack or two with a mallet and another jerk for good luck.

Tapering
Tapering the splice makes a neater job and a professional will tell you it also confers additional strength. This is surely true, but I have found tapering is by far the trickiest item on the list and the splice works well without it. Some fid manufactuers recommend leaving out the taper. The main thing for the average sailor is to be able to execute a good working splice, so I have not included a taper here.

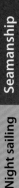

Night sailing

Some yachtsmen love the thrill and challenge of night sailing, while others shy away from it, fearful of unseen dangers. But with a little preparation you can enjoy the transition between day and night

Some people love night sailing, and there's no doubt that reaching bravely over an easy sea beneath the moon is a wonderful feeling – especially when the nearest land is a thousand miles away and you haven't seen a ship all week. It's a different story close in, with traffic, changeable weather, intricate pilotage and the intrinsic feeling that you're plunging along an unlit highway with no headlights. These concerns are not imaginary, so it's understandable that many skippers avoid a first brush with darkness for as long as they can. Sooner or later, however, we all must face up

to it because even in summer we aren't granted much over 15 hours of daylight. The rest is darkness.

With a view to sorting out some of the issues inherent in after-hours navigation, I went for a sail in the Solent with a couple of local chums. Rob Bell and David Kendall.

A leap in the dark
For someone like me who's been sailing night and day for a lifetime, it feels natural to go ahead into total blackness, confident that I won't pile up on some unseen horror. David and Rob have both dealt with the issue comparatively recently. Their

comments quickly brought home to me that an abstract anxiety about not being able to see where we're going is probably the most alarming spectre on the whole ghost train.

Talking it over in the cockpit at dusk, I realised that the answer is the same for all of us. It's a question of mind over matter. We've sailed in daylight, and we know that with the exception of navigation aids, charted hazards, the odd fishing marker and other vessels, there is nothing to hit. We could get unlucky and run into a stray container, but the chances of this are probably as remote as a tree falling on your car. More significantly, which of us can honestly say we're constantly scrutinising the seas for half-sunk perils on a daytime passage? Nobody can. Why? Because experience has shown that we don't have to.

The same truths hold good at night. The problem is getting over the primeval instinct that protects us from running down a rutted lane in pitch darkness. We three all found that we'd overcome it by firmly telling our fearful inner man that the sea isn't a lane, it's an open playing field. The only obstacles are either on the chart, well lit, or concentrated in areas we should sensibly avoid. As to the luck aspect, we agreed that if a stray tree trunk or oil drum has your name on it, you're slightly more likely to hit it after dark than in mid-afternoon, but the chances remain very slim indeed. David pointed out that if this were a genuine worry, you might as well give up the sea, leave your car permanently in the garage and be reborn as a couch potato.

Having dealt with the biggest hurdle, we slipped our lines and concentrated on finding a series of tips and pointers that can help us all out there in the darkness.

Navigation

The good news here is that navigation, as opposed to pilotage, is the same at night as it is in the daytime. Once you're well clear of the channels and buoys, you're dealing with fixes, estimates, distances run and courses to steer. The main difference after dark is that if you need a visual fix, you'll be using lights rather than headlands or distant church spires. Lights have the benefit of being unambiguous. You'll spot a north cardinal light long before you can confirm a topmark in daylight, even with binoculars, and unless the area is studded with them, the one you're seeing is generally the one you're looking for. Lighthouses are even less open to misinterpretation.

An EP remains a best estimate from your last known position. No need to eyeball anything other than log, compass and tidal atlas for one of these. The same applies to a course to steer. When it came to fixing electronically, none of us could come up with a single thing that daylight changes.

Harbour entries by night

For night pilotage, it's best to assume you'll discern nothing but the lights on navigation aids, unless you're expecting ambient illumination as you approach a town quay. If there are no aids and you've never been to the place before, my advice is to go somewhere else. My crewmates were interested in this point of view,

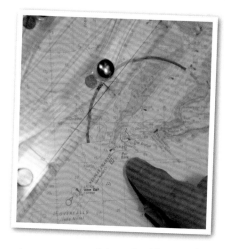

because one of them had been taken two miles up the unlit middle part of a river by his instructor after dark.

This can be a useful experience, but it's important to understand that it isn't a great idea if you've never been there before. I have 20/20 vision, I'm not noted for over-caution and I know the river well, but I'd avoid going up it after dark whenever I can. There are too many possibilities to come unstuck. In fact, I told the lads that after entering the well-lit port of Bilbao at 0100 many years ago in a sail-training vessel under my command, I awoke at dawn to see half the entrance encumbered with unlit debris. I'd been lucky, but I learned my lesson. Enter a strange port at night if you must, but be very careful indeed. Beware of assumptions such as, 'My chart is up to date,' and 'The fairway is bound to be clear.'

Ranging by eyeball

This can be nigh-on impossible after dark. A flashing buoy that seems far off can suddenly appear so near it looks like joining you in the cockpit. Watch out for this, and don't get too close, especially when the tide is swishing you on!

Ensign check

Make sure the ensign does not drape over a white stern light – turning it red

Pilotage plans and looking out

All three of us know our way into the river we'd chosen as well as we can recognise the path down to the local pub. Studying and writing up a pilotage plan therefore seemed like overkill. Coming in towards midnight and pretending it was our first try, we were left in no doubt that we'd have been glad of one. The sectored leading lights proved anything but easy to spot (the second only becomes visible among the shore lights when you're practically on it) and we were falling back on pile-hopping before they finally showed up.

Perhaps the most important lesson here was that the skipper (me) had to call on all hands to help him discern those lights. As an examiner, I hate it when the pilot peers alone into the darkness while the rest of the team does little more than steer or feel cold. Four pairs of eyes have a 400% better chance of finding a tiny flashing red.

The trick is to use the yacht as a gunsight. As you make a turn on your planned route, you should know the bearing of the next light. Steer the boat straight down this for a second or two, even if it isn't exactly the right course. Tell the hands, 'OK. East Cardinal buoy dead ahead. Who can see it?' Someone will, and it might not be you!

Four eyes are better than two

Remember that your night vision is best at the peripheries so try looking out of the corner of your eye if you can't pick up the object you're after.

Collision avoidance

What do you see?

You're out at sea with no lights visible, when a pair of whites rises over the horizon to port. They're about a finger's width apart and the one on the right is higher than the one on the left. They won't mean much to a beginner, but an old hand will say, 'Ten-to-one that's a ship's steaming lights. She's showing us her port side so there's no collision risk.'

It's all very well studying the books and flashcards, but there's no substitute for experience when it comes to vessels' lights. If you don't have any, try to make your early passages with others who do. If you can't manage this, just be extra cautious in places where shipping is dense, fast-moving and likely to be of tactical interest.

The fishermen in foreground are clear – but have you seen the ferry?

Take a look at the above shot. In the foreground is a fishing boat. He may well have the correct lights switched on, but he might not. In any case, they'll be obscured by his mega-bright working deck light. This is typical, and it's never in the books. But look behind him! Check out that cluster of lights among the shore clutter to the right of him. That's a ship coming our way, head-on. I had her clocked for what seemed ages before David and Rob picked her out. She's got red, green and two steaming lights almost in line. We're passing clear ahead, but it was easy to miss her while trying to suss the fisherman.

Track a ship's movements relative to static lights behind – binoculars can be a great help

Watch the background

Spotting ships is no problem far from land because the horizon is black. Close-in, it can be a different story. The only answer is to watch the line of shore lights and check for anything moving relative to the others, then sort out what it might be. Train your eyes to do this, and get your crew on the case as well. Don't forget the binoculars. They can make all the difference. Sometimes, they even gather enough light to show the form of the vessel.

Switch it off

Many modern yachts have all sorts of lights at their disposal. The Najad had the lot and we were careful to show the right ones. Motoring in, we passed a yacht dressed up like a Christmas tree with running lights (red and green forward, white stern light aft), a steaming light halfway up the mast, and, horror of horrors, her tricolour shining above as shown on the switch panel below.

Look around and you'll find this is far from unusual. We're all quick to complain about fishing craft, but this yacht was lit for lifting crab pots and bringing us all into disrepute.

Nav Lgt   Steam   Tricolour   Anchor   Deck

What not to do. Show either tricolour or running lights – NEVER BOTH

Collision avoidance (continued)

Tricolour or not

Under sail, Rob turned out his running lights in favour of his tricolour. Somewhat to his surprise, I suggested a different point of view. Tricolours are fine at sea, especially in waves. They can be seen at greater distances and, of course, they save amps.

Unfortunately, because they are sited high up, they don't help an observer sense how far off you are. For some reason lower lights are better, so in tight, calm waters I prefer to use the 'lowers' and take the hit on the batteries.

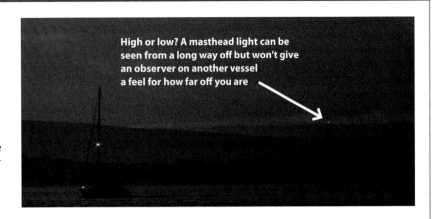

High or low? A masthead light can be seen from a long way off but won't give an observer on another vessel a feel for how far off you are

On passage

Keeping fresh

Full watch systems on small yachts only really start to work on passages of two nights or more. On one or half-nighters, nobody gets sufficiently into the swing of things to knuckle down to a formal arrangement. However, everyone needs rest, especially the skipper, so a régime needs to be established.

David had avoided night passages with his young family wherever possible, so we discussed ways of upgrading his wife's ability to keep watch while he managed enough shut-eye to be fresh when it counted – such as crossing shipping lanes and arriving in the dark. Building confidence gradually seemed the key.

It doesn't take much for a competent crew member to take a watch alone in open water and fair weather. Indeed, that remains one of my criteria for the qualification. Crew aren't much good to me if I can't trust them to steer and look out for a couple of hours, calling me if need be according to the agreed night orders.

Night orders

This is the crunch for any passage where the skipper goes off watch. The secret of a good kip is to be certain your watch-keeper understands when to call you. In my case, it's often a ship coming within the three-mile ring on my radar. If you don't have a radar, it might be any ship on a steady bearing, and so on. A change of wind, a nasty-looking cloud and, of course, the arrival at some waypoint pre-designated for a call. The

Give the crew clear instructions on when to call the skipper

final word must always be, 'Absolutely anything that leaves you in the slightest doubt, never hesitate to give me a shake.'

The whole system runs on mutual trust, and the obverse of the coin is that the skipper has to put a brave face on things if he's been disturbed for nothing. Even a muffled 'Tut' will make the watch-keeper hesitate next time.

Cockpit discipline

Harnesses

David and Rob were both well kitted up with modern gear. I didn't even have to ask them to put on harnesses on deck after dark. As skippers, they already knew. The point is that whether or not you use modern

lifejackets, if someone goes over the wall in the dark, retrieval can be an impossible task. The lifeline makes sure they don't, however inconvenient it seems.

Torches

A good torch in the watch-keeper's pocket is a must at night. It finds a thousand uses. I also keep a pocket strobe light which is passed on as the watch changes like a relay baton, so that anyone alone on deck has it. If he should go overboard and is not unconscious, as he probably won't be, he can activate it if need be.

ABOVE: Red light does not destroy night vision and should be used above and below decks when possible. LEFT: Hand torches are a must

Night vision

This is the stock in trade of all watch-keepers. It's up to them to remind 'torch-bearers' not to blind them. Of course, all attempts at maintaining night vision can be lost on one trip to the heads or to brew up. A useful tip here is to shut one eye firmly before you go below and keep it that way until you surface again. The irises work independently, and that peeper will keep its 'night status' intact.

Tidal curves

Mention the words 'secondary ports' and 'tidal heights' and most people recoil quickly. Yet they needn't be such cause for concern, and you don't need a degree in Advanced Mathematics to work them out

High Water at a secondary port can be 30 minutes earlier, or even 50 minutes earlier than at a standard port!

BEAULIEU RIVER

Max Speed 5 knots

If the Good Lord made tides to speed the prudent on their way and to float the unfortunate off the putty, the Devil made secondary ports to drive sane and courageous individuals to distraction, drink and despair. No two ports are exactly alike when it comes to rise and fall, but because there are hundreds of them, publishers watching their pennies and sailors wary of excess weight have no interest in promulgating individual tide tables for every single one. Until the merciful intervention of electronics, we were stuck with a workable number of 'standard ports' from which all others were calculated, and a list of secondary ports relating to them that was a lot longer than anybody's arm.

The handiest way to deal with a local secondary port is to grab a set of tide tables from the harbourmaster or a public-spirited chandler. Failing this easy solution, it's down to a chartplotter capable of the job, or the time-honoured wrestling match with the almanac, numbers and graphs, which is what we'll do here. Secondary ports should have been just a matter of applying simple corrections to the times and heights of HW and LW, but they aren't. The gremlins contrive to vary the differences between Springs and Neaps. These also change by different amounts in between, and they're extrapolated for super-Springs and mini-Neaps. You can see why they'd make people want to boil their heads. Happily, it doesn't have to be that bad! Ask five instructors and you'll get five ways of dealing with this – all no doubt very good. My own has worked for me for decades. I should add that I do not have a degree in physics and was obliged to resit O Level maths before any university would accept me to read something else altogether.

Getting started

TIME ZONE (UT)
For Summer Time add ONE hour in **non-shaded areas**

DOVER   LAT 51°07'N   LONG 1°19'E
TIMES AND HEIGHTS OF HIGH AND LOW WATERS

JANUARY		FEBRUARY		MARCH	
Time m	Time m	Time m	Time m	Time m	Time m
1 0333 1.7 0859 6.1 M 1614 1.5 2134 6.0	**16** 0332 2.1 0845 5.6 TU 1559 1.8 2119 5.7	**1** 0539 1.4 1051 6.1 TH 1813 1.4 2304 6.3	**16** 0459 1.4 1007 6.2 F 1725 1.3 2229 6.4	**1** 0440 1.7 1002 5.8 TH 1716 1.6 2214 6.0	**16** 0337 1.7 0900 5.8 F 1608 1.6 2123 6.1
2 0441 1.5 0956 6.2 TU 1719 1.4 2225 6.2	**17** 0428 1.8 0935 5.9 W 1652 1.5 2204 6.0	**2** 0629 1.2 1130 6.2 F 1855 1.2 ○ 2341 6.5	**17** 0551 1.0 1050 6.5 SA 1816 1.0 ● 2310 6.7	**2** 0535 1.3 1043 6.1 F 1801 1.3 2250 6.3	**17** 0434 1.3 0948 6.3 SA 1702 1.2 2207 6.5

LEFT: The standard port tidal heights we all know and use regularly in the almanac

BELOW: Heights and times are easily found in the almanac and anything not listed can be worked out from what's there

If you're thinking about secondary ports, it's likely you will know how to find out standard port tidal heights and times. I'll work through some of the basics below, but for this feature I'm assuming some knowledge of tidal tables and graphs.

Standard port data speak for themselves: you read the times and heights straight off the page. The illustration (above), from Reeds Nautical Almanac, shows part of a page that practically all British cruising sailors use regularly.

The next picture (below), also from Reeds, shows the entry for Folkestone, which also includes data for the unusual secondary port of Dungeness. I've chosen this one because few readers are likely to go there and thus it remains reassuringly theoretical. The first item of interest is the reference to the relevant standard port, which, in this case, is Dover. The arrow shows which way to turn the pages of the almanac to get there.

Where the table says High Water

(HW) and Low Water (LW), the times given refer to Dover. The time differences in the nearby secondary ports of Folkestone and Dungeness are listed below. So if HW Dover is at midnight (0000), HW Dungeness will be 10 minutes earlier (-0010) and so on. To the right, you'll see the height differences. These work similarly. If HW Dover is 6.8m, HW

Dungeness will be a metre higher (+1.0), at 7.8m.

The fun begins when the times or heights at Dover do not coincide with those listed here. The process of dealing with this is called interpolation and on its rock many an honest Yachtmaster candidate has seen his ship well and truly wrecked.

9.3.12 FOLKESTONE
Kent 51°04'·59N 01°11'·67E ※⊛⚓⚓⚘⚘

CHARTS AC *5605, 1892, 1991*; Imray C12, C8; Stanfords 20, 9.

TIDES –0010 Dover; ML 3·9; Duration 0500
Standard Port DOVER (⟶)

SHELTER Good except in strong E–S winds when seas break at the hbr ent.

Times				Height (metres)			
High Water		Low Water		MHWS	MHWN	MLWN	MLWS
0000	0600	0100	0700	6·8	5·3	2·1	0·8
1200	1800	1300	1900				
Differences FOLKESTONE							
–0020	–0005	–0010	–0010	+0·4	+0·4	0·0	–0·1
DUNGENESS							
–0010	–0015	–0020	–0010	+1·0	+0·6	+0·4	+0·1

The information for secondary ports Folkestone and Dungeness is listed here

Interpolating times

Inspect the figures for 'Dungeness'. Under 'High Water 0000' and 'High Water 1200' you'll see '-0010'. In other words, if HW at Dover comes at midnight or noon, you subtract 10 minutes to find the time of HW at Dungeness. This easy calculation works whenever local High or Low Water coincides with any Dover figure.

Inconveniently, this almost never happens. If HW Dover is at 0300, for example, you're left with an interpolation between the two differences given for 0000 and 0600. There are various methods for dealing with this by means of diagrams, but I find it's a lot easier and quicker to do it in my head.

For practical purposes, it simply isn't worth splitting hairs about fractions of a minute. All tidal data are, at best, only predictions. HW may well be a few minutes adrift in any case. The same system is used to interpolate LW times.

Dungeness may not be the yachtsman's ideal destination but it's tidal difference to its standard port of Dover make it a useful subject!

Times				Height (metres)			
High Water		Low Water		MHWS	MHWN	MLWN	MLWS
0000	0600	0100	0700	6·8	5·3	2·1	0·8
1200	1800	1300	1900				
Differences FOLKESTONE							
–0020	–0005	–0010	–0010	+0.4	+0.4	0.0	–0.1
DUNGENESS							
–0010	–0015	–0020	–0010	+1.0	+0.6	+0.4	+0.1

2

How to find the tidal time difference for Dungeness:
1 HW Dover is 1600.
2 Differences given for Dungeness are -0010 (at 1200) and -0015 (at 1800). The difference therefore varies by 5 minutes in 6 hours, which means it's changing at roughly a minute an hour. HW at 1600 will vary from the 1200 figure by 4 hours, which, in the case of Dungeness, we can calculate will be around 4 minutes.
3 Subtract this from the -0010 minute figure because we are moving towards -15 minutes.
Therefore, when HW Dover is 1600, HW Dungeness is around -0014 minutes earlier, at 1546.

Interpolating heights

The system for calculating time differences also works with tidal height differences, the only variance being that first you need to deduce whether you are on Spring or Neap tides. We all know how to do this – subtract the LW height from the HW height and compare the answer to the 'Spring' and 'Neap' ranges listed in a box on your standard port's tidal graph.

As with working out the time differences, I then simply use an intelligent assessment of the situation in my head.

The differences between Dover and Dungeness are modest. Some ports differ even less, while others change dramatically. Stansore Point, on the bar of Beaulieu River in the Solent, varies by 45 minutes or more. The principles remain the same and the more you work them, the easier they become. I've kept boats in the Beaulieu for years and rattling off a quick 'secondary port' to see if I can scrape in or not has become as much of a motor function as putting one foot in front of the other to walk.

Given an understanding of interpolation, a simple table is the best way to deal with secondary ports:

Here's an example for Dungeness. The question is to find the time and height for evening HW and LW on Saturday 17 March. Dover range is 5.3m, as you see (difference between High and Low Water). Spring range is 6.0, Neap is 3.2, therefore we're around ¼ the way down from Springs to Neaps.

You'll have noticed that I have been rounding hours and

With practice, a quick look at the information before you provides a useful answer without having to resort to complicated and time-consuming diagrams or graphs

decimal points of metres up or down. I make no apology for this. By doing so you are unlikely to be further adrift than, perhaps, five minutes out of a six-hour period, or more than 0.1m in height. Remember that local weather anomalies can and do affect the predictions. Expect a tide to be a foot lower (both at high and low waters) if atmospheric pressure is very high. Levels are generally greater when pressure is low, especially in times of strong onshore wind.

All tidal height calculations need to be treated with circumspection. Interpolating in your head rather than working to fractions on paper or constructing diagrams may add a small measure of the unknown but, so long as you bear this in mind, little is lost but stress, while the speed of the process, once mastered, saves precious time.

HW	Time	Height	LW	Time	Height
Dover	2207	6.5	Dover	1702	1.2
Difference			Difference		
Dungeness	– 0011	+0.9	Dungeness	– 0013	+ 0.2
HW Dungeness	2156	7.4	LW Dungeness	1649	1.4

Mid-tide level on paper

Whether you're working on a standard or a secondary port, the system for arriving at a tidal height is the same.

Simply fill in the tidal graph of the standard port, using the times and heights you have calculated for the secondary port. You'll find standard port tidal height graphs in the almanac.

I normally plot in the almanac with a 2B pencil, but if you're entering a port often, it pays to scan its graph and run off a few copies.

Once you have filled in all the secondary port information, use the almanac's tidal graph for the standard port as normal, remembering to add the extra hour for British Summer Time after the differences have been applied

Filling in a tidal curve

Each standard port is supplied with a tidal height graph which is published in the almanac. These look a bit fearsome if you're unused to working in this way, but they are extremely easy to use. Here's the procedure.

To find the height of tide at 2000 on Saturday, 17 March, at Dungeness:

First, find the heights of High and Low Water from the almanac, in this case 7.4m and 1.4m.

Mark those values on the top line (High Water) and bottom line (Low Water) on the graph. Plot line A between the points.

In the series of boxes along the bottom, fill in the time of High Water Dungeness (2156) and any subsequent or preceding times that are of interest to you.

To find the height of tide at a particular time, in our case 2000, plot line B from 2000 (which is HW-2) up to the curves. There are two curves. The solid one represents Springs and the pecked line is Neaps. We are one quarter from springs towards neaps,

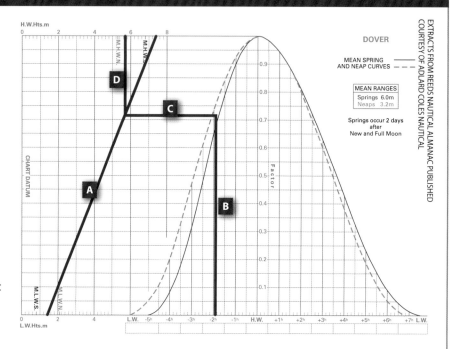

so choose a suitable point between the two.

From the point where line B joins the curves, plot line C horizontally to A, then plot line D upwards to the tidal heights

at the top. We can see the height of tide at 2000 is 5.70m.

To find the time of a given height of tide, just reverse the procedure.

Solent curves

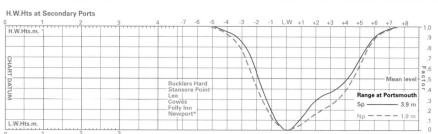

Because of the double-tide situation between Swanage in the west and Chichester in the east, it has been found unreliable to predict the time of HW in the Solent with any degree of accuracy. The time of LW is far more solid. Special curves are therefore issued (and are in the almanac) for all ports associated with the Solent.

Find the special Solent tidal curves in the almanac. Failure to use them can lead to disappointing results!

The tides at Bucklers Hard and elsewhere in the Solent have their own curves

Chartplotters

Most chartplotters now show tidal information for secondary ports

Zone time
Tidal difference data is presented in GMT (also known as 'Zone Time', or 'Zulu'), and not in any form of daylight saving time such as BST. If you are looking for accuracy, do the whole job in Zulu, then add on any sunlight hours at the end.

Any modern chartplotter worthy of the name incorporates tidal height data for most of the ports covered by its charts. The trick is to find out where it is. Raymarine units show a tiny 'T' in a diamond near the port in question. Hover the cursor over this and 'enter'. Basic data pops up, which can be converted to a fully dynamic graphic display by one more hit of the button. My small Garmin delivers a first-class result via the menus. Meridian PC software produces a clear tidal curve on demand, as does Seapro. Whatever your electronic choice, it'd be a sad piece of kit that didn't measure up these days. There's just one proviso: I have four plotters at my disposal. All deliver tidal graphs and all give slightly different answers. If it really matters, therefore, I revert to pencil and 'Mark I Admiralty', courtesy of Reeds, thank you very much.

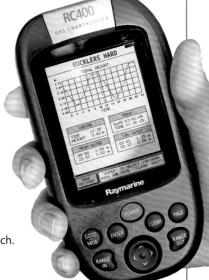

Staying safe with radar

Modern radar sets are becoming ever-more sophisticated. But as they do so, so the risks of potentially disastrous 'radar-assisted collision' are increased. Knowing how to get the best out of your radar is, therefore, crucial

The late Alexander Filatov, an instructor at the Moscow Cruising School, one of Russia's premier maritime education establishmen ts, sent me an email some time ago in which he voiced his concern that most radar manuals for leisure sailors concentrate on using 'head-up' displays, and tend to ignore the other options now generally available.

He cited the well-documented incident in May 2003, when the Moody 47 *Wahkuna*, en route from France to the south coast of the UK, was run down and sunk in fog in the English Channel by a 66,000-tonne P&O Nedlloyd container ship. The conclusion of the accident report was that it was a clear case of 'radar-assisted collision.'

As well as radar, *Wahkuna* was equipped with MARPA which, in case you haven't remembered,

stands for 'Mini Automatic Radar Plotting Aid'.

Inbuilt into many plotter/radar setups, MARPA should be a really useful tool, but not everyone finds it as handy as it sounds. My own boat is equipped with all this gear, yet MARPA had always given muddy results that I wouldn't care to trust with my life. Was it me, I wondered, or was my equipment not doing what it said on the box?

I first used radar on the bridge of a coaster in the 1970s. The unit was the size of a Las Vegas fruit machine. You had to stick your face in a huge sight guard, inside which the glimmering, green display offered 'head-up or nothing'. Today's daylight-viewable sets are far more sophisticated, but a can of worms lurks under the 'display options' button.

'Head-up', 'Course-up', or 'North-up'

is, as Hamlet might have observed, the question. Mr Filatov held strong views on this. As for me, I didn't really have a clue. Although I was confident with operating traditional radar, it was becoming clear that there were gaping holes in my understanding of my own modern sophisticated radar kit. I tried the manuals, but they were written on a different planet by a sub-species of *Homo sapiens*, 'Electronic Man'. I needed help, so I called my friend Alan Watson.

If ever there was an electronics guru, it's Alan. He started out as a young 'sparky' in the Merchant Navy. After countless miles under the red duster, he came ashore to work in radar and communications. He's now one of Britain's leading authorities. We met aboard his seamanlike Nelson launch.

Anatomy of a collision

Moody 47

In May 2003, the P&O Nedlloyd container ship was travelling at 25 knots in thick fog when the yacht *Wahkuna* was detected at a range of 5-6 miles on the port bow. The ship's master estimated the yacht would cross eight cables ahead. But at a range of 1.5-2 miles, *Wahkuna* slowed quickly.

The Marine Accident Investigation Board concluded two actions by the yacht and three by the ship caused the collision. There was a misunderstanding of the COLREGS. *Wahkuna*'s skipper thought he was the 'stand-on' vessel. Such a status does not exist during restricted visibility. In fog, the onus is on both vessels to 'take avoiding action in ample time'.

The inability of *Wahkuna*'s crew to use radar effectively was also cited.

The yacht had two radar displays. In the run-up to the collision, the cockpit display was monitored but many of the radar set's features (10-target tracking, selectable target vectors, target risk assessment with danger alarm, history plots, target speed, course, CPA and TCPA) were not used.

The ship's high speed in fog, plus too small passing distance and an undermanned bridge also contributed to the collision.

Yachtsmen should be aware of the alarming statistic from the MAIB report, which revealed that only one ship out of 19 in the vicinity of this incident reduced her speed because of the fog. They were all monitored by radar surveillance, by Jobourg Vessel Traffic Service.

FREYA

Pros and cons of display options

Alan began by making sure I was clear on the basics. I wasn't entirely surprised when his first action was to flash up the display options on his fully linked Raymarine E-series. The same results could have been had with my C-series or various radar sets from other manufacturers. Here, in a nutshell, is a breakdown of the main display options.

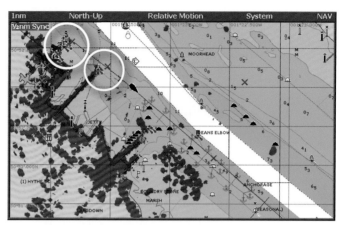

Radar overlay on the plotter. The illustrations below, showing head-up, course-up and north-up were taken with the boat at approximately the position shown. Top ring: Marina entrance. Lower ring: Hythe Pier

Head-up

The heading line points from the centre to the top of the screen and no external data are fed into the radar. It stands entirely on its own, assuming itself to be stationary with all other objects moving around it. Its reference point is the bow of the boat.

Plus points
The picture corresponds with what you see when looking straight ahead from the cockpit. An object off the port quarter will therefore be in the lower left quadrant of the screen, and so on. On the face of things, this makes orientation with the outside world intuitive, but there's more to it than meets the eye.

Minus points
If your course changes, the picture will appear to rotate. This can lead to considerable confusion. A further issue is that it is difficult or impossible to tell at a glance what another ship's aspect may be. All you can be sure of is where she is and, after a while, what her movements are – but only in relation to your own. A yacht yaws and wobbles in her course, so this mode is not ideal for collision avoidance because targets appear to zig-zag.

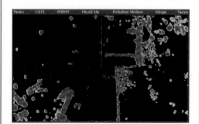

The head-up radar image with the boat travelling down the river. Note the markers for the marina entrance

North-up

A paper chart on the table with north at the top is said to be 'north-up'. To deliver a north-up picture to the screen, the radar processor takes in data flowing from a fluxgate compass, usually from the autopilot. Although the radar picture is stable with north at the top, the heading line follows your direction of travel. If you are steering 090, the heading line points to 3 o'clock.

Plus points
〉 Comparing the screen with the chart is simple and intuitive. The screen stays in the same mode no matter what, so if you change your heading, any targets you are monitoring do not alter theirs.
〉 Because the display is linked to the compass rather than the ship's head, it is said to be stabilised. This means that any minor yawing and pitching that upset the head-up display are, to a large extent, neutralised.

Minus points
North-up is sometimes awkward for comparing the screen directly with the outside world. If you are steering south, the top of the radar screen shows what is happening astern of you. This can be disconcerting.

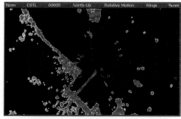

The north-up radar image. Note the immediate similarity to the chart with radar overlay, above

Course-up

On the face of things, this looks just like head-up, but information from the compass is used to stabilise the picture. Short-term yaw is thus removed, just as with north-up. In course-up, the top of the screen represents your course.

Usually, the heading line wavers from side to side of it, indicating where you have yawed to right now. Exactly what is meant by 'course' may vary with different radar manufacturers. Raymarine, for example, uses a priority order to work out which heading to stabilise to:
〉 Bearing from origin to destination (ie between waypoints).
〉 Locked heading from autopilot.
〉 Bearing to waypoint.
〉 Instantaneous heading (ie the course you are steering by hand).

Plus and minus points
These are similar to head-up with the important exception that because the image is stabilised by the sampling of compass data, the collision avoidance potential of a course-up display is more reliable.

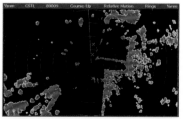

Course-up radar image: similar to head-up, image, but the display is stabilised against yawing around her course

How to avoid 'radar assisted collision'

Head-up

Wahkuna was run down by a ship in dense fog. She was abandoned, sinking, in an orderly manner and no lives were lost. Her radar appears to have been set to head-up. Could the collision have been avoided?

Alan began by pointing out that the first action on identifying a new target should be to place the electronic bearing line (EBL) on it. This line emanates from the centre of the screen (your ship). If the target stays on it and closes its range, it is by definition on a steady bearing and you are in a potential collision situation. What action to take may not be obvious, because without going into the laborious and somewhat academic process of plotting, you will not be able instantly to tell the aspect of the other vessel if you cannot physically see her. All you know is that she is tracking towards where you will be.

A common error is to assume that the other vessel is heading towards you. A classic example is when you are overtaking a vessel you assume to be closing from your port bow and showing you a green light. At least, however, the collision risk is identified.

On *Wahkuna*, the radar was in head-up mode, as it is by default on most yachts. It appears that the EBL was not deployed. The target in question seemed set to pass fairly close according to unassisted radar observation, so it was decided to take off way and let it pass ahead. Unfortunately, the ship was in fact passing almost a mile astern. This would be hard to judge by eye on the screen, but the EBL would have shown it within a few minutes. Had the yacht kept going, she would have been fine. When she took off way, she lost steerage and her heading began to alter. Naturally enough, the radar picture now seemed to indicate that the ship's bearing was changing. In fact, it wasn't. It was the yacht's heading that was swinging around. The ship, meanwhile, was powering straight for the centre of the screen, but from a series of apparently different directions, so that it appeared to be almost spiralling in towards them. In due course, it hit, with well-documented results.

North-up

My Russian correspondent was of the opinion that had *Wahkuna*'s radar been set to north-up she would have seen what was happening immediately and been able to take avoiding action.

Of course, in north-up, the target's heading would not have appeared to change as *Wahkuna* started to swing round. It would have been seen coming on in a straight line which, as it grew closer, would have represented an obvious risk of collision – even without the electronic bearing line. The stabilising effect of the compass input would also have made things a lot clearer than the head-up confusion. Alan agreed with this, but went further.

Course-up

Had *Wahkuna*'s radar been set on course-up, the picture would probably have maintained its orientation as she lost way – it would certainly have done so had she been on autopilot or been proceeding towards a waypoint. The question in my mind was, would the screen retain its orientation when all way, and hence perhaps the 'course', was lost?

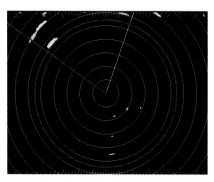

North-up or course-up?

Clearly, in this situation, either would be far safer than the unstabilised option of head-up. When I queried his logic, Alan pointed out that the advantage of course-up over north-up is that the picture is more instantly recognisable while way is still on. It could certainly be argued that with way off, the boat drifting, and the course stabilised to the last continuous heading, a course-up display might confuse an inexperienced operator.

The answer is that anyone using radar should know what these options are, understand what they mean, and remember which has been selected. Above all, he or she must be aware of the EBL and VRM (variable range marker) – and use them.

How MARPA works

With the choice of display options now clear in my mind, I asked Alan why I was getting odd results with MARPA. With MARPA switched on, you have only to select a target to set the program in motion. A minute or two later, when the radar and the processor have 'shaken hands', a symbol appears on the target indicating its course, speed and closest point of approach (CPA). Full MARPA data is accessed via a further click or press of a button, including the time to CPA and speed, potentially to ± 1 knot. The trouble is that, in practice, some of this information doesn't appear to make sense. I have passed a buoy in clear sight that MARPA proclaimed to be proceeding towards me at 6 knots. Results have also been unstable, apparently subject to the boat's yawing around, despite my having pricey gear to minimise this. It all seemed poor value compared with AIS, except, of course, that AIS only works when the target has it switched on, if it has it at all. Alan explained the errors of my ways.

True or relative motion?

Buried not too deeply in the radar menus is an option that's important whatever features you are using. If MARPA is running, the choice is critical. The alternatives are 'Relative motion' and 'True motion'.

Relative motion

Relative motion means that all targets move on the screen in relation to your ship. In this respect, it is equivalent to 'head-up'. Indeed, with the radar set to head-up, only relative motion will be available. With MARPA engaged and relative motion selected, all courses and speeds will be given as relative values. This accounts for the buoy cruising along on a course which is, of course, reciprocal to your own. For a ship heading across your track, the computations are more complex, but the bottom line is the same. The

With MARPA running, Tom twiddles a knob to select relative motion

MARPA LIST - True Data						
ID	Bearing	Range	Course	Speed	CPA	TCPA
1	298°T	9.647nm	091°T	21.2kt	2.821nm	00h25m34s
2	308°T	10.89nm	093°T	20.4kt	6.804nm	00h21m59s
3	331°T	8.237nm	092°T	11.9kt	6.041nm	00h21m30s
4	314°T	9.801nm	204°T	7.0kt	8.557nm	00h22m29s
5	300°T	11.12nm	098°T	19.6kt	4.260nm	00h29m04s
6	307°T	12.04nm	092°T	16.5kt	6.306nm	00h35m38s
7	353°T	8.153nm	081°T	9.9kt	7.512nm	00h12m07s
8	358°T	7.065nm	086°T	7.0kt	5.433nm	00h27m44s
9	012°T	7.434nm	088°T	10.1kt	7.057nm	00h10m15s
10	022°T	8.100nm	069°T	12.1kt	8.080nm	00h01m40s

Lollipops and electronic wakes

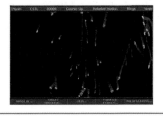

The fix and the lollipop stick
Using the EBL for an instant check on collision possibility can readily be augmented by fixing the target's position on the screen. The cross-bearing is supplied by the variable range marker (VRM). The VRM is an adjustable circle centred on your boat. To refer it to a target you've only to wind the knob or tap the arrow until the ring moves to the desired range. When it's on the target, it is crossing the EBL, and the two lines fix the target's position at that moment as surely as if they were pencil lines on a chart. The fix will stay where it is until you actively move one or other of its component lines.

As the target moves away from the fix, its closest point of approach to the centre of the screen can be estimated by placing a lollipop stick (or some other 'soft' straight edge) across it and the fix left behind it.

The target is effectively moving along the edge of the stick and seeing where it is going is a simple matter of visual extrapolation. Cheap, cheerful and totally reliable.

Confused by electronic wakes?
Most of today's radars can display an electronic wake, apparently 'astern' of a target. The usefulness of this in head-up, unstabilised relative motion is questionable, because of the risk of confusing this with the actual wake created by the vessel in the water. Change course yourself, and all the wakes take on a kink. They may even be coming out of the bow of a vessel being overtaken. Odd. In true motion, they show where the target is actually heading. You have only to lay the lollipop stick along the wake so that its extrapolation crosses your heading line to see what is going to happen, and whether this should concern you.

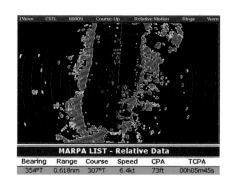

MARPA LIST - Relative Data					
Bearing	Range	Course	Speed	CPA	TCPA
354°T	0.618nm	307°T	6.4kt	73ft	00h05m45s

Relative motion and MARPA – the triangle is a buoy identified by MARPA as a target. Because it is being asked relative motion, it shows the buoy travelling towards the vessel at around 6 knots, which is the vessel's own speed

CPA may be accurate – or as accurate as it can be if your radar is on unstabilised head-up – but it won't be what is really happening.

Any attempt to use unassisted MARPA to determine the aspect of the other ship will be doomed to failure.

True motion

Once the radar picture is set on a stabilised course-up or north-up, it can be further clarified by opting for true motion. This uses the processor to show targets as they really are, rather than as they appear in relation to you at the centre of your own little world. It means that the movement

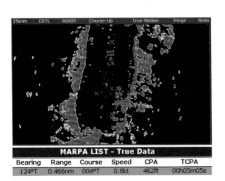

True motion and MARPA – the triangle is the same buoy in the previous illustrations, but the radar has been switched to true motion. The buoy now appears as it really is – stationary. For purposes of MARPA, anything less than 1 knot can usually be taken as zero

of targets is independent of your yacht's motion.

The effect on MARPA is immediate: a ferry is logging 20 knots, the buoy is stationary, and a yacht running parallel to you is making the same speed that you are, on the same course. The stabilised heading removes most of the problems of yaw so that, suddenly, this remarkable piece of equipment starts to earn its keep.

Whether you opt for true or relative motion, it is vital to have a firm grasp on what they mean, to choose in light of what you want to know, and to remember which mode is active.

Using split-screen radar to show both options

Opting to display a split-screen setup, with true motion on one half of the screen and relative on the other, is a sensible plan. Relative (with EBL) shows any targets

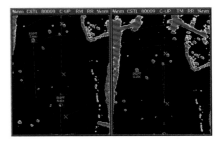

Split screen display to clarify true and relative motion. The target on the port bow is in fact stationary, but only the true motion display shows this unequivocally at a glance

heading for centre screen and draws attention to them.

The EBL cannot be used with true motion to determine collision, because 'collision targets' are not usually heading for centre screen. The importance of the true motion picture is that it indicates the aspect of targets, thus providing data that empowers you to decide what action to take.

Radar-assisted collision – could it happen to you?

Alan Watson observed that had *Wahkuna* maintained course and speed, the two vessels would have passed 0.8 miles apart. The ship was making 25 knots in zero visibility and thus was far from blameless, but this was a radar-assisted collision that the yacht could have readily avoided.

Like many leisure sailors, it seems probable that the yacht's crew were not privy to all the skills flagged up by Alexander Filatov. I wonder how many of us could raise our hands and say, 'I know all that. It couldn't possibly have happened to me....'

Compass deviation

Mobile phones, engines and even lead keels can affect the accuracy of your onboard compass. By using the simple technique of 'swinging' your compass, however, you can ensure your primary navigation tool is calibrated to pinpoint accuracy

Most sailors will, at some time, have peered long and hard into a compass bowl. For the best part of a thousand years, the compass has been the mariner's bulwark against confusion, pointing inexorably northwards no matter how the vessel may writhe beneath it. It never occurred to me that anything would challenge its sover-

eignty until a singular event a couple of years back.

I was on a coastal passage in poor visibility on a yacht equipped with a chart plotter and an autopilot. The plotter's projected track enabled me to see my course over the ground (COG) at a glance; the tide was with me so there was no significant cross-set. My arrival waypoint was clear on

the screen but the track arrow indicated I was off by a few degrees. I hit the 'minus 1' button on the autopilot once or twice and watched the track line swing across the chart until it sat over where I wanted to go. So is the compass redundant?

Not a bit of it. On any longer passage in a turning tide, only a compass course can make the most of the currents. If we use the plotter to stick to the rhumb line, or follow the waypoint 'GoTo' as the stream ebbs and floods, we sail a lot further through the water than we need. A yacht needs a compass like a flower rain, and a skipper piloting though shoals must use the compass to check transits, to establish bearings and for many other reasons. The compass, then, although its function may have shifted and been diluted by recent developments, remains a vital piece of kit.

How accurate can a yacht compass be?

A compass will always point to the vicinity of the North Pole, but it must be free from error. Any errors that arise from the planet – 'variation' – are tabulated on a navigation chart. More sinister is the 'deviation' induced by metalwork and other magnetic features within the yacht. Deviation may be non-existent, a degree or two, or as much as 180 degrees. Discovering and dealing with modest deviation lies well within the capabilities of us mortals, but coping with bigger numbers is the work of the professionals.

To learn more about compass deviation I borrowed *Sailfin*, a Bénéteau Océanis 43, and spoke to compass expert Ron Robinson.

Deviation
What is it?

Once, in the days before GPS, I found myself in the North Sea on a trip to Norway. When I plotted my first celestial noon fix, I found I was way to the east of where I hoped to be. The second day was worse. On the third day I began steering 'up' to lay off this oddity. My offset proved correct and on the fourth day I was on course. I'd found out by observation that the yacht's compass had a deviation on northerly headings. It was real, not the fantasy of some faceless writer of exam papers, and I'd compensated for it by experiment.

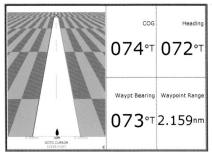

Has technology rendered the compass redundant?

What causes it?

Classically, deviation results from one or more lumps of on-board ferrous metal that can't be moved – usually an engine or even an iron keel – being too close to the compass. Deviation varies with the ship's heading because the aspect of the onboard metals changes as the vessel alters course.

Yacht construction

Neither plastic nor stainless steel affects compasses, so a typical modern production cruising yacht often pops out of the shrink-wrap with no deviation worth mentioning. Older wooden yachts with iron fastenings may not be so lucky, and a steel or a ferro yacht typically suffers significant deviation.

Extreme deviation

I'd been aware that deviation of cosmic proportions can be caused by modern equipment, but it wasn't until I talked with Ron Robinson that I realised the full extent of the madness. Radio speakers feature serious magnets. If a careless builder

Cockpit speakers and electric winches can deviate a compass significantly

or retro-fitter has sited one in your binnacle, stand by for extravagant effects. Even sited in the coamings, they can affect a steering compass. Ron considers deviations of 170 degrees by no means unusual.

Even an apparently innocuous piece of gadgetry can deviate a compass significantly. Almost five degrees resulted from our test with my mobile phone – and five degrees is a five-mile error at the end of a 60-mile passage.

However, the *prima donna* of deviation generators is the electric winch. Ron told us about one well-known manufacturer that sites these on each side of the cockpit, immediately outboard of the pedestals for twin wheels. Unfortunately, the motors are driven by monster magnets which drag a compass needle miles from its proper heading. If you activate the winch, the card literally spins round and round – the sort of challenge a compass adjuster relishes, but not what the navigator wants to see.

What to do about deviation

The best solution to deviation is to remove it, either by siting the compass far enough away from interference for it not to matter, or by adjusting the instrument. In order to tabulate deviation, the compass must be 'swung'. Many sailing yacht producers consider it unnecessary, or an owner's responsibility. Fortunately, you can do the job yourself.

Every compass should be swung for deviation. If this is small or non-existent, we can deal with it ourselves. If it is more than a few degrees, we owe it to ourselves to call in a compass adjuster.

How to swing the compass

Our Bénetéau 43 had two steering positions and two compasses offering different readings. At least one was subject to deviation. On a boat with a single compass things are simpler. The quickest way of determining whether or not a compass is free of in-yacht error is to check it against the handbearing compass. This presupposes that the handbearing unit is unsullied by interference – if, for example, it is being used by someone standing beside an electric winch. To make sure the handbearing compass is reliable, here's a trick I learned from a lifeboat coxswain – and endorsed by Ron Robinson.

1 Take the yacht into quiet open water with a distant (at least three miles) object in clear view and a buoy of some sort close at hand to verify your position.

2 Position your mate on the boat where magnetic interference

will be at a minimum. The mate observes the distant object – we chose a tower – with the handbearing compass.

3&4 Once your mate has a clean bearing on the tower, drive the yacht slowly round in a complete circle. The mate turns on deck as you go, continually taking the bearing of the distant tower. I made sure I didn't stray more than 50 yards or so from my buoy.

5 Because of the distance to the tower, its bearing would not materially alter while we made our circle, so the reading should remain constant. If it did not, it would indicate deviation and we'd then have to repeat the operation with the handbearing compass somewhere else on board. As it was, positioned near the stainless steel backstay the result was good. The handbearing compass was proved.

6 All that remained was to execute a series of courses and to compare the steering compass reading with one

taken on the handbearing compass looking dead ahead. The tower was now redundant – we could do this anywhere at any time. Discrepancies would mean deviation of the steering compass. If it read 205 when the handbearing compass said 203, for example, the deviation was two degrees west on that heading, and so on. Given that the deviation figures were low, eight headings were sufficient.

The Bénetéau's two steering compasses

Heeling error and on-passage checks

A mobile phone can deviate a compass by as much as five degrees

On a longish leg of a passage it's worth using the proved handbearing compass to check the course. A yacht that is well heeled over – with the iron keel out to one side – may be subject to considerable compass errors. Take a look. If in doubt, trust the handbearing compass. Granted, you haven't proved the instrument for all angles of heel and on every heading because that just isn't practical, but it is the best check you have.

A yacht that is heeled over may be subject to considerable compass errors

Radar and AIS

Combining radar with an Automatic Identification System provides an extra level of information about shipping movements in your area, and can be a vital resource to have on board when navigating at night or in fog

During a recent summer cruise, my boat limped into a marina after a rough North Sea crossing. I was reflecting on the increasing levels of commercial traffic in the area when I started talking with my neighbours, Colin and Fiona Martin, who'd arrived from Holland a few hours earlier on their Westerly Oceanlord *Pirate*. It turned out we both had modern chartplotters with radar overlay and MARPA. Despite this, and being fully equipped with the eyes our mothers gave us, we'd all had a rough ride with the shipping.

Visibility hadn't been great although we hadn't suffered any fog. I'd been using my radar, but Colin was singing the praises of his new AIS equipment. I'd only a vague idea as to what this was. Some sort of device whereby ships could tell you automatically who they were, how big and where bound, perhaps? Fascinating, no doubt, but all I wanted to know was, 'Is he going to

hit me?' As Colin began explaining, I realised that this was something that could make life a lot easier, and that it was high time I sorted out my act. Colin suspected he wasn't getting the best from his radar, so we agreed to share a day out on *Pirate* and compare notes.

Jargon buster

AIS – Automatic Identification System
MARPA – Mini Automatic Radar Plotting Aid
EBL – Electronic Bearing Line on a radar screen
VRM – Variable range marker on a radar screen
SOG – Speed over the ground
COG – Course over the ground
CPA – Closest point of approach in a ship-to-ship encounter, often expressed in miles, decimals, and time to go (TTG)
IMO – International Maritime Organisation
ROT – Rate of turn

What is AIS?

Ships over 300 tons are now obliged to carry an AIS transmitter and to have it switched on, though there are exceptions to this rule. AIS consists of a processor which gathers position, SOG, COG and ROT from the ship's GPS. It transmits this 'dynamic information' via VHF to anyone within range who has the kit to decipher the signal. Also broadcast is static information – the ship's call sign, name, IMO identification number and dimensions. Voyage-related material is appended, including draught, cargo, destination and ETA. Much of this is of

only general interest to yachts, but the ship movement data can be solid gold when related to your boat by your own receiver.

What does a yacht's AIS receiver do?

A typical yacht's AIS receiver does not transmit anything, so it doesn't help ships 'see' her. Instead, it reads out all the AIS data arriving from any ship within VHF range. By relating her position, course and speed to your own, it can immediately give your CPA to the vessel in question, and at what time this will occur. Accuracy levels are, for all practical purposes, very high.

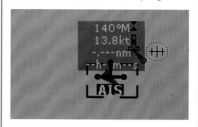

How does AIS display its information?

AIS data is gathered by an 'engine' (a black box the size of a video tape tucked away somewhere) and overlayed on the chart of a compatible PC or chart plotter.

If you don't have a plotter, you can instal a stand-alone unit with a screen

for surprisingly little money. The display looks like a simple radar, but of course it only shows vessels that are sending AIS signals. It shows nothing else. Most systems feature a menu which allows you to activate projected track vectors.

AIS targets can also be displayed on

compatible radar screens, making contact identification unambiguous.

Land your cursor on an AIS contact and the only thing you won't know is what the captain had for breakfast.

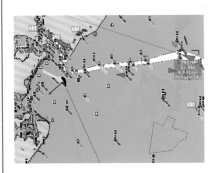

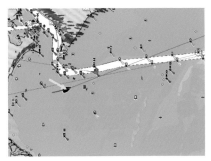

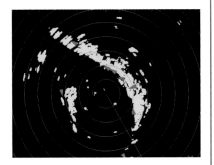

Installing AIS

Installing AIS is just a matter of buying a suitable receiver and wiring it up. A stand-alone set needs power and a VHF aerial. A plotter-compatible unit also needs plumbing into the 'bus' wiring or the plotter itself.

Conflicting views exist as to whether a dedicated VHF antenna is required for an AIS receiver. Some people say it is cheaper, easier and equally effective to use a 'splitter' on the existing aerial lead. Older-style splitters may cause problems. In addition to sockets for VHF and AIS, the unit carries a bonus socket for your FM radio antenna.

The little black box that contains the AIS 'engine'

AIS in practice

It can be hard to tell which is the bow and which the stern of some modern ships

Was this container ship turning towards us? A glance at the AIS told us all

When I arrived to meet Colin and Fiona, the AIS had gone down.

'Highly unusual,' said John the electronics engineer who'd manfully arrived to bail us out. Nice to know, of course, but we three had given up a day for this. John kept his cool. The most likely cause seemed to be the dedicated aerial, but after further diagnostics, John decided that the only answer was a new unit. He rustled one up like a bunny from a conjurer's hat while the rest of us had a bacon sandwich.

Out in the small-boat channel south of the buoyed 'fast lane' into the port, we shut down the engine and were reaching easily when we switched on the kit chartplotter/radar and AIS. Entering the channel to seaward was a hefty container ship which binoculars revealed to be the MSC Marta. AIS was 'on' and radar 'off' when I peeped into the plotter. A series of unmistakable triangular ship icons were dotted around the chart – notably alongside the container berths – but there up ahead was our man. Colin flipped the cursor over the icon and a box popped up with COG, SOG and CPA.

Just what I'd always wanted to know. A second click delivered data on the ship herself. Identifying her as the Marta and seeing her MMSI number would have simplified calling her up on VHF DSC radio for collision avoidance. Her rate of turn reassured me that she wasn't about to do anything unexpected, and I could envisage circumstances when information on where she was bound might help me assess her probable actions. I couldn't have cared less about her IMO number, and it was a safe bet that the huge pile of containers on her deck contained cargo, but it was an impressive performance.

Further vessels we clocked included a trawler and a fast-moving pilot boat. A second fishing vessel had no AIS transmitter, or hadn't turned it on, which served as a reminder that even this wonderful tool is not foolproof.

Of course, we were merely conducting an experiment on a pleasant morning. In real life inshore like this on a sunny morning I'd have been out on deck using my eyes, as Fiona was. In poor visibility, however, AIS used with radar could prove a lifesaver.

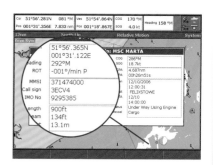

The AIS readout for MSC Marta shows her ROT as a negligible -001°

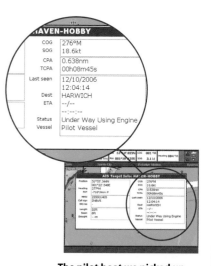

The pilot boat we picked up was making 18.6 knots

AIS & MARPA

MARPA is an acronym for 'Mini Automatic Radar Plotting Aid'. To activate it on a suitably equipped radar, you place the cursor over a contact and tell the system to 'acquire' the target. It will then analyse the data from this blip, reproducing its findings numerically and as a projected track on the screen. Numerical data include COG, SOG and CPA.

Colin hadn't made much use of his MARPA so far. Mine sees a fair bit of action. Part of our trade of skills had been that I'd walk him through this. MARPA shows a ship's COG, SOG and CPA, but they're deduced from a radar scanner tossing about on a yawing platform. Despite a gyro-enhanced fluxgate compass upgrade, my MARPA readouts do not measure up to Colin's

AIS. They still 'wander', so while they're useful for deciding whether a long-range target is of interest, my crew never use them as the final arbiter when a ship is coming closer. By comparison, AIS information straight from the ship's GPS is completely stable as long as the information being broadcast is accurate. Remember that many targets will not be transmitting AIS information so MARPA is all you have. However, for assessing collision risk, I have found a small-boat operator better served by using radar's excellent (and simpler) range and bearing facilities.

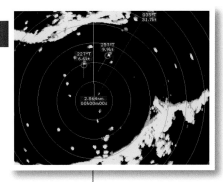

The yacht is in the centre. Lines coming from the MARPA targets show their projected positions

'Traditional' radar features

This was where I was able to give Colin and Fiona a quid pro quo for the heads-up I had just received on AIS.

The first radar set I used was on a coasting cargo vessel in 1978. It was almost steam powered but it did have an adjustable bearing line. The ship was in the centre of the screen as usual, so all I had to do was turn the knob that swivelled the magic line onto the target. If it approached straight down the line it was, by definition, on a steady bearing. Anyone who has eyeballed an approaching ship knows this means she's on a collision course. If I was in doubt about whether a target was moving, I could wind the variable range ring in and out until that sat over the target as well. I then had a cross which was as good as any fix I could plot with a compass.

Today's electronic yacht radars

feature electronic bearing lines (EBLs) and variable range markers (VRMs). Learning how to set them up is a matter of reading the manual, but once you've cracked it the job rapidly becomes intuitive.

Colin's radar has a second pair of lines he can deploy so as to monitor two targets, and I would far rather trust what a ship is doing relative to these than put my faith in small-craft MARPA.

My own crew enjoy using the VRM and EBL. If unsure about a ship in visual range, they click them on to double-check their impression of its activity before calling me. In poor visibility, of course, the setup is a Godsend, as it is at any time for a target that is not transmitting AIS data.

If AIS is connected to a radar, perhaps via a plotter, overlaying it onto the screen makes target ID an issue of the past.

Use the radar regularly and you'll be up to speed when you need to rely on it

The purple line can be rotated to show a target's bearing, the ring expanded to show its distance

AIS without radar

Standalone AIS screens are neat and very affordable. They are marketed as 'AIS Radars' and at a quarter of the price it is tempting, especially if you're not rolling in readies, to think of them as an alternative to the real McCoy. This would be a mistake. Combining AIS with radar is the best of both worlds. The AIS-only option is a good one, but don't be fooled into thinking that because the screen looks like a radar it can see more than it can.

Conclusion

As we sailed home, Colin praised the way AIS gave him an extra 'onion skin' of safety. I liked this concept, and he's absolutely right. Yacht collisions with ships have been in the news recently. There will never be a substitute for looking out in the old-fashioned way, but as ships' profiles diverge ever-further from the classic form, their dimensions and direction of travel are growing increasingly tough to call by night and even sometimes in daylight. In poor visibility we still need all the help we can get to stay well out of the way. My day aboard *Pirate* convinced me that AIS represents a huge leap forward. When you start thinking about value for money, it seems hard to beat.

Sail trim tips

Correct sail trim is extremely important if you want to get the most out of your boat. An increase in boat speed of just a quarter-knot can reduce an overnight passage time by an hour

C ontrary to popular opinion, many cruising yachtsmen maintain a lively interest in extracting the most from our boats. We might not choose to extract it very often, but when there is a tidal gate to catch or a pub that might shut, we want to give the job our best shot without resorting to the engine. And after all, a quarter-knot gained can be an hour saved on an overnight passage. Without going mad about it, this is best achieved by a bit of informed care in sail trim.

John Brighouse and his bold crew – Mike, Peter and Gary – are a group of cruising and dinghy sailors who every year charter a cruiser-racer to

do some racing in. Although there is no doubting their experience and general competence, they had been consistently finding themselves in mid-fleet. Try as they might, they could not persuade their boat to keep up with the leaders. My job was to find out why.

Five areas define who wins a yacht race. In no particular order, these are starting skill, tactics, boat speed, making less mistakes than anyone else, and good old luck. Starts, tactics and avoiding errors are definitely outside my remit; luck – or lack of it – is a matter for the gods; but plain-sail boat speed was right up my alley for the day.

The Mainsail

Our Jeanneau Sun Fast 37 had a partially battened, radial cut mainsail and a powerful 19/20 fractional rig with double spreaders and an adjustable block and tackle backstay. This arrangement would allow us to tweak to our hearts' content.

As soon as we were out of the harbour, the crew hoisted the main. Their set-up looked very flat to me in the gentle airs, so I decided that our first job was going to be shaping it to deliver more power.

Kicker tension – The kicker has a vital function in maintaining leech tension, but when closehauled on something other than a full-on race boat, much of its work can be done by the sheet. When the sheet is eased to set the sail on a reach, the kicker becomes the vital controller of leech tension, and this must be checked frequently if the boat is to go as fast as she is able.

Luff tension – Choosing the right tension in the main halyard or, in this case, the 'cunningham', adjusted the sail's maximum curvature to where we wanted it. For most mainsails, the best point of greatest 'camber', or curvature, lies between 35 and 50% of the way aft from luff to leech. The crew had been deciding on luff tension by feeling the luff itself rather than by observation. Looking aloft supplied a far better answer.

Leech tension – With the camber set up as a starting point, we next tightened up on the mainsheet to shape the leech. We rough-hewed this by keeping the top batten parallel with the boom when sighting up from the aft end of the spar, then we fine-tuned it by easing and hardening until all the leech tell-tales flew free.

Main clew outhaul – The outhaul is often left permanently tied off on a cruising boat. Given a decent sail, this is a shame. Hauling the clew aft as the breeze hardens flattens the lower part of the sail. The flatter sail can sometimes be set a touch further from the midline of the boat, which increases forward drive and eases any weather helm which may well be dragging way off.

Mainsheet traveller – Using the mainsheet traveller can sometimes seem a black art. Our race team were doing it full justice to spill wind in gusty conditions, but had not really grasped its function in lighter going. Once the sail has been shaped up with luff, leech and outhaul tensions, it can be thought of as a sculptured board that is trimmed by using the traveller when closehauled or close reaching so as not to compromise its form. As soon as the sail needs trimming out beyond the end of the traveller, the sheet must be eased. The kicker then comes into its own as the main tool for keeping the leech in order. Trimming closehauled, the traveller car may safely be pulled to weather of amidships in light airs to keep the main from being backwinded by the jib, so long as the boom itself stays on the midline or to leeward of it.

Sunsail Sun Fast 37

Practice makes perfect

Balancing act: With the parameters set for sail shape, the whole team had fun tweaking and watching boat speed rise and fall. In the end, it became obvious that unless we were all to sail this particular yacht every day, there would always be a trial-and-error factor, but at least we now knew what we could work on and what, essentially, we were looking for.

Heavier airs: Our crew's history suggested that they were doing better in stronger airs than in light going. I suspected that this was because in such conditions they were getting things right by flattening the sail with luff, leech, outhaul and kicker tensions, setting the traveller some way to leeward, then letting it slide down all the way in the

gusts to dump power and keep the boat on her feet. This is a sound policy as 'reefing time' approaches.

Keep tweaking: Our sails were brand new but if yours are older and prove less receptive to treatment, don't give up. Every little helps, and remember, any old salt can make a yacht fly when it's windy. It's in light going that class will out!

The Headsail

Up at the sharp end we had a tall, narrow, roller-reefing jib rather than an overlapping genoa. The sail set wonderfully and the boat pointed significantly higher than the average cruiser, which goes to show that size does not always matter. When it comes to headsails, brute force may be confounded by a perfect shape.

Luff tension – We first unrolled the sail in about 8 knots of apparent wind, and even in so gentle a breeze it was obvious that the camber was too far aft, producing more drag than lift. The only means of tensioning the luff to pull the draught forward was the halyard. This was coiled and stowed at the mast, but we gently twanged things up by dropping the coil and leading it to the coachroof winch. The effect was dramatic. If some kind soul would buy me a dinner for every boat I have sailed with a slack roller jib luff, I doubt I'd ever eat on board again.

Sheet tension closehauled – As we sailed closehauled under the lee of the shore, the breeze dropped somewhat and John complained that the boat had gone dead on him. A glance at the jib showed that it was suddenly very flat indeed. The deeper the camber of a sail, the harder it pulls, so it wants all the shape it can get in light going. Easing the sheet by only two or three inches powered it back up again immediately. The boat accelerated, John started smiling again, and we didn't drop a single degree off the wind. As the breeze came back on, the sail bagged out and the boat pointed a few degrees lower, so Peter cranked the sheet in and we slipped back into the groove once more.

Forestay/backstay tension – As soon as the breeze picked up, it only took John a glance up the headstay to see that it was sagging alarmingly to leeward. This is bad news any time, but the effects are multiplied if ever the jib is reefed. These days, forestays, or headstays, are generally hardened up by tensioning the backstay, and the *Sun Fast* had a powerful backstay tackle. A strong pull on this and the boat pointed perceptibly higher.

Sheet leading on a reach – Closehauled, the headsail was sheeted on a track well inboard of the shrouds. A second track was sited outboard. As we bore away onto a reach, Mike pointed out that the jib was back-winding the mainsail even with the sheet trimmed correctly. We attended to this by attaching a spare sheet to the jib clew and leading it aft via the car on the outer track. As the original sheet was eased, the new, outer sheet was hardened to move the clew progressively outboard. This opened the slot between the leech of the jib and the mainsail and boat speed increased noticeably. This process is called 'barber-hauling'. As the breeze frees further, the outer sheet carries more and more of the load until the inner one becomes redundant. A barber-haul can often be rigged to advantage on a cruiser with a perforated alloy toerail.

What we learned

Skipper John Brighouse comments:

'Most of our sailing has been dinghy racing or cruising where the key aspects of set up are to make passages as comfortable as possible and to ensure that the crew lying on deck has a clear view of the sun! As we started racing yachts we recognised that we had to hone our skills to get the most from a bigger boat.

'Balancing the tensions from the main halyard, the outhaul, the Cunningham, the kicker and the mainsheet had dramatic effects; not just on sail shape but on the speed we attained. Knowing how to use mainsheet and traveller together to shape and trim the sail is clearly vital.

'Most importantly, we noted that as soon as the set up has been perfected, the wind has changed and it's time to do it all again!

The harder you work at sail shape the faster you go and half a knot makes a big difference whether in passage time or race placing.

Sheet leading closehauled – When we came closehauled, I watched the crew slide the jib sheet cars into position on their tracks by following an imaginary line down at an angle from about a third of the way up the luff. This is a sensible starting point, but not good enough to extract 'the max', because even with the luff tight and the stay under control, the luff tell-tales were not all lifting together, as they should, if we steered above 'the edge of the wind'. This showed that the twist of the sail was out of order. If the car is settled a hole or two forward of the ideal, the leech will be too tight and the bottom tell-tales on the weather side of the sail will break first. Further aft than ideal, the top ones will 'lift' early as the foot is stretched. In either case, the boat loses power and doesn't point as she should. We experimented with various positions until all was well.

Conclusion

The overriding conclusion was that by having fun 'serial tweaking', we undoubtedly increased boat speed. We had also learned that while some adjustments are universal, a crew of switched-on individuals will often find more than one way to boost performance. The answer is to practise when we can, experiment, and make notes when we get it right. This trip reminded me why I love sailing for its own sake. In these days of reliable auxiliary power and cruising deadlines, it's all too easy to forget.

Tacking and gybing

Tacking and gybing may come as naturally as walking and talking – but like all aspects of sailing, techniques can be improved on and made more slick, if you follow a few basic rules

We all tack and gybe almost every time we go out. It's as familiar as changing gear in the car. So why waste pages in this book on it? Here's the answer.

Gybing was in the news a few years ago following an incident involving a charter boat skipper, who contrived to injure two of his crew seriously on consecutive gybes. The authorities have since suggested that all professionals undertake a risk assessment for so 'safety critical' a task. The truth is that gybing doesn't have to be dangerous at all. In many ways, it's easier than tacking, so long as it's

managed expertly which is far from difficult. More of that in a moment. What about tacking?

The decision to include tacking here was sealed following a sail on a modern 35ft sloop. Like many winches on yachts of her ilk, the primaries hadn't been too big when she was new. Now that the turning blocks were worn and things had stiffened up a bit, however, I found myself winding in the genoa with my eyes popping out of my head. I needed all the help I could get and the skipper wasn't delivering much.

I'm a big chap. I'm not in the first

flush of youth, but I've been winding winches all my life and I can throw my weight effectively. Imagine a 7-stone lady who spends only two weeks a year on board faced with the same job. 'No, thank you very much,' is going to be the understandable reply to a brisk, 'Ready about.'

It doesn't have to be like this, even if the gear isn't great. As with so many manoeuvres, happiness lies in the way the lucky one relaxing at the helm wiggles the stick or the wheel.

To tackle these issues, I borrowed an X332 from a local charter company. I'd asked for a lively boat with a tiller and a conventional mainsail. They and their boat did us proud. I haven't had so much fun on the water for a while.

Tacking

The answer to contented tacking is to steer the boat quickly through the wind, then hold her 'above' close-hauled while the crew brings in most of the new sheet. That way there's no wind in the sail so there's nothing to fight. If you are lucky enough to have a self-tacking foresail none of the following applies. Move straight to 'gybing'. Sadly, most of us outside Scandinavia are still groaning under the stress of full-on genoas. Here's how to make the big job easy when you're only two-up.

'Ready about' – helm

Check to windward

❯ Take a look over your weather shoulder. You're about to turn suddenly through 90°, and not everyone out there will understand why.
❯ If you're not very experienced, note some features on the background (or a handy cloud if you can only see the horizon) at 90° to windward from where you

are now. That's roughly where you'll end up steering after completing the tack, although you won't go for it straight away.
❯ Take a glance at the crew's preparations. You've a good overview from where you are. Don't start your tack until they have all responded, 'Ready'.

'Lee-Ho' – Helm

Make sure you have a decent amount of way on, then, on the order 'Lee-Ho!', steer hard into the wind, watching your crew and the headsail all the time. If they're struggling, slow down your turn, but don't let the genoa come aback. It spoils the sail, kills your precious way and ruins any chance of a neat tack.

Keep turning briskly through the breeze until the boat is almost on the new tack, but not quite – say around 30 degrees from the wind. Hold her on this heading. She won't sail properly, but she'll carry more than enough way to steer.

'Ready about' – crew

> Secure the mainsheet traveller – very likely this is already done, but a swift visual check can save someone getting a nasty knock.
> Flake the lee genoa sheet clear to run – no need for anything fancy. Don't coil it on any account. Start at the knot and run the sheet through your hands all the way up to the winch. Let it fall as it will. It'll run off like a greyhound out of the trap.
> Load up a whole turn on the new winch and pull all the slack out of the sheet to prevent it snagging.
> Leave the winch handle somewhere you can grab it when you're working the new winch.
> Tell the helm that you really are, 'Ready'.

Flake the sheet with the tail clear so that it can't get tangled

'Lee-ho!' – crew

> 'Lee-ho' means that the helm has started the turn. It does NOT mean, 'Let go the sheet!'. Sailing with my close family or friends, I just say 'OK', because we all know what's happening.
> Watch the luff of the headsail as the boat swings into the wind. Once it starts collapsing, but well before it comes aback, let go the working sheet. The best way to do this smartly is to remove carefully all but the final turn as the load eases.
> With the lee sheet away and running free off its flake, move smartly across to the new winch. Grab the sheet you've already loaded and rattle it in hard and steady. You may be delayed for a second or two as the clew sorts itself out at the shrouds. If so, wait for it to clear, then heave again until you can't pull in any more.
> Quickly lay two more turns onto the winch barrel and, if it's a self-tailer, pop the bight into the jaws on top.
> Grab the handle, whack it in and crank home the last few feet of sheet. If your shipmate at the helm got it right, you'll hardly wind the winch at all on a boat under 32ft. Bring the sail in until the leech is a few inches off the spreader or shroud. That's the job done, except that you may have to bring the sheet in a few inches more as the boat gathers way and the apparent wind rises a notch.
> If the winch isn't a self-tailer, hang onto the tail as you deal with the handle, then tail it yourself if you can. If you can't, hand the sheet to the helm.

Ease off the turns

Watch as you wind

Here comes the big secret: keep steering 'high' of a true closehauled course (just to windward of the mark you identified to tack onto) while the crew brings the genoa in. Don't bear away onto a true closehauled course until the sheet is right home. They won't have to fight a sail full of wind, and they ought to be very grateful.

Once the sheet's in, crack away to fill the genoa and watch her go. It may not feel like it, but the tack will actually have been quicker than one leaving the hands gasping for resuscitation.

The ghastly grunt

This time, I've steered too quickly through the wind and ended up 'below' a closehauled heading. Miles, my crew, is left with yards of sheet to haul in and is half-killing himself. The drinks will be on me tonight!

The mainsail leech has just started to flip over. That's the sign that the boat's gybing. Get ready to put 'opposite lock' on.

Gybing

Gybing can be the easiest of all manoeuvres. My crew prefer it to tacking because, whether you're sailing a giant schooner or a 22ft sloop, it requires no effort beyond pulling in the mainsheet. Like tacking, however, there's a simple trick that makes all the difference. The early instructions that follow are the sort of 'good practice' most of us employ without thinking. The two jewels come near the end. I didn't learn either of them by intuition. Somebody had to tell me, and there might just be something there for you.

'Stand by to gybe' – crew

Secure the traveller then haul in the mainsheet

> On the order, secure the traveller amidships. It really matters this time, especially if it's in the cockpit, because if it slams across it can do as much harm as the boom itself.
> Heave in the mainsheet until it's virtually amidships (above). Make it fast with the jammer or, if there's an old-fashioned cleat involved, take a whole turn.

Flake the main sheet

> Flake the mainsheet ready to run (left).
> By now, the boat should be just 'off' dead downwind. Stand by the mainsheet and DO NOT let go the genoa sheet.

'Stand by to gybe' – helm

> When you're ready to gybe, steer downwind until the genoa collapses behind the mainsail, then give the order, 'Stand by to gybe'. The crew will heave in and secure the sheet and traveller.
> If your crew are inexperienced, remind them to watch their heads.

The wind will be about 20° on your quarter as you set up for the gybe

'Gybe-ho' – helm

> Once you're satisfied the boom is contained, call 'Gybe-ho!' and ease the boat towards a dead run. Ignore the genoa's antics. It won't go far because the crew has not let off the sheet on pain of rum stoppage.
> Looking aloft at the mainsail and any masthead indicator, steer the stern carefully across the breeze until the leech of the mainsail flops across. On a conventional main, it'll do this before the body of the sail follows it.
> As soon as the leech flops, the boat will start thinking about taking matters into her own hands and rounding up hard towards the wind on the new gybe. This is the wicked broaching tendency which most fore-and-aft rigged boats suffer, and now is the time to show her who's boss. Steer hard back towards the way you've come for a second or two as a pre-emptive strike. It's like applying 'opposite lock' to a car in a rear-wheel skid or the hip-shimmy of a classy centre three-quarter's body swerve. If you over-do it, the boat will gybe back again. Just give her enough opposite helm to keep her travelling in a straight line. The rest of the main will follow the leech into the gybe and she won't deviate from her downwind heading.
> Steer ten or fifteen degrees off the run and tell the hands to let out the sheet.
> For practice, it's fun to steer dead downwind with the main pinned in, gybing from one side to the other and back again without deviating more than ten degrees or so either side of the run.

Steer stern through the wind. Keep an eye on the leech of the mainsail

The main is going over. The genoa is left well alone

Put 'opposite lock' on as soon as the leech flips through the wind

Now straighten up onto the new course

'Gybe-ho' – crew

> Once the main has gybed and you're sure it will stay that way, let the sheet out for the new heading. Doing this as smartly as you can will help the helm keep her going straight because the boat won't be trying to broach so viciously. Set up the traveller as required.
> By this time, the genoa may well be aback against the shrouds or flopping about of its own accord. What it will not be doing is wrapping itself around the forestay, the hateful result that awaits those who let fly the sheet on the order, 'Gybe-ho!' If you've a full crew, by all means ease it across with the main, but most cruisers are short-handed. Wait and be patient.
> Take up all the slack on the new lee sheet

Stay in control of both genoa sheets when gybing the headsail

(one turn around its winch) and, keeping this one as tight as you readily can, ease away the old working sheet so the sail passes across to the new lee side, under control all the way. Set it for the new course, and put the kettle on.

Sailing up river

You don't have to start your engine as soon as you enter a river. Sailing up a narrow waterway can be a challenging experience but, if the conditions are right, it is well worth the effort

Sailing full-sized yachts in rivers was meat and drink half a century ago. Today's reliable engines have revolutionised our seafaring, but there's no gain without pain. Firing up the machinery as a matter of course every time we enter a river delivers short measure when it comes to satisfaction.

The skills of working up a narrow water-way under sail alone are fun to master; the sense of fulfilment is priceless.

There is, of course, a time and a place for everything. These days, short-tacking up a popular river at 1600 on a summer Sunday is like driving a hay-cart the wrong way down a motorway, but when it is quiet with a steady breeze and a rising tide, it seems almost rude not to sail. Two friends, Miles Kendall and James Troup, and I, recently arrived at the entrance to a local river in a Feeling 36, with enough flood tide to beat up the three and a half miles to the nearest village for a lunch-time pie and a pint. The wind was a light northerly with a slice of west thrown in.

Lining up the entrance

As we came in to the river entrance from seaward the stream in the offing was running to leeward, so our main concern was not to end up in a downwind position. With this firmly in mind, we hardened up early, lining up the bar dolphin with an unmistakable beacon on the foreshore. Trimming continuously to keep on track we squeezed around the corner and set about sailing up the narrow confines of the river.

The bar dolphin lined up 'casually' with a beacon...

Near HW it was deep enough, so...

...we kept the transit 'on' until we squeezed in

Crossing the bar

I once examined a group of fast-track Yachtmaster candidates who complained of unseamanlike practice when I asked them to beat across the entrance to a river. I don't doubt they'd have made the same remarks about any river. While they blundered to and fro in their modern 35-footer, an elderly lady came tacking past us in a bilge-keeled Westerly Centaur with a cup of tea in her spare hand while her husband worked the headsail sheets puffing his pipe. The place can look a bit tight to anyone without the experience to give it a go, but in truth, it's not difficult. It's just a matter of keeping way on and maintaining a positive mindset.

With a knot or two of favouring tide all our helm had to do was make sure he came about before we hit the invisible line joining the beacons on either side of his necessarily brief tacks. As we rounded the first bend he found he could almost lay the straight sea reach, so on we went, fetching the next bend with two long tacks and two short ones.

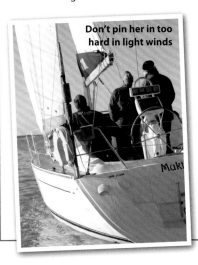
Don't pin her in too hard in light winds

1 First tack in, trim and steer for speed.

2 The second tack a short one, but don't worry. Just don't pinch!

3 Losing way behind the trees. Point higher than she'll sail now, and it's all over!

4 Safely round for another short one.

5 And again – note headsail is not pinned in too tight.

6 Last time. Lots of draught in the sails to power out of the tack.

Take no chances on a lee shore

When you're beating in a river one tack is generally favoured, and it's this one which ends its progress on the lee shore. Near the top of the tide as we were, avoiding any risk of running aground goes without saying, but special care must be taken on the long tack because if you touch at the end and lose way, then by definition you cannot sail off. You are now reduced to the sorry options of starting the engine or, if you are feeling purist, launching the dinghy and laying out a kedge.

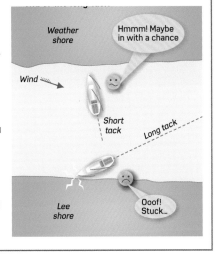

Going aground

If you do touch near the end of a tack, it is critical to steer hard to weather immediately, keeping the headsail sheet made fast. If you have enough residual way for the yacht's head to pass through the wind, the jib will fill aback, helping her round dramatically. She will also begin heeling again. There is now every chance she will sail straight off into deep water. Fail to react instantly, and you're stuck!

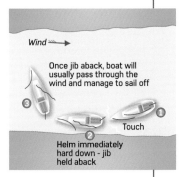

Keep well to windward

On a long reach, always keep well to windward when it's a safe option, ready for that heading gust.

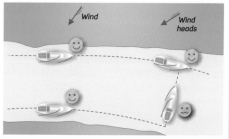

Wind

Wind heads

Sailing free along a straightish reach of a river, it pays always to keep up to windward. Allowing the boat to sag away to the lee side invariably ends in tears because if the wind can possibly head her, you can be sure that it will. Then you'll be faced with an unnecessary tack. If doing this places you on the 'wrong' side for

COLREG purposes, you'll have to make a judgement call, but it's surprising how other sailors respect your position. A wave of acknowledgement is usually enough to let folks know you haven't taken them for granted and that you appreciate them giving way to you. If you're confronted with a fleet of motor cruisers all ploughing

down the 'correct' side of the river when you want that water to keep up to weather, you are probably best advised to drop to leeward and take the consequences on the chin. Not all the other skippers will understand your situation.

Pinching and keeping your way on

It's a natural reaction when looking down the gun-barrel of a tight tack to try to win an extra yard or two by pinching above a proper closehauled course. Unless you are lee-bowing (see below) or huffling (see opposite), don't do it! When a boat comes above close-hauled so that her sails begin luffing, she will start sliding sideways as soon as her speed drops below a critical level – typically around 2 or 3 knots. This means that although you are pointing to where you want to go, you are actually sliding to leeward of it. The answer is that you must be cruel to be kind.

Steer full, get the sails drawing strongly, and gather way. Once the boat is sailing positively, luff her gently but persistently and you'll be amazed how high she'll point. You can even shove her head to wind for a short time if need be, so long as you don't lose that critical way. Try it from a standing start or at slow speed, though, and you're a dead duck.

It takes confidence to steer downwind of something you really need to lay, even for ten or twenty seconds, but watch an expert, and you'll note he's doing just that, yet he's laying the marks against all the odds.

Maintaining proper steerage way is especially important if you are faced with lots of truncated tacks. The worst-case scenario is that you don't gain enough way to come about. Then you've had it, so keep her moving sweetly even if you don't seem to be pointing very high.

LEFT: If the sails start luffing, you'll slide sideways

Wind   Wind

NO PINCHING

By getting plenty of way on, *Go-er* is able to luff around the mark and carry on. *Pincher* never gets moving and ends up head to wind with no way on

'Pincher'   'Go-er'

Lee-bowing

Beating against a contrary current (which we were not), there are sometimes occasions when you can steer so as to place the tide on your lee bow. As soon as you do this, the boat will begin drifting up to windward. As a bonus, the mysteries of geometry also free the apparent wind, so you are winning two ways up. Grabbing a lee-bow when it's offered can save whole tacks and can occasionally repay even the otherwise primeval sin of pinching.

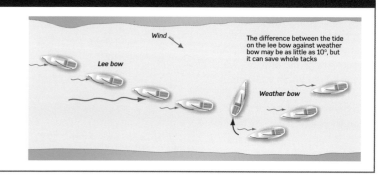

Wind

Lee bow

The difference between the tide on the lee bow against weather bow may be as little as 10°, but it can save whole tacks

Weather bow

'Huffling'

An old trick of the river sailor is to 'huffle' at the end of a tack. Thames Barge skippers perfected this, calling it 'The Gravesend Hitch'. It doesn't often work at sea because of the waves, but in flat water with plenty of way on you can often shoot head to wind for several boat's lengths as you come from one tack to the next. This gains valuable distance, especially among moorings where the boat must be placed with great precision.

The downside of huffling is that if you lose too much way, the boat will stall as she falls onto the new tack. You'll know this is happening because she develops lee helm as she fills away. If she does, you've over-cooked it. Less huffle next time!

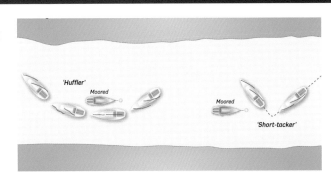

In flat water, with plenty of way on, try 'huffling' – shooting head to wind at the end of a tack and so gaining several boat lengths for free

Transits

We had a good flowing tide under us as we beat up through the moorings, so we had to be doubly vigilant about where the boat was going. This, of course, was generally not where she was pointing. The only real answer is to line up the moored boats with their background and make sure both ends of any craft you're approaching are moving in the same direction. If the stern's gobbling up the background and the bow is spewing it out, you're passing clear ahead, and so on. If the stern and bow are both eating background, you are on course for a guaranteed 'T-boning'!

Keep an eye on your masthead

On a windy day with lots of heel going on, make sure you don't foul any other boat's rigs with your masthead. It's easy to become obsessed with sea-level transits and forget the main event going on aloft.

Think ahead

With a tide running, you should always be thinking at least one tack ahead – preferably two. Don't be over-ambitious, and the policy will keep you from fetching up at the bitter end of a blind alley.
Use all the available water. The flooding tide means this boat's not so close as she looks.

Sailing alongside

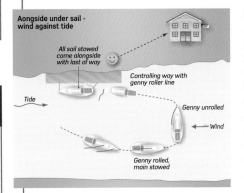

During this trip we were presented with a perfect set-up. The tide was running along the ancient dock below the pub and the wind was as near opposite as the doctor could have ordered.

Rule 1: Wind against tide – drop the mainsail, then approach the berth downwind and up-tide under jib only. As things panned out, we rolled up the genoa completely before luffing to stow the main. Bringing her head to wind, we let go the main halyard and the sail fell into its stack-pack. I steered the boat across the breeze towards the dock using the last of her way, then unrolled a little genoa to bring her back under steerage. All that remained was to organise warps and fenders with emphasis on a stern line to stop her if need be, then trundle in, controlling speed with the genoa furling line and the tide, instead of a throttle.

As I rolled away the last of the canvas, she settled into her berth as neatly as my granddad used to sink into his chair by the kitchen range. The pint was a beauty!

Handling a spinnaker

Spinnakers can be daunting sails to set and handle, yet with a bit of experience and a step-by-step approach, even the most hard-nosed cruising yachtsman can be converted to the joy they bring

I f you're thinking, 'Spinnaker handling has nothing to do with me. I'm a cruiser,' please don't turn the page yet. I worked with spinnakers as a race trainer when I had just returned from a long ocean cruise in a gaff cutter. Nothing could have been further from the world I knew, yet as I grew in expertise it dawned on me that handling spinnakers safely depended on the essentials of seamanship – the sort of skills that cut across class, creed and calling. It's all about relieving big strains with a spare line in order to deal with the one that's loaded, hiding one sail behind another to snuff the power out of it, and running downwind

instead of luffing up when the action turns on hot. Read on, and I hope you might agree. At least, it might make sense of what those maniacs are doing at the leeward mark on a Sunday morning when all you want is to sail past unmolested.

There's one more thing. Broad reaching under spinnaker is a bit like drinking really good rum. Once you've felt the yacht take off and go weightless, it's akin to sampling the real McCoy – things are never quite the same again.

After helping a crew of occasional racers get to grips with sail trim and increase boat speed (see p102–105), it was time to look at spinnakers.

It turned out that the boys had had one or two 'moments' with the spinnaker and were unclear about trimming it for best performance. Also, the thorny question of gybing had been lurking in the shadows like a bed-time bogeyman.

Up went the helm, out rattled the mainsheet, and a potentially confusing array of spinnaker gear began spilling from our lockers.

Packing the spinnaker

Without a good 'pack', any attempt to hoist a spinnaker is doomed to wretched nastiness. Start at the head of the sail, which usually has

Hoisting the spinnaker

These days, race boats hoist spinnakers in various ways, but because our team were not practising together every weekend, we stuck with the bullet-proof, time-honoured seaman's solution. The secret is to get the sail up without a twist before you let the wind have a look at it. The method uses the old trick of hiding the action in the 'shadow' of the mainsail until you're ready to reveal it.

Here we go:

❯ Keep the genoa up so that the spinnaker cannot take a wrap around the forestay
❯ Attach the open spinnaker bag to the lee foredeck rail
❯ Clip on the sheets and guys
❯ Take the halyard in hand, look aloft to make sure it is led clear, then clip it to the sail from outside the genoa
❯ Attach the pole uphaul and downhaul and secure the pole to the mast
❯ Raise the inboard end of the pole so that the outboard end is resting on deck inside the forestay
❯ Pass the bight of the weather guy through the bayonet fitting at the pole's outboard end
❯ Raise the pole until it is parallel with the deck, keeping it to weather of the forestay. Leave the downhaul slack
❯ Run off the wind and hoist the sail in the lee of the main
❯ When the halyard is mastheaded, and only then, pull aft on the weather guy, thus squaring the pole. This will expose the weather corner of the sail to the

Principal lines

Uphaul
Guy
Downhaul
Sheet
Block for guy

• On port tack the pole is rigged to port of the forestay
• The lazy sheet and guy have been omitted for sake of clarity

wind, where it will begin to fill. Take up the slack on the pole downhaul
❯ Haul on the (leeward) sheet until the sail fills completely
❯ Lower the genoa, get on course and trim the sail

a swivel. There will be a red and a green tape running away down the two sides. A pair of crew can now flake each tape, keeping them in the hand, until the bottom corners are reached. Without letting go the flaked sides, the body of the sail is stuffed into the bag with the edges on top, leaving the three corners uppermost, ready for the sheets and halyards.

Reeving the gear

When we hauled out the gear, we found what looked like four sheets, all with snap shackles on the ends. In fact, these are sheets and guys, one pair of each, which is where a yacht spinnaker differs from that of a smaller craft. A dinghy spinnaker is set with a single sheet on either side. Where the sail is more powerful, however, seamanship starts to enter the equation. One sheet and guy will be attached to each bottom corner of the sail so that, for certain manoeuvres, or if all else fails, the rope with the weight on it can be relieved by its partner. The active guy leads aft from the windward corner of the sail (nominally the tack), and it is run through the outboard end of the pole. Under no circumstances is the sail itself attached to the pole bayonet. The active sheet leads aft from the free corner of the sail (the clew). The guys are shackled to rings on the outboard end of the sheets, thus securing both together.

In our case, the spinnaker was to be hoisted on the port side (starboard tack), so the sheets and guys were shackled in readiness to the guardrails on the port bow. Sheets were led back to the cockpit via blocks on the quarters. The guy blocks were at around the point of maximum beam, siting the lead further forward to exert a degree of downward pull on the pole.

All sheets and guys are led 'outside everything'.

Trimming

This was an area of some confusion for our crew, so we tackled it systematically. Starting with the pole.

Trimming the pole

❯ Using the guy, and always maintaining control with the pole downhaul, set the spar so that it is approximately at right-angles to the apparent wind

❯ Eyeball the free clew of the sail, and raise or lower the pole so that the two clews take up the same height relative to the deck

❯ Adjust the mast end of the pole to keep it parallel to the deck

❯ On a close reach, the pole can go as far forward as an inch off the forestay

Trimming the sheet

❯ With the pole set correctly, the sheet is eased progressively until the luff (the weather edge of the sail) begins to curl. At the right setting, the

Look out for the weather edge starting to curl

Sheet in until the sail fills then start easing again

luff is just suggesting that it's about to do this. As soon as it shows signs of falling in, the sheet is hauled smartly aft to re-trim

❯ In light winds, the trimmer on a yacht up to 36ft can trim by hand with a turn on the winch. As the wind rises he will need a crew member at the winch handle. The command, not surprisingly, is, 'Wind!' (to rhyme with blind)

❯ On a reach, the trimmer may prefer to stand on the sidedeck for a better view

❯ As the boat comes up onto a closer reach, the foot of the sail will end up snagging on the forestay. If it hasn't been done already, this is the sign to ease the pole forward

Gybing a spinnaker

Gybing a full balloon spinnaker with no snuffer can be fraught. In windy conditions it demands a full crew, good technique, sound teamwork and a general reluctance to panic. It is best practised on a calm day or, at least, a nice steady breeze. Let's assume we're shifting from starboard gybe to port.

❯ Run the boat square off the wind. The helmsman must keep her there no matter what betides until the gybe is complete. Anything else, and all hands could be forgiven for sending him to buy the first three rounds when the survivors finally stagger into the pub

❯ Ease away on the starboard (weather) guy (the one through the pole) and take the weight of the sail equally on both sheets. The sail is now effectively flying free, independent of the pole

❯ The bowman grabs the bight of the port (leeward) guy

❯ Next, he unclips the pole from the mast and pulls it across the boat, opening the bayonet fitting on the port side and slipping the port guy into it

❯ When the starboard end of the pole reaches his hands, he opens the bayonet to release the starboard guy, then clips this end of the pole to the mast

❯ The slack of the port guy is taken up so that the spinnaker clew is pulled snugly to the pole. The lazy port sheet is then let off

❯ The spinnaker is now gybed. All that remains is for the helm to flick the stern across sufficiently to allow the mainsail to come over. The mainsheet is let off rapidly and the boat trimmed for the new course

❯ Depending on the results, either give the helmsman a nice cup of tea, or confine him to his bunk until further notice

The skipper must maintain his concentration as the pole is unclipped from the mast

The pole is led across the bow and the port guy clipped into the bayonet end

The starboard guy is released and the new pole end is clipped to the mast

The slack of the port guy is taken up, pulling the clew to the pole

The dip-pole gybe

This technique is used when the pole is essentially asymmetric. This is the way of things when the downhaul and uphaul attach to the outboard end, while the inboard end has a dedicated mast fitting.

The helming technique and general strategy are identical. The difference is in the action on the foredeck. The issue is that because the pole cannot be detached from the mast, a different method must be found for getting it across the boat.

> As with an 'end-to-end' gybe, the boat is run square off the wind and the weight of the spinnaker taken on both sheets,

thus releasing the guys for the action

> The bowman takes hold of a bight of the leeward guy, ready to transfer it to the pole as the spinnaker drifts across. He then moves right forward with it to the pulpit

> The old guy is taken right off the winch and the uphaul is eased. This allows the pole to swing forward and down as the sail floats free on its sheets. It may be necessary to slide the pole heel fitting further up the mast to gain the necessary clearance

> As the pole approaches the forestay, the bowman grabs it. The crew on the uphaul watch carefully and allow the pole to dip just far enough to pass inside, or under the forestay

> The bowman releases the old guy from the bayonet and pops in the new one. Good technique is needed here, or the new guy can be slotted in with a half-twist. I've experienced some highly creative cock-ups in this department, but 'Rubber Ball', one of the great foredeck men of my time in racing, never missed. I think he turned his hand upside down somehow as he did the job. Clever stuff!

> As soon as the guy has been transferred, the pole end is lifted again and the new guy is winched in, taking the weight off the now lazy sheet as it comes. Attention must be paid to the downhaul at all times, making sure the pole is under control as the main gybes and the boat sets off on her new course

> The success of this manoeuvre, in common with so much else on board, is good planning and making sure everyone knows what their job is and when to do it.

DIP POLE: STEP BY STEP

WIND

1. Bear away on to a run

2. Weight of sail taken on both sheets, pole forward and dipped, release old working guy from pole

3. Keep the mainsail and spinnaker centred while the new guy is introduced into the pole end

4. Gybe the main, pull the pole aft with new guy while raising it with uphaul

5. When guy has pulled tack of sail to pole end, ease off lazy sheet on that side. Trim the spinnaker

Dropping the spinnaker

The lads had had their worst moments dropping the spinnaker so, once again, we avoided fancy racing drops and concentrated on a fail-safe approach.

> Flake the halyard ready for action
> Run the boat square off the wind
> The crew who will gather the sail now grab the bight of the 'lazy' (leeward) guy and take it to a suitable place near the companionway
> Ease the pole forward, taking up the slack on the downhaul
> The sail now collapses in the lee of the mainsail
> The bowman can 'pop' the tack snap shackle if it can be reached, releasing the sail from the pole. Watch out for the pole trying to spring back and brain you!
> If the tack is out of reach, let the active (weather) guy and its lazy sheet run
> Ease the halyard down fast as the boys pull the sail in under the boom with the lazy guy and stuff it down the companionway
> Don't forget to turn off the cooker first…

37

Conclusion

Our crew promised to go out and practise on the back of our training session because, unlike the man who thought he might be able to play the violin but had yet to try, they recognised that without taking the time to sort out who did what, who was going to steer and who would call the shots, there would be no progress.

Handled in a seamanlike manner by a crew who have considered the teamwork aspects, a spinnaker is a source of joy and satisfaction. The trick is to use the lazy sheets and guys to remove strain where required, and to blanket the spinnaker at critical moments with the mainsail. When things go wrong, it is usually better to run off than luff up, just as it is in a cruising boat when something breaks.

Cruising chutes

Cruising chutes are an invaluable addition to any sails wardrobe, and can transform downwind sailing. Rigged with either a snuffer or roller furler, they are also straightforward to set up and handle

Cruising chutes. Nothing to them! Some would agree, but plenty more might not. I meet all sorts of sailors in my professional capacity, and I'm often consulted about choosing and using one of these marvellous sails. People who have them swear that in light weather they can make the difference between motoring till you're deaf and sailing the passage under canvas. There's certainly no doubt that once you've experienced how a boat comes to life with any sort of spinnaker – which is what a cruising chute really is – downwind sailing is never quite the same again.

My own knowledge of chutes is extrapolated from racing with full-on spinnakers, but I've never been shown by a sailmaker how, specifically, to deal with the cruising version. So, I met up with sailmakers Paul and Roger Lees, on their Comfort 32, and away we went.

'We've a choice of two chutes here,' Paul announced, rigging the tack downhaul through its turning block on the stem head. 'There's the 165% bomb-proof cruiser – that's 1.65 times the area of the genoa – or we've a lighter, 180% version for the sportsman…'

1. Rigging the cruising chute

A surprisingly modest bag was passed up. We ferreted out the tack, the head, and the single sheet that was sensibly already attached. The rest of the sail was entirely subdued inside a light nylon tube a foot or so in diameter called a 'snuffer'. We attached tack and head to downhaul and halyard, making sure the whole shooting match was to leeward of everything, then ran the sheet outside the shrouds, the mainsheet and the guardrails to the lee quarter block. From there it was led to the now-vacant headsail winch. The tack downhaul came aft from its block to a winch on the coachroof and was set up with a few feet of slack at the business end so the sail could drift well clear of the pulpit.

FAR LEFT: The tack runs through a block forward of the forestay.
ABOVE LEFT: The line that hoists the snuffer runs through a block at the head of the sail. ABOVE RIGHT: The sheet is led to a block on the lee quarter

2. The Hoist

Before hoisting, the lines for working the snuffer up and down were loosely attached so as not to lose them. Once the halyard had been mastheaded, the boat was steered onto a broad reach and the snuffer was hove up to expose the sail.

It blossomed forth as if by magic. As the snuffer went into a 'crumpled ball' mode at the top, the tack was pulled down to within a couple of feet of the pulpit and the sheet was rattled in. The sail filled with a gentle 'pop', the boat woke up and

speed jumped from 3 to nearly 6 knots. Paul demonstrated how close the sail could be set to the wind if need be, but was at pains to point out that, as any race skipper knows, there comes a point of diminishing returns.

The cruising chute is safely hoisted in its snuffing sock, which is then drawn up over the sail

The snuffer has a flexible rim which prevents it snagging during the hoist

As the wind fills the sail the snuffing sock is pushed up over the sail

The sock forms a concertina above the sail. The snuffing lines are made fast on deck

3. Sheeting the sail

'It's a bit like sailing a gaff-rigged yacht really,' Paul observed. 'You can often make them point higher than they'll sail...' I was digesting this profound remark, noting that the chute was still full even though the sheet was cranked hard in around the back of the mainsail with the tack winched tight down on the bow, when we noticed dramatically diminished boat speed. As we bore away to put the apparent wind back on the beam we cracked the tack a foot or two to round up the luff and eased the sheet to open the leech. The boat literally leapt ahead.

Like all spinnakers, the cruising chute is best set with its luff just short of curling, so the sheet is eased as far away as it can be to achieve this happy state. Doing this has the dual effect of speeding up the boat and easing the helm considerably. As she approaches a run, easing the tack still further enables the luff to peep around the weather side of the rig and grab some of the wind that the main is missing. Like most sails, however, it won't set dead downwind in anything other than a flat sea without goose-winging it onto a pole.

Above: The tack is eased as the wind comes aft. Trimming from the shrouds allows you a clear view of luff and leech. Below: Harden up to create some apparent wind if the breeze fades

The tack line is tightened when going to windward. We're pinching, the sail is oversheeted and not drawing well

Bear away a few degrees, ease the sheet and watch your speed climb – even in light airs

4. Gybing a cruising chute

Gybing a cruising chute proved so easy it was almost embarrassing. All we did was bear away, trot forward and snuff the chute, gybe the main, walk the sheet round to the new lee side, then unpeel the snuffer again. The alternative would have been to rig two sheets instead of one, the lazy sheet being led outside the forestay. When the boat has been run well off, the chute tack is then eased a couple of feet to soften the luff and make more space for the sail to pass around the forestay, then it is gybed before the main. It's important to make sure the lazy sheet takes up all its slack as the old working sheet is eased, otherwise the sail can drift round the wrong side of its own luff and flip inside out. Not a problem if you concentrate and make positive movements, and useful if you're club racing, but it's a lot easier to plump for the single sheet and 'snuff gybe' as we did.

Gybing a cruising chute is child's play if you take the easy option and snuff or furl it before leading the sheet around the forestay and to the new leeward quarter. If gybing conventionally, ease the working sheet as you go onto a dead run and pull in on the new sheet

5. Dropping the cruising chute

Barrelling along as we were, the harbour entrance soon loomed up and we had to lower the sail. This has always been the crunch for spinnakers, and I've had many a lively session when a rising breeze said 'dropping time' just as the cook served up the cocoa.

The snuffer kisses those horrors goodbye. Dousing the chute under full control is just a matter of easing the sheet then heaving down on the snuffer line. Our snuffer whisked down over it with the ease of a pirate slipping his peg leg into a well-greased seaboot. All that remained was to lower away the halyard and stow the now full sock, ready for the next hoist.

Ease the sheet to depower the sail and haul on the snuffing line. The sock is drawn over the sail, which can then be dropped behind the main

6. Roller furling system

On our second run, Paul produced a bigger and lighter 180% chute controlled by a roller-furling system. The sail comes out of the bag, wrapped around a Kevlar stay with a Facnor furling drum, which is secured to the stemhead or bow. The tack is secured to the stemhead by a strop. Its height can be adjusted by running a strop line through a block to the cockpit. The head of the sail is attached to the Kevlar stay and it's the head that starts furling first. When unfurled the chute flies free of the stay. An alternative system to the free floating chute is a sail which is cut much flatter and has a Kevlar rope sewn into the luff. When this is rotated the sail furls around it.

Paul and I felt a snuffer would do the job just as well – though furling systems are excellent if short-handed, as all lines can be led aft and the sail can be set and furled from the cockpit. A snuffer's lines can also be led aft to the cockpit for single-handed furling.

The furling drum with a separate tack line lead aft, via a block, to the cockpit

The furled sail is hoisted – preferably with a spinnaker halyard – and then unfurled

The sheet is led aft via a block on the rail. For cruising you can rig a single sheet

Unfurled and under way – but you'll need to furl the sail to gybe or risk a wrap

The free-floating furling chute. Cruising chutes are also available with the Kevlar furling luff rope sewn in

The bottom of the furling stay is thicker than the top to increase purchase on the sail as it furls

The head starts to furl first and the rest of the sail follows

The sail needs to be furled before the boat is gybed

Hardware requirements

Halyard: To set a cruising chute you will need a spinnaker halyard that hoists from outside, or above, the forestay at the masthead. Many boats already have one of these. If yours has internal halyards but nothing for a spinnaker, she will almost certainly have a mouse in place to install one and a point at the masthead plate to hang the block. Where a halyard just can't be rigged internally, don't despair. There is no law against external halyards; easy to rig and entirely free of problems. Just make sure you frap the ropework away from the mast at the end of the day!

Tack block: A cruising chute sets from a tack line that is passed through a turning block somewhere near the stemhead. The line is then led aft either to a spare winch (the lazy headsail sheet winch will do if there is nothing else), or a long handy billy set up on deck. Just where and how you site the turning blocks depends on the boat, but it should ideally be shackled to a strong point so that the tack line can run free of chafe between block and sail. Perfection is often unachievable, but a sensible compromise usually does the trick.

Sheet blocks: The sheets pass through turning blocks somewhere on the yacht's quarter.

Ropework: You'll need either a single sheet 1.5 times the yacht's length, or a pair of sheets twice her length (see gybing the cruising chute). Also a tack downhaul at length x 1.5.

If the snuffer fouls

This is actually not a problem, so long as you do the right things:
> On no account come head-to-wind
> Run as square downwind as you safely can to shelter the chute behind the main
> Flake the halyard and tack downhaul
> Ease the tack
> Grab the bight of the sheet between the sail and the quarter block
> Ease the halyard away fast and pull the sail in under the boom by the sheet
> Let the tack away when the halyard is in hand
> Stuff the sail away down the companionway after first extinguishing the galley stove!
> If the snuffer fouls at half-mast, just release the halyard and gather it all on deck

Reducing weather helm

Most modern yachts are well balanced, but if conditions get windy, some are not, and prove very heavy on the helm. With a few tweaks to the rig and sail trim, however, significant improvements can be made

John Gilbert sails *Salty Stella II*, a Feeling 1040, with his regular crew Roger Parsons. He's owned her for two seasons, although his background is with heavier, long-keeled yachts. John loves the accommodation (so did I) and he'd been hoping *Salty Stella II* would be a useful cruiser, but what seemed like bad manners in gusty weather were making him wonder if she was really right for him. Was the fault irretrievable, or could something be done about it?

I joined John one weekday morning to see if I could help solve the problem. Force 4 and a bit was forecast – just what the doctor ordered for once – plenty of wind to show us the problem. We'd pile on a bit more rag than she wanted, then see if she flew into a strop or took it like a lady. After all, every one of us sometimes ends up harder pressed than the designer intended, but that's life, isn't it? We don't want boats that can't cope when we need them to perform!

RIGHT: The rudder churns up the wake as it fights to keep the yacht from rounding up.
FAR RIGHT: The sharp bows dig in

What is weather helm?

Weather helm is the requirement inherent in most sailing craft for the tiller to be set to windward (wheel turned to leeward) to keep her going straight. A good boat needs a touch of it to remain balanced. Too much, however, and life is not only a misery, it's also very slow because the rudder drags off way. A traditional yacht of moderate beam rarely has a problem with weather helm unless she has a serious design flaw or has been altered in an ill-informed way.

Many modern yachts are similarly well balanced, but when it gets windy some are not.

Where a designer has been prevailed upon to install two large aft cabins in a boat that isn't really long enough to support them, the hull lines can become distorted. As such a yacht heels, the extreme buoyancy of the stern sections causes them to rise up, while her sharp bow digs in and makes her 'gripe' to windward. In extreme cases, the rudder stalls and the closehauled boat tacks herself when a gust hits her. The only way to deal with this is to bring her upright again by dumping the mainsheet, which also serves to shift the centre of effort of the rig forward. The question with John's boat was, 'Is she irretrievably sulky, or can we make adjustments that will really help?'

Mast bend and weather helm

'Weather helm,' you think. 'Either the boat's a lemon or she's got a mainsail problem!' But if the mast isn't set up as it should be, any attempts to tune the sail will be as useless as trying to wash it in your friendly boatyard laundromat. As I hopped on board, I toddled up to the spar and eyeballed straight up its track – the best way to see what's really happening. Try it. It can be revealing, to say the least. It certainly was here. Above

A look up the mast track can be very revealing

the upper spreaders the mast was actually bending towards the bow. This is opposite to how things ought to be, with a sweet, gentle curve sweeping forward in the middle like a flat longbow, and the cap a touch abaft the heel. The forward curve is called 'prebend'. I asked John if the backstay was set up, and he said it wasn't usually touched. The mast had been installed by a yard and John had reasonably assumed that that was an end of the matter. In fact, its bend was,

as riggers say, 'inverted'. Starting with our speciality of stating the obvious, we tightened the adjustable backstay tensioner. This brought the spar more or less into 'column', but there was still no healthy pre-bend. In addition to the stays and caps, the deck-stepped rig was supported by pairs of forward and aft lower shrouds attached at the lower spreaders. All the lowers were slacker than I'd have wanted, so we decided to take it

Don't be frightened of adjusting the backstay

easy, go for a sail and see how it all looked under load. You might think that by raking the top of the mast further aft, I was increasing weather helm, but seen in the big picture the adjustments would have little effect on the centre of effort of the rig as a whole. I was more interested in getting it working properly so we could shape the sails better for more drive and less heeling effect.

Under sail & before treatment

As soon as we got under way, closehauled with full main and full genoa up, we could see that the forestay was sagging badly to leeward, so Roger wound on more backstay. It helped a little, but the main was a horrible shape and the mast track had begun to nod forward again. I was steering as the first gust hit us and away we went, broaching to windward in the finest traditions of the fat-sterned yacht. The rudder stalled with a veritable rooster tail gushing off it, and up we came, head-to-wind.

OK, we could have eased the main, but who wants to do that every time there's a puff of wind? Unless John's boat was a terminal case, there had to be a better way, so we turned our attention back to the mast.

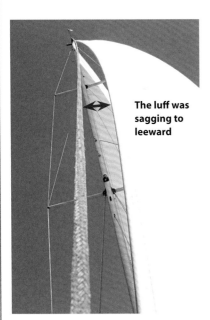

The luff was sagging to leeward

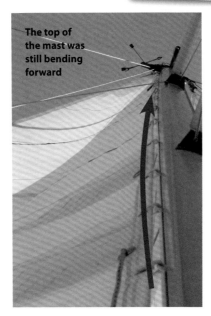

The top of the mast was still bending forward

ABOVE: Tom looks up the jib luff and calls to Roger (TOP LEFT) to tighten the back stay

The mast – remedial action under way

First we attacked the lack of prebend. The leeward lowers were now far slacker than they ought to have been so we knuckled down to tightening up the forward pair to try to induce some bend. With care, in sheltered water and not much traffic, there is no reason why this should not be attended to at sea. The plan was to initiate some prebend into the spar to load up the forestay and persuade the masthead to stop nodding forward. To do this, we hove the boat to under backed headsail with the main idling closehauled to leeward.

The wheel was lashed hard to weather (had it been a tiller, it would have been hard 'down'). This took off all way and

left us with no load to speak of on anything.

Roger now pulled the split pins out of the bottlescrews and tensioned the lee forward lower to take out about half the slack, counting the turns. Then we tacked, hove-to again, and did the same on the other side. This had hardened up the aft lowers by default, and we got under way again.

We'd made some progress, so we repeated the operation until, as if by magic, the mast came into line. Even the forestay tension had improved.

Looking up the track indicated that the cap shrouds now required attention (the

We hove-to and tightened the forward lower stays

masthead was curving to leeward), but since the bend didn't look dangerous we left it until we returned to the pontoon where we set about it with the spanner and screwdriver. For now we had a spar we could work with.

Five steps to a well-set mainsail

Even with the mast sorted, the fully hoisted main continued to look sorry for itself. The foot was baggy, the leech was hooking up to windward and the whole sail was horribly full – a sure guarantee of weather helm when it's nearly time for the first reef. Here's how we set about cheering it up:

A heave on the clew outhaul flattened the lower portion of the sail.

With the outhaul well on, it was time to crank up the halyard a bit harder.

Next came a good heave down on the mainsheet, not forgetting to winch the slack out of the kicker as we did so.

Looking up at the seams, we could see the sail was flatter. The hook in the leech had also disappeared. To set it closehauled it was now time to use the mainsheet traveller to present it at the best angle to the wind. The traveller would also be the 'tool of choice' rather than the sheet for dumping the sail if need be.

Avoiding a broach

Keep your wits about you and you can often avoid a broach. The key is to respond to the helm proactively the instant you feel the boat starting to gripe to windward. A quick adjustment will allow to you to keep powering along but leave it another second and she'll be on her way and you'll have to dump the main.

Mainsheet traveller

A traveller on a modern yacht must be easy to operate under load if needs be. The one John had inherited was a disaster area. He and Roger had been hoping that I might have some miracle cure, but I didn't. The wretched thing could never have worked unless the crew boasted the finger strength of an adult male gorilla in full rugby training. None of us did, so adjusting it quickly – vital on this sort of boat – was impossible.

When we returned to the marina, John and I looked for an example of a good traveller on nearby yachts. We found one, so John is now ordering the parts!

Some of the neighbours didn't even have tackles on theirs. That might be OK on a gaff cutter, but on a modern sloop with a big stern it is ludicrous. Because of this shortfall, we set the traveller a short way to leeward and lived with it as best we could.

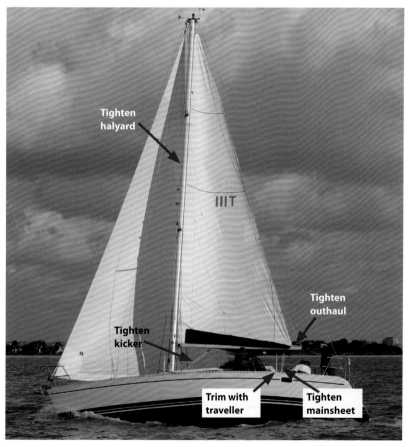

Tighten halyard

IIIT

Tighten outhaul

Tighten kicker

Trim with traveller

Tighten mainsheet

A decent traveller is essential – this one was poorly designed and wrongly set up

Reefing the main and keeping it flat

By the time the wind began gusting up further we had made serious inroads into the weather helm. The main looked good and the genoa was standing up far better. The lazyjacks were interfering with the main, but this wasn't too serious and we had other things on our minds. In the rising breeze it was unfair to expect the boat to balance any longer. She needed a reef.

The reefing system was two-line, with one for the tack of each reef and a conventional one on the clew. Both led aft to the cockpit. I like this arrangement and it worked a treat, except for one thing. The boom had a set of fittings under the aft end, which John and Roger had assumed were for the reef pennants. Perhaps they once were, but not any longer. The pennants had been tied off to these before leading up through the leech reef cringles, aft to the boom-end

turning blocks and so forward through the boom to the winch. Had the fittings been in the right place this might have served, but they were too far forward.

The sail was being pulled down but not aft and therefore reefed with a baggy foot and, guess what, loads of weather helm was the result.

As it happened, the main had small eyelets in its foot through which the pennants were meant to pass before being tied around the boom with a running bowline. The sailmaker had these eyelets in the right place and as soon as we shifted the pennants to them, the sail reefed like a gentleman and the weather helm backed off.

It was also clear by looking at how the reefing lines ran through it that the mainsail stackbag should be shifted half a foot aft – another tweak to get everything shipshape.

ABOVE: The reefing pennant did not pull the clew aft. BELOW: Re-rigged and secured with a running bowline

Leech lines

The breeze dropped off a notch and we shook out the reef. The leeches began 'motoring' in a manner calculated to drive a sensitive sailor directly to the brandy bottle without passing 'Go'. Since all else was in order, I tweaked the leech lines. The genoa went to sleep for about 10 seconds until the line began dragging through a worn-out cleat that looked too big for it.

A flutttering leech is a dead giveaway for a sloppily run boat but as a rule they need a light touch. Tune them like the 'squelch' on a VHF: pull till the flutter goes then pay out a smidge.

BELOW: Adjusting the leech line was one more minor adjustment

Briefing your crew

A bad briefing can leave your crew bored or terrified before
you've even cast off from the marina – a good one will help
them have a safe sail that is enjoyable for everyone

One of the things I like about being a freelance writer is that nobody says, 'You must do it our way!' This suits me because I've learned that at sea there is usually more than one way to achieve the desired end. From splicing a braidline eye to brewing the tea, a good skipper's techniques are often modified by circumstances, and this is never more true than when briefing the crew as they join the ship.

As someone who's been involved with training since sailors wore canvas smocks, I've heard all sorts of briefs dished out. At one end of the scale, I've seen people taken to sea without being told if the yacht has any lifejackets, much less where they are. They seemed happy enough, but they wouldn't have been if they'd been run down at 0100. At the other extreme, I've sat through a two-hour session officially called a 'safety briefing' where everything that could possibly go wrong was addressed in terms of kit that can be bought off a chandler's shelf. That crowd had no doubt that the sea was a dangerous place and that their professional skipper's most important task was to keep them from harm. This was the 'Anyone caught having fun will be sent to the headmaster's study for six of the fruitiest' school of yachting.

Somewhere between the two lies the right answer. To find some input, I got together with Alan and Wendy Butcher on their Hallberg-Rassy 36. They've been sailing long enough to have it worked out, but we also invited Peter Chennell, a sea safety expert.

Who gets which brief?

I often ask myself who should be told what and Alan pointed out that when he and Wendy went off for an evening sail, they didn't bother with briefings. Obvious, you'd think, but can your number-two send a distress message? This raised a whole issue about how much regular and family crews need to know, and how much skippers may wrongly take for granted. We decided to address that

important question on another occasion. Today, we'd deal with briefing a crew of comparative strangers to the boat; taking the neighbours yachting, for example, or cousin Egbert, or even a few mates from the rugby club.

What's needed for the day?

Wendy observed that if she and Alan were just taking a few chums for a sail on a summer's afternoon, she'd want to sort out the lifejackets and the loo, but she'd be inclined to give the harnesses a miss. It takes too much time and starts to sound heavy, she said. I was right up for that and so, to my surprise, was Peter. 'It's your duty to keep people safe,' he said, 'but you've also to remember that we're supposed to be having a nice day out. If you suddenly decide you're going to need to clip on, you'll be able to anticipate and hand out the harnesses under way. If you're intending to cross the English Channel in the dark ... that's a different matter.'

Peter's realistic approach had uncovered the secret of a successful briefing – 'Now, or later?'

When to hold a briefing

The answer to avoiding the dreaded hour-long briefing is confidence in your own experience. You know that everyone must understand the heads. You also are well aware in your heart that you ought to be telling at least someone about how to send a distress message in the event of you falling overboard. The differ-

ence between the two is as follows.

The heads? Everyone needs it. Many will be embarrassed to ask and will 'put it off' if nobody shows them how. Someone may even be bursting to go as you speak. So do it now, in a light-hearted way. If your bulkheads are thin, make a joke about the noise issue, and so on.

A distress message? For your own safety, you must have someone able to do this. What the crew doesn't require is to be sat down in a row and talked through the VHF syllabus. Unless your luck is really out, you won't all fall overboard or suffer heart attacks together so, in all honesty, it's only necessary to have one person who can give a shout if you're the victim. Chances are that you won't die or take a tumble in the first half-hour or so. You might, of course, but if you're of a nervous disposition, consider the chances coolly. Once you're under way and you've a mug of tea in your hand, take the most likely person aside and explain quietly what to do.

Single skipper or skipper and mate?

Taking on a novice crew when you are the sole competent person is very different from doing the same thing with a mate you generally sail with. If your partner knows where everything is and what to do, much of your briefing to the new crew can go by the board. You'll still have to deal with some things, but what they may be is up to your judgement.

Distress messages

I suggested advising my 'lifeline person' to call '999 – Coastguard please!' on their mobile. After all, they are familiar with that and it'll probably work, won't it?

Peter had a different perspective. He told us that the rescue services by far prefer a VHF message, even if it's not a formal one. 'The thing is, they can initiate a 'DF' [Direction-find] on a VHF signal, so if the casualties can't describe their position or read it off a GPS for whatever

reason, we can still locate them.'

Mobile phones are a perfectly good backup, he went on. The rescue services have no quarrel with them, but the truth is that they don't always work. There are coverage black holes aplenty around the coast, and they don't pick up far offshore either. So how do you train someone to use the VHF in two minutes?

'Ideally, have a distress procedure posted on the bulkhead and show them

how to read the GPS position,' said Peter, going on to note that with GMDSS, anyone can be shown how to press and hold the red button.

'At worst,' he continued, 'if someone remains calm, picks up the handset and says, "Help! Will someone talk to me please. I'm in distress!" the rescue services will spring into action. I don't think either of them will be concerned about lack of proper radio procedure!

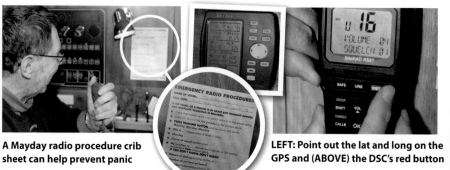

A Mayday radio procedure crib sheet can help prevent panic

LEFT: Point out the lat and long on the GPS and (ABOVE) the DSC's red button

What to include and how to put it across

What follows is suggested guidelines only. Every boat is different and so is every crew. What's important is that you as skipper have worked up your own policy.

The formal briefing

These topics are best mentioned in a formal session before you set sail.

> **Hand out lifejackets** – Give everyone a lifejacket, then it's theirs for the rest of the trip. I like crew to keep it with their kit so they'll know where it is.

> **Adjust it** – Make sure everyone has adjusted it to fit – normally over oilskins.

> **When to wear it** – This is up to you. Rescue services like all hands to wear them at all times. My own crew have other ideas. Decide on your rules and explain them now.

> **First-aid kit** – Explaining where the pills and bandages are only takes a second or two. You might as well do it now. Some people like a label on this and other lockers. Others hate it. Suit yourself, but if there are no marks make sure your crew know what's what.

> **Heads** – An absolute 'must', and you really have to demonstrate the action. It's a good plan always to pump the

thing at least a dozen times. Beginners can be content with a mere disappearance, while we know that 'out of sight' may not ultimately be 'out of mind'. A meaty flush diminishes the odds on the unspeakable.

> **Cooker and galley safety** – Make tea while you're briefing and use the operation to explain how it works, complete with gas safety. You can do this in a relaxed but clear manner, so as not to degenerate into a didactic 'gloom and doom' session.

> **Awareness** – A new one on me, this, but Alan and Wendy said they always tell inexperienced crews not to be afraid to mention anything they've seen. Nice one! 'Have you got this large ship 50 yards astern, skipper?' Oooops!

> **Seasickness** – If I'm going offshore, I advise everyone in advance to start taking Stugeron according to the maker's instructions a day before they join, and go on taking it until they leave (assuming it's only a few days). That's the brief done

– and the seasickness dealt with in most cases. Where we're off for a jolly on a gentle day, I don't even mention it. No point in putting ideas into worried heads, is there?

> **Cold** – If this seems likely to be an issue, tackle it right from the start. If it's not going to be a problem, leave it out!

> **'One hand for yourself** – and one for the ship' is great advice. It only takes a couple of sentences, and it's easy to give it up front (or perhaps as you go up on deck) in a light-hearted manner while still hitting the spot. As Wendy said, you don't want people falling overboard.

> **Heeling** – There's nothing so alarming to a novice as feeling the ground tilt beneath the feet. Tell them that it will, then remind them it's about to happen when you hoist the sails. Forewarned is forearmed. Given the brief beforehand, a quick 'Whoopee!' as it actually comes to pass can work wonders.

Explaining how to use the heads (LEFT), where the first aid kit lives (ABOVE) and how to use the stove (RIGHT) should all be part of the initial briefing

Later briefings

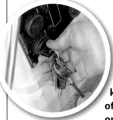

LEFT, ABOVE & RIGHT: Decide who needs to know how to set off flares or turn on the engine

BELOW: Show crew how to use a winch when it's time to hoist the mainsail

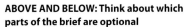

ABOVE AND BELOW: Think about which parts of the brief are optional

These are all the items that need mentioning, but that you might decide to leave for later to keep the initial brief light, short, and to the point.

> **Starting the engine** – Someone should know how to do this. Show anyone appropriate the procedure when you actually do it. And remind them to shove the stop button all the way in if the beast won't fire up!

> **Distress calls** – As we've decided, this is a classic for 'later'.

> **Flares** – When you're out for an afternoon, you can always find a minute to show someone where they are and chat about how they work 'for interest'. On a more serious trip, you may feel it's worth briefing all hands before the first night.

> **Fire extinguishers** – I pick my moment to advise about these. Almost more importantly, I state the ship's policy about fire. Typically, this would be, 'If you find a fire, let everyone know (no shouting! It winds people up) then get all hands on deck. Grab an

extinguisher and fight your way back in.

> **Winches** – These can cause some nasty injuries, so make sure everyone knows the basic safe procedures. The obvious time to explain this is when you first use one. A halyard winch is less lively, so I tend to choose that for the full demo, then advise about differences with sheet winches, demonstrating them when the time comes.

> **Liferaft** – Here's one that can usually wait for a suitable moment under way. If you need the thing in the first hour or two you can usually opt for the superior alternative of sailing up the nearest beach.

> **Harnesses** – 'As and when', unless it's going to be heavy weather or dark, right from the off.

> **Boom** – This certainly needs comment, and the time is when you're hoisting the mainsail. Make a point of advising what can happen, but beware – this is another area where its easy to get heavy and negative. There's nothing dangerous in a boom so long as it's under control and

everyone knows what it can do.

> **Action for MOB** – Once you're sailing along nicely, give the drill for what to do if anyone goes over. Here's mine:

If it's a crew member, call 'Man overboard!', point at him and keep pointing no matter what, and steer through the wind. The skipper will be up soon enough if he's not there already. If it's me over the side, they steer through the wind, throw the MOB kit overboard, hit the GPS MOB button and call for help, in that order. They also point, point, point.

Later, and given time, I might show them how to initiate a recovery procedure, but for now, that'll do nicely.

ITEM	NOW?	LATER?	ALL HANDS?	ONE PERSON?	EVERY TRIP (E), OR AT DISCRETION (D)?
Hand out Lifejacket	✔		✔		E
Show adjustments and brief on when to wear it	✔		✔		E
How to start the engine		✔		✔	E
Operating the VHF for distress calls		✔		✔	E
Flares – where they are and how to use		✔		✔	E
First aid kit – where is it?	✔		✔		E
Fire extinguishers		✔	✔		E
Heads	✔		✔		E
Cooker and basic galley safety	✔		✔		E
Using winches safely		✔	✔		E
How to launch liferaft		✔	✔		D
Harnesses		✔	✔		D
Beware of boom		✔	✔		E
Keep aware (looking out)	✔		✔		E
The value of a round turn		✔	✔		E
Seasickness	✔		✔		D
Dangers of cold	✔		✔		D
Action for crew in event of MOB		✔	✔		E
One hand for yourself and one for the ship	✔		✔		E
Heeling for novices – forewarned is forearmed	✔		✔		D

Conclusion

Sailing is mainly about giving ourselves an enjoyable time. A certain amount of pre-emptive explanation can make unpleasantness less likely, or help novices deal with it should it arise despite our efforts. The trouble is, if we try to cover everything we know about what passes for 'safety', we risk starting the day with a negative impression. We also waste good yachting time. The answer is to find the compromise that best suits us, our boats and our crews. Careful preparation can ensure all hands are safe, almost without realising it.

Cruising with children

Sharing the joy and fun of sailing with children is no mean feat, particularly when they are young, but get it right and they'll love the water for the rest of their lives

I've been aboard two yachts recently sailed by families with young children. One crew were as busy as bees in a hive when I poked my head down the companionway; the kids mobbed me to show me their latest efforts at trashing Dad's ordered chart table with painting books. A happy ship if ever I saw one. On the other boat, the youngsters were surly. Mother looked as though she'd had enough, and Father was clearly wishing he'd invited the rugby team instead. The problem might have been superficial, but I doubt it.

The contrast was so stark that I started wondering why my adult daughter still wants to come sailing with us even though she's now living a life of her own with her partner. It occurred to me that for once my wife and I had probably got something right. Then I thought about my neighbours, David and Chloe Kendall, and their daughters, Ellie and Aasta. They're out sailing every weekend. In the summer, they all play truant with praiseworthy cynicism, and recently, when I popped round after breakfast to borrow a spanner, I got short shrift from Ellie, aged 11, who saw me as an obstacle between her and the road to the marina. It was when five-year-old Aasta came shuffling happily through the hall, oilskins in one hand and battered cuddly horse in the other that the penny dropped. If ever I'd met two experts, it was David and Chloe. They should be a national authority on making children want to go cruising, so I asked them if they'd give us a day on their boat to tell us how they do it.

Make kids feel valued

I learned my first lesson as soon as I stepped on board the Kendalls' Najad 331, *Splash*, at 0900 one windy morning. David was taking the cockpit tent down, Ellie and her

LEFT: David and Chloe Kendall with Ellie, 11, and Aasta, 5. RIGHT: Tom invests some time with Aasta and is well rewarded

mother were stowing victuals and generally sorting stuff out, but Aasta was lurking in the saloon eyeing me up as a potential victim.

'Come and see my book!' she commanded. I looked around me. My instinct was to offer my services to the skipper, but he didn't really need me. Besides, Aasta was treating me like a human being. I owed it to her to respond accordingly, so I did. And therein lay the key to the whole secret.

The book concerned a group of toys living together in some sort of commune. A trip to the seaside was proposed by Big Bear and you can probably guess the rest. Lots of inconsequential stuff about sand castles, buckets and spades until Little Bear somehow got himself in deep water and was saved by a fluffy seal called 'Splash' – same name as the boat you'll note. High drama, but all ended well and I was awarded a coffee by a grateful mother.

Two points here: The first is that Aasta might have been feeling a bit left out. Everyone was busy, and because she is so young there wasn't a lot she could do for the immediate cause. She's quite a character and some children might have played up to demand attention. By talking with her 'man-to-girl', I had made her feel as valued as in fact she is. Thereafter, she was perfectly content to potter about on her own until we cast off.

The second point is that at five, she was reading phenomenally well and she was enjoying it. Reading is a great way to pass time at sea, for adults as well as children, but a child like Aasta will positively devour books on board as the years go by. Encouraged by parents who look out a good mix of books, this means that she will never, ever be bored.

Working together

Among my own family, I normally drive the boat in tight quarters, so I was most impressed when Ellie took the tiller as we slipped out of our berth. Her Dad tactfully opted to man the sternline, which placed him handily to assist if need be, but basically, he left her to it. At one stage he leant down, quietly offered a piece of advice and eased the throttle, but Ellie brought us astern off our finger berth, swung the boat round, manoeuvred to the lock and laid her alongside. Now, you might be thinking, 'Oh, Little Miss Wonderful. Obviously a multi-talented child…' Actually, that's not how it was. In fact, she didn't get it quite right and the boat biffed the lock wall. Now came the real crunch. I don't know how I'd have coped with seeing my nice new boat bashed, but David didn't blink an eye. He just peeped over and declared no major damage. Then he got on with helping his daughter secure the stern line he'd grabbed from the lock wall. She knew she'd boobed, and they discussed why, but her confidence wasn't dented. She'd be ready to try again another day. There was no atmosphere, and the scratch would be made good with a bit of polish.

Meanwhile, on the foredeck, Chloe and Aasta were manning the boathook to grapple the bow line. I was touched by the sight of the tiny blonde girl, properly kitted up in lifejacket and oilies, brandishing a long alloy boathook while her mother looked on, trying hard not to relieve her of the load until the last possible moment. Somehow, Chloe contrived to give Aasta the impression that it was she who had done the job, while teaching her how to

Ellie's on the helm and loving it

Time to take *Splash*, the Kendall's Najad 331, to sea. Mum and Aasta work the foredeck while Ellie reverses off the pontoon. Dad tends the sternlines so that he's on hand if needed

**ABOVE: There's nothing like getting afloat on their own to keep children happy.
LEFT, RIGHT AND BELOW: Take the time and make the effort to allow children to do jobs on their own. It's a small investment that will provide great returns**

take a turn at the same time. There was no shouting and no running around. Because the parents had obviously given the matter fore-thought with the children in mind, the whole thing seemed to happen in slow motion. The net effect was one of modest mutual accomplishment.

Once we were under sail, Aasta decided it was time for a kip, just as my own daughter often would at that age. She'd been fully involved until now, she knew she was valued, and she needed to go off watch, so she snuggled up to the horse and disappeared into her private bubble for a while. Ellie steered while David hoisted the main. Indeed, she carried on at the helm after we'd set course. She'd obviously done it

before, because she knew where to go. Her mother went below to brew up and her dad was freed so that he and I could talk about grown-up stuff.

Parental fears & anxieties
In my notes, I headed up this section as 'stress management', but really it's back to anxiety again. The commonest sign of parental anxiety I can think of is the old cry, 'Don't go near the edge, Johnnie!' Actually, Johnnie, aged 8, has a lower centre of gravity than his Dad. He's also prob-ably fitter and he'll certainly have a well-developed sense of survival. He's no more likely to topple over than an adult. It's just that the adult is so ill at ease with the surroundings

that he is transferring his own fears to the child, who then becomes up tight and bolshy.

The answer to this issue is simple. It's like the Yorkshireman's advice to the boy confronted by an angry sheepdog – 'Whate'r tha does, lad, don't show fear!'

Parents need to be competent and confident. If they aren't, they owe it to their offspring to try to look like it, or at least not to make a fuss if things go wrong.

Make sure young Johnnie can swim so that if he does fall in – as fall in he surely will if he's having fun in harbour – it'll be, 'Oooh! It's cold. Look Mummy, I'm swimming!' as opposed to screams of panic.

At sea, parental fear can be defused

by a strict régime of movement. Ours went like this:

> No horseplay on deck.
> At sea, if it's rough, stay in the cockpit.
> If it's really rough, clip on in the cockpit. The parent is the final arbiter of what's rough and what isn't.
> If you want to go forward at sea, clip on, and only do so if an adult is in the cockpit (to keep an eye on you!).
> Very young children may need an adult up forward with them as well.
> When my family was small, lifejackets were not so comfy as they are now so we clipped on rather than insist on them. Today, it's worth considering whether to make the lifer a rule on deck unless it's very calm.

Jobs to do on board
Navigating
While Aasta was minding her own business, Ellie explored the chartplotter, learning all the time about chart orienteering, and how to plot the lat/long fix on the paper chart. She also masterminded the logbook.

Watchkeeping
Ellie is now at the stage my own daughter reached at a similar age. She's dying to take a night watch. We broke our girl in gently as she and her mother took the first watch after dinner, so that she could see darkness fall, help maintain the plot and, most important, look out and fill in the logbook. Theoretically she was woken up to share the middle watch, but she rarely made it. By 15 she could stand her own watch reliably.

Duties
Aasta is just big enough to handle fenders, and she is starting to be 'fender monitor'. Our daughter took charge of ensign discipline, which was unpopular early in the morning, especially in the teenage years, but ran like a charm in the evenings. Pride, again, in small things. Learning a few knots makes a child feel more useful, as they can secure lines. Trimming sails can be the children's job, once they have learned how tell tales work. Boys love winching and watching the speed build in response to their efforts. If Dad comes on deck and finds the genoa stalled, he can stop the crew's grog, which is always good for a laugh because the only boozer is likely to be him.

Seasickness
Don't be afraid to send a child below if he is going green. The bunk is the best place for a seasick sailor of any age, but a good cockpit singsong can keep nausea at bay. If you aren't used to live music, this can be a bit embarrassing at first, but once you've got the hang of it, you'll love it. The laughs are endless as you make up dodgy verses about each other to old sea shanties.

Cockpit word games are another winner. Ellie and Aasta are still at the 'In my suitcase I packed….' stage.

In harbour
Learning to row
Ellie and Aasta have an inflatable canoe that they paddle contentedly around the place. We encouraged

our daughter to scull and row our hard dinghy, first on a long string, then going 'solo' to a neighbouring mooring buoy, where she would secure the painter and enjoy a picnic lunch with her bear. The important thing, especially for boys, is to row, not to use the outboard. Any self-respecting lad wants to get stuck into the outboard because he's not old enough to drive a car, but small boys buzzing around aggravate the neighbours and end up with the subversive impression that they are masters of the universe. A rowing boat teaches them that the tide and wind are stronger than they are. It also shows how it feels when your strength starts running out.

Music in harbour
Making music is a wonderful way of binding the family together. Ellie plays flute, her Mum (a cellist) is learning the guitar, and Aasta is a dab hand at banging things on the table. Dad, meanwhile, studies the level in the whisky bottle.

Off watch and at anchor
Aasta and Ellie have their own space on the boat. They keep their toys there, express themselves by hanging up their stuff, and play games together, many of which they invent. Visitors are encouraged to enter this den of delights, which means the girls are proud of their ship and their place on board. A healthy sign indeed. A child who doesn't invite you to see how it lives may not be in such good shape.

Conclusion
Given half a chance, children love living on boats. They need attention, respect, involvement, routine, some freedom, and a clear idea of what is acceptable behaviour. Oh yes, and they can also do with a little calm and a lot of love. All these are evident on *Splash*. I hope they ask me out again soon.

Sailing with your partner

Sailing with your spouse can often turn into a battle of the sexes, but if you both play to your strengths and lay down a few simple rules and well-defined roles, sailing can be a harmonious experience

Judith and Martin choose jobs they enjoy that play to their strengths

If you ever sail two-up with just your partner, take a look at these scenarios for a trip from the UK to France followed by a 10-day cruise. It's likely that one of the caps will fit. Even if you only sail on short hops in daylight the principles will hold true.

1. You're the man, your lady has decided for some reason that she doesn't like passage-making, so you sign on a couple of mates and run the leg down-Channel as a sort of rugby-club trip. Your partner then flies out for the sunshine. She doesn't take much interest in the sailing, but puts up with it for the holiday.

2. You plan and execute the whole trip together as a small team of equals.

In my experience, most of the men who fall into the former category would really prefer to live in the latter, but somehow they just can't make it work. Even those of us who do sail regularly two-up don't always manage to get it as right as we'd like.

It was an issue that I thought was worth investigating, so when Martin Oldfield and his partner Judith invited me to talk about it with them on their brand-new Dufour 385, I hopped on board with enthusiasm.

General considerations
Who does what?
When I arrived on board, there wasn't a breath of wind, so we took a protracted coffee break around the saloon table. Martin and Judith have been sailing together for a number of years and my wife and I have been cruising as a couple for longer than I'd care to admit. We found a lot of common ground. Regardless of any predetermined ideas of 'man-woman' roles, we agreed that it's fundamentally important for both partners to settle with the jobs they want. It's a safe bet that these will also be the ones they do best.

As we passed the biscuits round, Martin and Judith provided me

with an object lesson of people thinking freely about these issues. In general, Judith said, Martin steers the boat during manoeuvres at sea or in harbour. Partly, this is because like most men – me included – he enjoys doing it, while she doesn't mind either way. More importantly, it's because Judith is nimbler about the deck. She can therefore get things organised quicker and with less danger of taking a tumble. If she were to fall overboard offshore, Martin's greater strength would give them a better chance of unassisted

Judith is nimbler than Martin so normally tends the sheets unless it's blowing really hard

The skipper

When it comes to skippering, the bottom line seems to be that with only two on board, there doesn't have to be an official captain. If one party is more experienced at navigating, he or she will probably take the final decision on matters of piloting. The driver of the boat in close quarters will dictate what happens in berthing situations, but it doesn't necessarily have to be the same person. The important area of victualling will fall to anyone who prefers to cook, and so on. However, successful strategic choices

about such questions as where to go and when will always come down to give and take. If they don't, something is seriously wrong and discord will be the sure result.

recovery. In easy conditions at sea, the powerful winches on the Dufour more than make up for any shortfall in physical 'oomph', but if things get too much for Judith in heavy going, they reverse roles, accepting that Martin will deliver more pull.

This sort of talk gladdens my heart in a world where people are pushed into responsibilities that don't come naturally because of some half-baked ideas about politically correct equality. If I was still harbouring any doubts about lurking 'task sexism', they were dispelled by Judith as Martin popped over to wipe down the galley top and she filled up my coffee.

'Martin's not interested in engines at all,' she told me, 'so I do all the checks, the oil and so forth. I quite enjoy it really. He doesn't mind washing up, and over the years we've settled into that arrangement.'

Say no more.

As we continued to exchange ideas, we realised that we'd all seen couples sailing where the boat was clearly the male's world into which the female was theoretically welcomed, but in fact was virtually excluded from all but the domestic areas of influence. The lady becomes bashful about asking how things work while the gentleman takes on an ever-more dominant position. She becomes frustrated and he may be less comfortable with his new situation than he appears.

The result is unhappiness and, ultimately, the rugby-club delivery trip situation. The answer is the sort of honesty I was seeing from my hosts. No preconceptions, going with the flow and, above all, communicating in a straightforward way.

Working together at sea

Two heads and bodies are usually better than one, even if they aren't equal in knowledge and strength. Working together sympathetically is a great way of imparting skills from one to another without the sort of didactic 'instruction sessions' that are so difficult within families. Ever tried teaching your daughter to drive?

Preparation
I was interested to note that Judith stowed everything below while Martin sorted out the deck and took care of passage planning. When they thought they were ready, they cross-checked each other's work. This earned them a gold star from me for mutual acceptance, because I could well imagine some people reacting badly to the partner peering at their efforts, but their no-baggage attitude is great if you can manage it.

The autopilot
The big Dufour was the first boat Judith and Martin had owned with a really effective autopilot and I felt they were a bit slow to set it running. It came as something of a surprise to them when I flashed it up inside the harbour. Once set up properly, a modern autopilot is pretty reliable. There wasn't much traffic on our weekday morning, so I had no hesitation in using it to free all hands to deal with the sails.

On a powerful boat best handled by two, it really does make all the difference. Discipline is vital, however, because it's easy to become obsessed with freeing that mainsail track while forgetting the small yacht you're about to run down. The best answer is to develop a 20-second alarm clock in your head that reminds you to glance around.

Out at sea, a good autopilot or windvane is critical to all short-handed work.

Working together at sea

Communication

Anchoring and mooring, one partner is invariably at the sharp end while the other is doing the driving. It's too far for civilised conversation, especially if it's windy, and we've all heard the dreaded 'Back off, darling!' shouts, followed by crunching fibreglass.

My own answer is to develop a system of sign language for 'left', 'right', 'on a bit', 'take way off now,' etc. On my boat we use discreet finger signs. With luck, nobody else in the anchorage is aware of what's going on.

Take it easy

The Dufour has a big mainsail. So does my boat. Just looking at it and knowing we are only two-up can be enough to upset my stomach, so we often reef before we really need to just for peace of mind. A decent boat will go well enough in a bit of a breeze even if she is a bit short of rag.

Piloting together

Even though I've written books about pilotage I feel far more confident if my wife is up there with me supplying a second perspective on an unfamiliar shore. The pilot should brief the partner about what he or she is looking for, then the shipmate can use the binoculars to find it. A woman normally has 100% colour vision. Some men have a shortfall without being catastrophically handicapped by it. Typically, a woman will see a red light before a man who may have some degree of deficiency, even if he doesn't know it.

Piloting two-handed rapidly develops skills in the 'non-navigator' which raises his or her level of job satisfaction as well as making the ship a safer place.

Tips to make sailing easier
Like many yachts with no winch to roll up the genoa, Judith was finding the Dufour's headsail a handful if she allowed it to flog. The answer was to make sure we had sea room when it counted, then run off to hide the sail in the wind shadow of the main. A child could have rolled it away then. Another useful trick for weaker crews is to steer onto a close reach when reefing, then ease the sails right off to spill most of their wind. This slows the boat down and makes going forward a lot less alarming. It also renders life more pleasant by killing the apparent wind.

Watchkeeping
Martin and Judith had no worries about taking a watch below and leaving the other in charge. For full satisfaction of both people as well as successful passage-making this is important. It's not easy to muscle up to your first solo watch, so the 'senior partner' must make sure that it's not in the middle of a North Sea shipping roundabout, or when a thunder squall is looming. Choose an easy one first, leave clear instructions about when to call for assistance, and always be happy to be called. A single grumble can blow a week's hard-won confidence clean out the porthole!

Navigation
Modern kit makes it easier for an untrained person to take an interest in the navigation. Even if they aren't up to speed with the back-up requirements for failure, using a chartplotter is something anyone with basic computer skills can manage. Knowing that the less experienced partner understands the ship's position and is keeping the logbook up to date helps give the navigator a peaceful watch below.

Radar
Modern radar with all its bells and whistles was new to Judith and Martin, whereas on my boat we use it a great deal. To be properly effective in thick weather, radar needs to be monitored on a continuous basis. I suggested that both worked towards identifying targets that are of interest, having one of them at the screen while the other looks out on deck.

In general, I've found that a more experienced partner can become obsessed with the fact that he or she may have done more radar work and will hog the screen. We all need to fight this.

Train your 'oppo' in good weather so that when the chips are on the table you have confidence in one another's abilities.

Berthing
Berthing is the commonest area of discord in small crews, and Martin and Judith dealt with it by pure organisation. Judith had fenders and lines rigged both sides long before she arrived in a strange berth, leaving her ready for whatever came.

This freed up Martin to concentrate on bringing the boat in sweetly. On the berth we were using – a typical marina – Judith hopped off and made the head fast first, then moved smartly aft down the finger pontoon to take a stern line from Martin. She dropped a pre-made bowline over the cleat and he snapped in the slack to finish the basic job. Under different circumstances they might have used a short midships spring, but the important thing was a system they both understood and had practised. No stress. No shouting.

Conculsion
One or two simple rules became clear on my day with Judith and Martin. Apart from basic competence, of course, the secret seems to be that we must communicate without 'baggage', share as many tasks as we can, and not arrive on board with preconceptions as to which sex will take care of a particular job.

If you're a man and you like cooking, run the galley and be happy. If you're a woman and you suspect in your heart that your partner has better spatial awareness, encourage him to berth the boat while you hop off with the lines. Do what you do best and, above all, do what you like doing.

Keeping your crew happy

If you crew isn't happy, then your boat won't be either. But keeping the crew content takes as much thought and skill as any other element of seamanship, and shouldn't be ignored

David Oliver runs a one-boat charter business. He is an international consultant in human relationships and motivation, so when such an authority asked me to compare notes on skippering, I was apprehensive about how my own techniques would shape up under the microscope! I climbed over our Bénéteau Océanis 36 *Cool Running*'s guardrails to be greeted by David, his one-man crew and a glass of champagne.

After a chilly motorbike ride on a road populated by homicidal maniacs, this hit the spot far more than a standard safety briefing. By David's own admission, he felt he wasn't always an expert skipper, which, with his business background, meant we had lots to talk about. The bottom line was: what could we learn from one another, having agreed that nobody is the Ultimate Fount of Knowledge on everything.

'Good', I thought. 'Give and take. There's lesson one!'

A warm welcome (and a glass of champagne) will make the crew feel at home

'Safety' briefing

When we'd washed up our champagne flutes (glass, not plastic I'm delighted to report), our brief for the day was a positive affair lasting only a few minutes. We were kitted up with lifejacket / harnesses, we discussed how the galley and heads worked, then we gathered round the chart to plan where we'd go, how long this might take, and what conditions we'd be in for. The theme was positive all the way through. 'Downers' were minimised but touched on sensibly, with gas taps noted as part of an overall 'how to put the kettle on' scenario, rather than a finger-wagging frightener about explosions. The great time we were going to have was maximised. And we did indeed have a lovely day.

Forewarning novice crew

Skippers easily forget their first day in a sailing boat. When she heels, you feel as if the world is falling over. You're also psyched out by the noise of the flapping sails before they fill. I've found that telling new crew what to expect is the key.

'See that yacht over there? Well, when we're heeling and you think life is ending, it's only really leaning as much as that. Plus, we've got three tons of lead underneath us that makes it impossible for the boat to fall over and tip us out.'

It works like a charm!

Their pace, not yours

David was exemplary in the discipline and patience needed to run manoeuvres at his crew's pace not his own. He always made time for their comparative lack of competence, which set me thinking. The previous weekend I'd been cruising with my family, who are highly experienced but don't sail all the time as I do. It was their first trip of the year and I'd planned to weigh anchor under sail – not easy in my 20-ton gaffer with a hundredweight of ground tackle to bring aboard. Normally, they'd have relished the challenge, but because they were rusty and I hadn't given this proper credit, we bungled it. My fault, not theirs. I shouldn't have assumed they were 'on the pace' after a winter a long way from the sea.

Keep your voice down

David is naturally soft-spoken. I'm anything but. He has no worries about unsettling his crew by raising his voice. In my case it's an issue. It's not that I want to shout at people out of frustration or anger. I don't. It's just that they may be 50ft away and if it's windy I get loud to make myself heard. Bad idea. A raised voice can be misconstrued by someone who's feeling nervous and inadequate. We skippers can easily forget that our crews may be precisely in that state.

Personal skill levels

David once had a bad experience trying to set his cruising chute in a lively breeze. His crew hated it and he didn't rate it himself. He didn't mind asking me to show him how to hoist it in front of his crew. As it happened it was blowing Force 5, the Bénéteau was already edgy on the helm and I judged that the chute might send her into a series of broaches, so we gave it a miss.

David hadn't been too proud to share a specific area in which his experience fell short. Good for him!

Accentuate the positive

This was an area where I watched David as closely as he was watching me, but he managed the last word. Approaching harbour in a strong cross-set, I encouraged our crew to sail a transit. Satisfied that he was on the ball and that David was looking out, I went below for a few minutes. When I came up we were on track and I did the right thing, but I honestly can't say I was thinking about it. I was very pleased with David's email comment:

'My crew had been instructed in his first-ever transit (he thought it was a Ford van!) and was doing well in a chop. Tom popped up his head from visiting the special seat below and says, "You've held that transit like a true pro". I watched the helmsman's self-esteem build almost visibly and a big smile cracked his face for the first time in the day.'

It doesn't take much to praise somebody, but a little well-placed acclaim goes a very long way. Try an objective look at your own performance. Are you encouraging the team enough?

Lead from the front

It's axiomatic that a good skipper will never ask a crew to do what he or she is unwilling to tackle personally. Less obvious is to take the lead on domestic issues. Someone who's hanging back from washing up, cleaning the heads or sweeping out can be a drag on general happiness. You could tell them straight, but an easier option is to start doing the jobs cheerfully yourself. This sort of leadership can leave them with such a bad conscience that they take up the slack voluntarily.

Delegating

I noticed that after David had instructed his crew on coiling and stowing, he left him to it even though the result wasn't as neat as it might have been. It takes a firm grip on yourself to keep your nose out. I often find it trying myself, but do it we must – and sometimes speak well of a less-than-perfect job – if our crew are to have a satisfying day.

The importance of good communication

When skippers don't make themselves clear, crews are often too shy to ask for clarification. They then do their best but fail to carry out what the boss thought he had told them. I was skippering *Cool Running* as we shaped up towards a mooring buoy. The tide was running hard, but the wind gave the option of a closehauled approach straight into the stream. An easy pick-up, so long as you chose the correct tack.

Although David had been obliged to practise this for his Yachtmaster exam, like many skippers he hadn't bothered since. He was helming and I gave what I imagined were clear suggestions. His remarks were:

'One of the less satisfying moments was trying to pick up a mooring buoy. Tom thought I understood the way he wanted the approach to be made but a basic communication went wrong. I discovered afterwards that Tom wanted me to stand in shoreward of the buoy, then go about between the shore and the buoy and hook up.

'In my mind I was processing the tack the opposite side of the buoy.

Tom's instructions, and my interpretation were not in harmony, I missed the buoy and we sailed on to try again. This time I made it my business to ask and keep on asking until I was clear about the approach required. We made it!'

I'd wrongly assumed that as the highly competent skipper he was, David would have realised I meant him to head into the tide for the pick-up, rather than choose the tack with the stream walloping across the buoy. Here's my reply to David:

'The initial failure to grab the buoy was, as I now see it, clearly down to my lack of detailed briefing. You understood everything I said all day, so I think I must have assumed you'd realise we needed

the "offshore", up-tide tack to make the approach. I was a step or two ahead and you were gent enough not to say, "If you'd just told me…" Many thanks for that. I had a similar incident not so long ago, and you've helped me identify what I now recognise as a personal shortfall creeping up on me. It was worth coming for that alone.'

The skipper's duty

When the burdens of being skipper weigh heavily and others start looking downcast in reflection of your mood, remember David and his glass of champagne. However bad things seem on the boat, the world out there is full of much more concrete horrors. Yachts are for fun. Our duty as skippers is to run a happy ship.

Make yourself clear

When you're off watch, people must fully understand their responsibilities, especially someone left alone at night. Noting your orders down helps a lot. Do they call you for any ship, or just one on a steady bearing? What about wind shifts? And how much sugar do you take in your coffee when they give you a shake?

Self-justification

The superficial conclusion from the incident with the buoy is that I have isolated a technical area in which I can improve – I have been forgetting to insist that orders are repeated by the recipient to remove any possibility of ambiguity. Less obvious but equally important is that I have faced up to a personal shortfall and considered what I can do about it. When I'm examining, I often find candidates making excuses for something that just hasn't worked. Self-justification is as natural a reaction as kicking your knee up when the doctor hits it with a toffee hammer. It has its places, but the deck of a boat isn't one of them,

and it's worth taking a few minutes alone after a passage to debrief yourself. Were you pleased with your performance? Were there areas where, deep down, you know you could have done better? I'll bet there were. I've found that it's only by facing myself honestly like this that I can improve my act. Sometimes, after the internal argument with 'Captain Justification', I have to admit to myself that I was wrong. As soon as I've accepted this I can forgive myself, analyse the problem and learn the lesson without angst. What's more, I can have a beer with the hands knowing that things can only get better.

Running aground

It can happen to any of us: one minute you're happily
sailing along and the next, you're hard aground. In most
situations, the quicker you react, the quicker you'll float
free, so knowing the right techniques is crucial

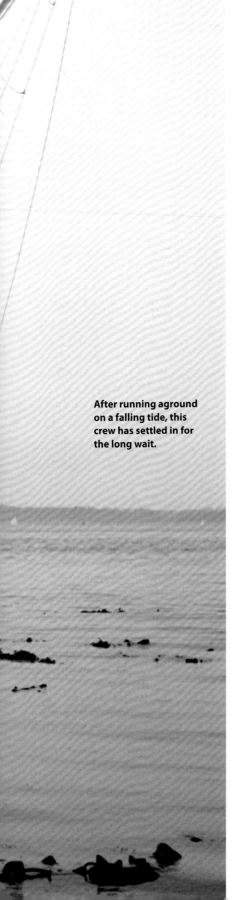

After running aground on a falling tide, this crew has settled in for the long wait.

RIBs have powerful engines, but a heavy old fishing boat with equivalent horsepower will have much more pulling power

If I had a pound for every time I've touched the bottom I wouldn't be able to retire in comfort, but I'll bet it would pay for a decent meal. Ask any sailor who's been around the block a few times. It's always the same story.

One season I spent an uncomfortable hour on a well-marked rock following an unpredictable incident during a race. It was all rather more public than I'd have liked, but the tide was rising and the traditional boat had one of those full-length lead keels made to absorb punishment. We brewed tea, served cakes, and in due course the flood lifted us clear. No drama, no damage and no problem beyond a dent to the ego, which does none of us any lasting harm.

A grounding can be a catastrophe involving loss of ship and even life, or it can be a minor event hardly worth logging. Which it is depends on where you ground, the prevailing conditions, and what you do about it. The latter might be an instant reaction that saves the day, it could be a measured assessment of the situation resulting in a plan to extricate the yacht without assistance, or it may be a decision to ask for help. At worst, it's remedial action if you're unfortunate enough to be stuck fast.

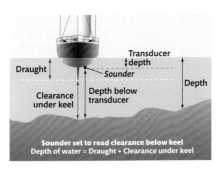

Sounder left uncalibrated
Depth of water = Transducer depth + Sounder depth

Transducer depth
Sounder
Draught
Clearance under keel
Depth below transducer
Depth

Sounder set to read clearance below keel
Depth of water = Draught + Clearance under keel

Transducer depth
Sounder
Draught
Clearance under keel
Depth below transducer
Depth

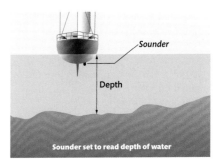

Sounder set to read depth of water

Sounder
Depth

Likely hotspots for grounding

LEFT: Stuck fast – time for damage limitation measures. ABOVE: Grounded on a river, this cruiser need only wait for the tide to float off.

The best answer to the potential horrors of grounding is to anticipate and avoid. It's a salutary lesson, however, that the officers of almost every big ship that strands on an isolated shoal imagine they know their position and are surprised when she hits. Recognising the sort of places awaiting the unwary is nearly all of the battle. Here are some of the favourites:

Shifting channels and swatchways

Some areas of the coast are notorious for shifting sands. I once bought a new, corrected chart of an area on the day I put to sea, only to find it seriously out of date when I arrived there 48 hours later. The notes on such charts advise about unreliable depths and channels. So do the pilot books. Unless you're sure of what's what, run your eye over the words of wisdom and leave a fat margin for error.

Harbour entrances

We all tend to relax our vigilance near the end of a passage, especially when we're tired. Sloppy chartwork follows, then the silly mistake that puts us on a shoal.

Rocks, reefs and offshore sandbars

If these are well buoyed, missing them should present no challenge to a prudent navigator. Places such as north-west Ireland, where isolated rocks are unmarked except by their own resident breaker, are more difficult. A chartplotter helps, so long as its datum is correct, but however deeply you trust the survey, there is no harm in giving a little extra clearance just to be sure. GPS has not diminished the number of yachts going ashore.

Amazingly, this yacht suffered no damage

Marina sills

Every year, yachts ground nastily on locked marina sills. Just because the gate has flapped open does not mean there's enough water over the lip. Charts are often not specific. Only the pilot book is a sure arbiter, unless a tide gauge tells you what you need to know. But is it reading tide height, or depth on the sill? They may be very different.

River edges when tacking

This one's my own best banker for picking up a dinner tab. Tacking up rivers is great fun. To succeed, we often push our luck. See below for what to do when you feel her slowing down.

A time and a place

I can't say I ever enjoy grounding, but some places and conditions are a lot worse than others. Like so many things at sea, they vary with wind and tide.

Height of tide

This one's pretty obvious. Sailing into a soft mudbank on a rising tide is rarely a serious problem. But the experienced skipper always knows when the tide is falling and, this being the case, avoids risking a grounding like the plagues of Egypt. A rapidly dropping tide gives very little time to act, and you're soon facing the question of calling for help before you dry out completely. One of the worst times to run aground is on top of a big Spring, with the following tide a foot or two lower. Tread as though on glass, otherwise you'll be 'neaped'.

Sea state

Calm water gives your best chance of escape from the grip of the seabed. In a swell, when a boat starts pounding on rock or sand, it feels as though she'll knock her bottom out. With a bolted-on fin keel this is not unlikely, so take no chances when there's a sea running.

Soft and hard bottoms

With a muddy bottom there's every likelihood of backing off the way you came in, and damage is improbable. Sand sounds soft, but it isn't. It feels as unyielding as concrete when you hit it, while even a smooth rock will often lift the boat out of the water a few inches as she rides up, leaving the engine with an uphill battle to heave her off. A poor start for extricating yourself.

Weather and lee shores

No sailing boat can manoeuvre off a lee shore without outside assistance of some sort. This may be a kedge, a

Blown onto a dangerous lee shore

tow or an inboard engine, but once aground with the wind blowing you on, there's no point in trying to sail off. On the other hand, beating up a river with a long and a short tack on a rising tide, you can usually try your luck on the weather shore. Getting off the mud there should be a piece of cake.

First actions for a minor grounding

However hard we try to avoid getting together with the bottom, it happens to everyone sooner or later. Hitting the mud isn't the end of the world. It's what happens next that counts, and few of us have a lifting keel or centreboard we can whip up before anyone has noticed.

Tacking in a river: Whichever side of the river you're on when the boat suddenly loses way, the reaction must be to shove the helm hard down instantly. As you steer into what you hope will be a tack, don't let go the jib sheet, but keep it secure so that the sail comes aback as the bow swings across the wind. Once she's filling on the new tack, let draw and it's 10:1 that you'll

sail straight off. If you don't, you'll certainly be able to drive her off under power. Any hesitation with the helm at that critical moment, however, especially on the lee shore, and you're hard on.

Crash-gybe: If she won't tack, either in a river or in wider waters, the vital thing remains to get the wind onto the other side. If there looks like room, therefore, you might want to try gybing round. This shock tactic may deliver the goods. If it fails, you're further on than you were. You're also downwind, so only use it if you must.

Full power astern: You were floating when you arrived in this predicament so if you can muster enough power to move

back out the way you came in, you'll be floating again fairly soon. If you can't flip round and sail out, therefore, the answer is usually to drop the sails and motor off astern. There's a catch, however. Many propellers don't deliver full thrust astern, so you may have to consider the spin-around.

Spin and go out ahead: A deep-fin boat can often pirouette on her keel by shoving the helm hard over and running the prop ahead, perhaps with a little help from a backed headsail. The rudder shoots the water out the side and, with luck, round she goes. So long as the tide hasn't fallen more than an inch or two, you've every chance of powering off now. Fin keels often draw more at their aft end, which means they're much more easily dragged across the seabed when going ahead than astern.

A minor grounding in calm weather. Whether you motor off, kedge off or get out and push, do it fast if the tide's about to ebb

Climb off and push: I once shoved a 22-footer off a shallow spit. I just climbed out (she drew 3ft or so) and pushed her head round. The trouble was, she almost left me behind because the only person on board didn't know enough to spill wind. We live and learn, but the message is clear. On a small yacht in calm weather, manpower is hard to beat.

Accepting assistance

On a falling tide, the time to accept assistance is as soon as possible. If it's offered and you don't take it, insurers may adopt a dim view of any resulting claims. The best option is the lifeboat, but you may feel things are not that drastic, or maybe a passing boat is offering a tow.

Salvage: The law of salvage lies beyond the scope of this book, but it is a well-established custom that if you accept someone else's rope, it may come with a possible salvage claim. Therefore, before taking a tow from anybody you do not know, make sure there is no misunderstanding. 'Bottle of Scotch OK?' is a tactful way of opening negotiations. If it's not all right, your saviour must respond accordingly. More than likely, he'll say, 'No charge. It might be me next week!'

If a pull from deck level doesn't work, try a masthead tow

Well-meaning amateurs: Towing a grounded yacht is not always as easy as it seems. Shallow-draught towboats tend to skid sideways and big outboards don't deliver as much grunt as an equivalent fishing-boat diesel. Before you know it, the scene has escalated from a simple grounding into one with you still on the putty, plus a dory alongside with a line around his propeller and his crew nursing a major rope burn.

The big heel: If a direct pull doesn't free you, rig a tow to a spinnaker halyard and carefully heave down on the mast with the towing vessel. She may well drag you off sideways. It's dramatic and everything below decks must be secured first, but it often works, always assuming there's an intelligent seaman in the towboat. This technique can also be employed with a kedge and a winch.

Well aground but still self-helping

If none of the actions on the previous page see you sailing merrily away, it's time for sterner stuff.

Reduce draught: Literature is full of incidents such as Hornblower throwing the guns over the side, or H W Tilman and his crew carrying eight tons of ballast ashore from a pilot cutter stranded at the north end of Spitsbergen. For most of us, things don't have to be so drastic. It may well be enough just to heel the yacht, or to alter her fore-and-aft trim.

Trim: Many fin-keeled yachts draw slightly less if trimmed well down at the bow. There's little buoyancy at the sharp end, so having all hands perch on the pulpit can lift the keel off the ooze. This easy solution is often the best.

Heeling: If the sails pull the boat over for you, so much the better – but they may already be down so as not to drive the boat further up a lee shore, or maybe you

Reduce draught by heeling: hang anchor, chain or full water cans on boom end

Alternatively, get the crew to hang out from the shrouds

motored onto the shoal in the first place. Heeling will reduce the yacht's draught, so try having all the crew lean over the rail at the point of maximum beam. If this fails, or your friends are skinny and few, the boom makes an excellent lever arm. Hang every heavy item you can think of (anchors, fuel cans and so on) on the end, then swing it out abeam.

Crew weight: In these well-fed times, there are 12 average adults to the ton. Put four into the dinghy and you may reduce the draught of a small yacht by an inch or two.

Kedge off: When you're stuck fast, a pull on

a big winch can be worth as much as a push from the engine. Root out the kedge – or the main bower anchor if you can manage it – lower it into the dinghy together with all its chain or rope, then row it out as far as you can in the direction you want to come off. Heave it over the side, making absolutely sure you aren't entangled with it, then get back on board and take up the slack. Lead the rope to the biggest winch you have, haul it tight carefully until the anchor is biting, then really give it some stick. Keeping one hand at the winch, gun the engine and take whatever steps you can to reduce draught. The chances of success are high.

5ft
30ft
Row the kedge out as far as your cable allows. You're laying it in deeper water and the more scope you have, the better the anchor's holding power is likely to be.

Kedging off: the anchor warp led to a primary winch

South Sea Salvage
In 2006, on her second voyage around the world, Sir Francis Chichester's *Gipsy Moth IV* was stranded on a reef in the South Pacific Tuamotu Archipelago, after a navigational blunder. Salvage experts flew in from Holland and 'jacked' the hull up to put a plywood patch on the hole. Planks of wood were nailed over this as a sacrificial 'sledge' so she could be dragged off the reef by a tug boat (inset).

Drying out on a falling tide

If all efforts have failed and you're stuck on a falling tide, two issues come to the fore. The yacht must have the turn of her bilge protected against sharp debris on the seabed that could harm or even puncture the hull. She must also be rendered proof against downflooding. This occurs where an otherwise buoyant hull has its watertight integrity compromised by openings which, in normal operation, would never be anywhere near the surface of the water. Cockpit lockers are typical. A number of active steps can be taken to minimise these dangers.

A comfortable berth: If she's going all the way over, probe underneath her with a boathook to check for ugly boulders before the turn of the bilge gets there. Stuff in cushions, fenders or an inflatable dinghy. A fender board, if you have one, is best of all.

Heel uphill: When you're stuck fast on the edge of a channel, or any sort of uneven bottom, every effort must be made while

there is still time to have her lay over with her deck facing uphill. If you manage this, downflooding may not be an issue. If you fail, read on …

Downflooding: Close every seacock, including the cockpit drains, then seal up everything that could allow water in. The job doesn't have to be perfect or permanent, so a roll of gaffer tape (sometimes called 'duct tape') is usually enough. If you don't carry any, it's time you did, for this miracle product has a thousand uses. While you're proofing the boat against downflooding, don't forget any external tank breathers. It's a classic way to get seawater in your diesel.

Some recommend sending the crew ashore once the yacht is sealed up. This makes sense when the refloating might be dangerous, but I'd want them standing by to come back aboard via the dinghy to pump, heave, shove and do anything else that may be required. While waiting for the tide, of course, I'll grab the deck brush and treat the old girl to a free scrub off.

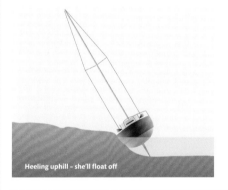

Heeling uphill – she'll float off

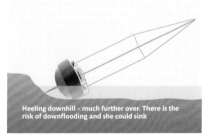

Heeling downhill – much further over. There is the risk of downflooding and she could sink

Bilge keels

Skippers of twin-keeled yachts, which can take the ground upright, are understandably more sanguine about grounding than the rest of us. However, bilge-keel skippers should be aware that their yacht's draught increases when she's well heeled, sometimes by as much as a foot. And if dried out precariously on a sloping bank, a twin-keeled vessel can fall over – potentially sustaining more damage than a fin-keeler that settles gently with the tide.

Afloat once more

Haul out and check after grounding

In any but the lightest of groundings, we have to face the possibility that the boat may have sustained invisible damage.

The first action is, of course, to check the bilge. If it's dry, you can take it that things probably aren't too bad. Check the rudder as well, so far as you're able. Watch the water separator in the fuel line carefully for a while after a major grounding. Finally, remember to open the seacocks and to 'burp' any deep-sea seals on propeller shafts. These are water lubricated and don't enjoy drying out. Just grab the carbon ring around the shaft and compress the rubber bellows. You'll see water flowing in, telling you all is now well.

If the yacht has taken any sort of a pounding, have her hauled out as soon as convenient. With luck there will be less damage than you imagine: perhaps a little gelcoat to make good, maybe a few dents in the lead that a hammer and some car body filler will fix, but maybe things will not be so pretty. Fin-keelers are prone to damage at the keel joint if they hit rocks hard, so have this checked thoroughly.

Also have the keelbolts looked at, especially on a fin keel. You want the boat as strong as she can be. There may be a next time.

149

Freeing a fouled propeller

Catching a rope or net around your propeller can lead to
a difficult situation. Knowing how to free it could save you
an embarrassing emergency services call-out – or even
save your yacht from sinking

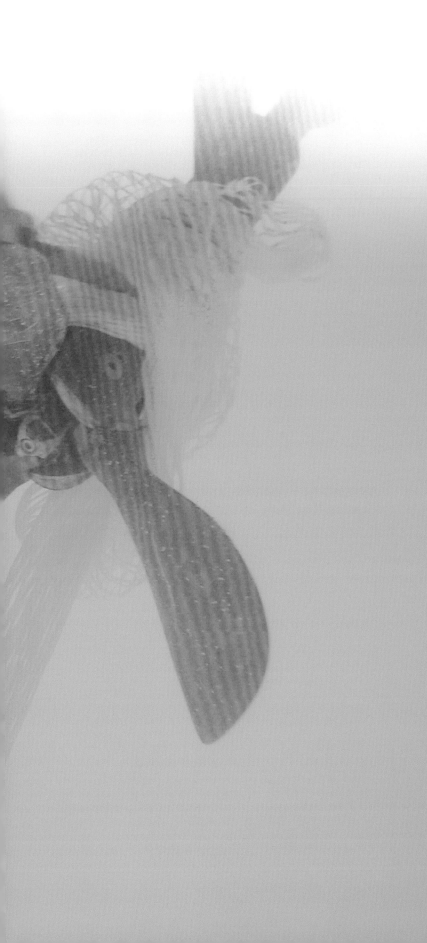

Everyone does it once. In the early days of our sailing, we have a lot to think about and stray ropes are not high on the priority list. Nothing stops a diesel engine so suddenly as a rope round the propeller, however, and once the wretched results have been experienced, nobody wants to let it happen again.

A fouled propeller spells, at best, no engine until it's cleared. At worst, it might mean a vessel moored by her sterngear in a strong current, attached well below the water to an object on the seabed. For a sailor with a fair breeze, the former is no worse than a nuisance. The latter can be catastrophic, involving water ingress and potential loss of the propshaft.

One way and another, there's a plenty of know-how about unwrapping propellers, but a good deal of hot air blows around the subject, too, so I borrowed a 40ft yacht in Majorca to take advantage of the warmer water and try a few ideas for real. 'Be gentle with the shaft,' was the owner's only stipulation, so we used a long length of lightweight fishing net and wrapped it round enough times to make a reasonable simulation of the real thing.

Our exercises were conducted while anchored in calm, warm water. In real life, conditions are likely to be much more demanding

How props get fouled

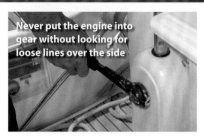
Never put the engine into gear without looking for loose lines over the side

Ropes from your boat

The first point about ropes and propellers is that most of the rope caught comes from on board the boat: a classic own goal. It's a sound plan never to start the engine without looking for loose ends over the side, then take a second glance before you put it into gear.

One of the most common foul-ups is a dinghy painter that has been tied off slightly too long. You forget you're towing it, and as soon as you go astern to slow the boat down – when approaching a pontoon, for instance – it sinks and gets sucked straight into the prop. If you use a floating line, such as the type used by waterskiers, this will never happen.

The rogue line

These are typically caught in harbours. They are a special favourite in places where large numbers of yachts moor bow- or stern-to, such as the Mediterranean or the Baltic.

Pick-up lines for moorings and other peoples' anchor warps are the most common culprits. The only answer is to be eternally vigilant.

Look out for rogue lines in harbour

Picking up a free-floating net at sea is pure bad luck

The free-floating menace

Picking up a length of discarded fishing net or floating polypropylene line out at sea is pure bad luck. It can happen to anyone. A modest length of light stuff is no problem for a sailing boat because you can always sail to the nearest calm water and try cutting it free at anchor where there's a decent chance.

If you pick up something so heavy that it seriously impedes your manoeuvrability, you may have to dive or attack it from the dinghy, but this is a last resort unless it's very calm.

Dangers in the dark

Some areas are notorious for lobster pots. In places with fast-flowing tides, these may well be sucked below the surface. We can't always know everything, but a good pilot book should advise about such dangers, and local knowledge is well worth noting if you can find any. The answer is, don't navigate in these regions after dark. If you can't avoid it, keep well offshore. In daylight, maintain a good lookout. Tangling with fishing gear is the worst scenario. The only response is to cut free as best you can before serious damage ensues. If you can buoy what remains so the fisherman doesn't lose his gear, you're a hero. Read on to find out how we fared with the cutting process.

Unwrap from the cockpit

If you suck one of your own ropes into the propeller, the chances are it will be something like a jib sheet or a halyard that someone has kicked over the side, very likely when the engine's going astern. So long as you can grab hold of the bight of the rope leading onto the propeller, there's a fighting chance of unwinding it. This also applies if the culprit is a rogue line that's long enough for you to catch with the boathook.

We didn't try the unwinding techniques with the borrowed boat – we would have had to wrap the prop up hard, with the risk of damage to the shaft. However, I have achieved success with the first method we described here and I'd be willing to give the second method a try. The trick is to turn the shaft in the opposite direction from the one that caught the rope. This doesn't mean trying to run the engine in gear – that is far too dangerous. The ideal method is to rotate the propeller slowly by hand, making sure the engine doesn't fire up.

Best method

The surest way of doing this only works on engines with decompressors and starting handles. With these, the whole engine can be turned under control:
> Decompress the engine and pull the 'stop' toggle to make certain it can't start
> Have a strong crew member heave on the offending line
> Put the engine in gear in the appropriate direction and wind the handle
> If the shaft has not been locked up solid, the rope will now unwind and you're away

Modern engines: Many modern engines do not feature decompressors. If yours doesn't, the technique is more drastic and the chances of success lower, but anything beats diving if you don't have scuba gear:
> It's vital that the engine doesn't start, so pull out the stop toggle if you have one
> Engage astern or ahead as appropriate
> Activate the starter motor while someone heaves the rope
> You need to be gentle here, because trying to crank the engine with the electrics when it doesn't want to turn can burn out the starter motor as well as flattening the batteries in short order.

Alternative method

It's a long shot, but before trying the starter motor method, it's kinder to put the gearbox into neutral, grab the shaft inside the boat if you can reach it, and see if you can turn it while someone on deck tugs the rope. You could even try mole grips on the shaft to get it started.

Cutting away the problem

To dive or not to dive? I once caught my own propeller in a massive, free-floating fishing net far out in the North Atlantic. I was young, fit, and I dived over the side in a 4ft sea because I had no option. I managed to saw the net clear using a full-sized hacksaw. Now in middle age, I feel the difference in my own performance and can report without shame that I would no longer fancy my chances of success in similar circumstances. Unless you're used to swimming and are in your prime, diving under a boat without scuba gear in anything other than calm water must remain very much a last resort.

Knife or saw?

Some sort of line on your cutting tool is essential if it isn't to disappear into the murky depths the first time your grip slackens. I've always used a wrist lanyard, but make sure it's not so tight that if the blade gets stuck in the obstruction on the shaft, you still have enough slack to free it and are not in danger of being trapped under the boat. The choice we made was to either use a slacker lanyard, or hitch the knife to a line from the diver's belt.

All sailors should carry their own sharp clasp knife, preferably one with a locking blade.

I'm advised by my local police force that so long as I'm obviously bound for the boat and the blade isn't more than 7.6cm (3in) long, I won't be arrested for keeping it about my person. A keen knife or multi-tool blade may be your best bet for cutting free, but bear in mind that a slip underwater could result in a nasty injury. Since a saw-edge seems to do the job more readily than a straight one, I favour either a robust bread-knife or a hacksaw. Both are less likely to inflict horrible wounds in an accident and both will hack their way through nets, rope that's welded itself together into a lump, or that villainous feature of modern life, the plastic fertiliser bag.

① ② ③ ④ ⑤

Choose your weapon:
1 Diving knife
2 Bread knife
3 Sailing knife
4 Multi-tool
5 Swiss Army knife

Boat types

On a long-keeled boat, like mine, the propeller is generally tucked out of harm's way in an aperture between keel and rudder, well aft and in the narrowest part of the yacht's underbody. On a 30-footer, you can almost reach one of these from the surface if you're a swimmer with long arms. Even on a bigger boat, the dive factor is minimal and you don't have to pluck up courage to swim under a large flat surface.

This arrangement is prone to fouling, but the anode should prevent the shaft falling out

By comparison, the modern-yacht operator with his saildrive or P-bracket out of sight under the widest part of the vessel is going to have a sorry time of things. If this is your lot, you'll just have to bite the bullet.

On a very beamy yacht, before you start hacking away underwater, you may find it useful to run a line from the front end of the cockpit, underneath the hull and back to the cockpit on the other side of the boat. The diver can use this to haul himself along and to guide him to the prop.

Traditional long keels keep the prop out of harm's way... most of the time

Diving kit

Mask, snorkel and fins
Every boat should have these on board, and whoever is going to be the diver must have tried them in advance to made sure they work.

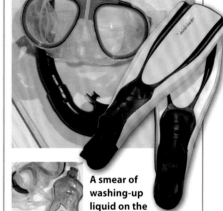

A smear of washing-up liquid on the mask lenses stops them fogging up

Lifejacket
We had a strong crew, a good swimmer and a controlled situation so we didn't use one, but if in any doubt, wear one deflated. If you have selected the auto-inflate type, that's a shame…

Hypothermia
It's surprising how rapidly the body loses heat in cold water. Even in the Med, I started to feel the pinch after half an hour. The best bet is to carry a basic wetsuit aboard, or at least a neoprene vest, 'pending the day'. If you don't have one, wear a tight-fitting T-shirt and long trousers while you're in. They will help trap a small amount of warm water next to your skin.

Don't lose your shaft

Some experts advocate fitting a spare shaft anode onto the propshaft, either inside the boat or just forward of the P-bracket, as a stopper, to prevent a fouled prop dragging its shaft clean out of the boat.

Putting theory into practice

The dinghy

This, in theory, is the soft option, so I grabbed it. First, I lashed a short breadknife to our extending boathook. I used a couple of frapped seizings (see illustration) for this, and despite a quarter-hour of hacking about, the arrangement didn't budge a millimetre. The only chance of getting near the propshaft was to lie in the boat with my arm right in the water. The question was, after I'd groped around and found the shaft, do I try to cut up or down? I'd assumed that 'up' would be best, but in practice, on this boat, 'down' proved the superior option. I had enough purchase to do some cutting and there was plenty of space above the shaft, but it was literally a hit-and-miss affair. In real life, I'd have been in with a chance, but I could well have been at it all morning.

It occurred to me later that perhaps I'd have done better to have taken the plunge, stayed out from under the boat and used my lash-up from alongside. I might have had a decent view of the proceedings via my face-mask while the boathook got the knife into the job without me having to hold my breath and submerge. Sadly, we didn't try it. Next time...?

The frapped seizing didn't budge a millimetre

Tom could only reach the tangle lying down with his whole arm in the water

HIT!

MISS!

Using the boathook was a hit-or-miss affair

Carry bungs on board

You have to be really unlucky for your propshaft to fall out at sea – but it does happen. Make sure you have a hardwood bung on board that fits the propshaft's exit hole – ideally secured with a lanyard next to the sterngland. If you ever need it, you can be sure it will be an emergency!

Rope cutters

You could save yourself a cold swim – and a hefty repair bill – by fitting a rope cutter to deal with rope, nets and plastic bags that would otherwise cause a wrap. They have been around since the early 1980s and have proved their worth many times. There are three types: scissor, disc and shaver. Scissor cutters have two, three or four plain or serrated blades attached to the shaft between the prop and the cutless bearing, and a fixed blade on the shaft tube or P-bracket. Disc cutters rely on a single circular blade fitted around the shaft and shavers have a fixed blade, like that on a lathe, which shaves the rope as it wraps tighter around the hub. Most can be fitted without removing the prop but you'll need to drill into the shaft to attach the cutter so the boat must be out of the water. Not all are suitable for saildrives, some are suitable for outboards.

Clearing a fouled prop under the water

The boat was anchored in calm water and I stood by as look-out to assist if necessary while our diver entered the water. It was instantly obvious that the problem was the shape of the yacht. A certain amount of 'bottle' was needed to dive under the boat's broad, flat aft sections, where the instinctive 'up to safety' was not possible. Once used to this idea, our diver managed to get into a position where he could carve away with the knife of his choice, a locking clasp knife with a serrated blade. He developed a rhythm: up for breath, down for a quick hack, up again, and so on.

His efforts destroyed our 'Mickey Mouse' net without difficulty and the diver felt he would have coped with a modest rope equally well, always assuming it hadn't been drawn into the rubber cutless bearing. If that happens, you've no option but to sail to a slipway or boat-hoist to access the problem on terra firma.

The diver developed a rhythm: up for breath, down for a quick hack, up again, and so on

Conclusion

The best way to deal with ropes around propellers is not to let them get there in the first place. Any boat with a P-bracket or saildrive should be equipped with a rope cutter on the shaft. When the shaft can't be cleared by somehow winding the obstruction out backwards, diving is the best bet, but you must be properly equipped and it's not recommended in a seaway.

People worked sailing craft around our coasts without engines for thousands of years. If the 'iron horse' is disabled, we're still better off than they were because our boats sail far better than theirs ever did.

The only situation where we may need assistance is where we're moored to the seabed by a heavy line, or have picked up an obstruction so unwieldy that it prevents the boat from sailing. If we can't free ourselves, either of these scenarios could become life-threatening. In a genuine emergency, the rescue people will be more than happy to come and sort us out.

Taking a tow

Sooner or later, we all become involved in a tow.
You can avert disaster by accepting a tow from
someone, or vice versa, but you can run into a lot
more trouble if you get it wrong

Lifeboatman
A lifeboatman may
be put on board to
help while under tow

Crew
Keep weight aft in
the towed yacht. If
you have steerage,
centre the helm but
aim for the tug's
stern if you start to
veer off course

Contact
Have one crewman
your dedicated contact
point with the 'tug',
monitoring the VHF
radio and watching the
tug crew

Drogue
Cleat the drogue off
on an aft cleat so it can
be easily slipped in an
emergency. The load on
the drogue line is huge,
so keep all fingers well
clear once underway

SHADOWFAX
OF
SOUTHAMPTON

Speed
The nature of the towed yacht and the general conditions will decide the speed of the tug

Tow line
Use as much line as you have. Most lifeboats and tugs will use their own line and generally find no reason to weight the rope with an anchor or other object to avoid snatching. There are, however, many examples of successful tows that have used this method

It has been said with justification that we learn more from our own mistakes than from any manual, and when it comes to towing, I'd agree. I'd pottered about boatyards towing odd vessels astern and alongside for years before I came face to face with the ugly truth about towing offshore. My rig was disabled, the boat had no serviceable engine and I was 60 miles from help down the coast in Rio de Janeiro, so I accepted a tow from an old pal. My saviour, a sometime Greek ship-owner, had a 60ft motor-sailer of huge power. On the day in question he wasn't quite himself on account of a broken toe incurred during a misunderstanding with his somewhat feisty cook the previous night. The cook had subsequently gone ashore and left him single-handed. He hooked me up with a long length of whatever we could muster, swallowed a handful of painkillers, and away we went. With the autopilot set for the Sugarloaf Mountain, he selected 9 knots and promptly passed out. As we surged through the big seas left behind by a cold front, the Samson posts on my classic wooden boat, standing in for the mooring cleats of a modern yacht, began taking their leave of the foredeck. The seams were gaping to letter-box proportions before I hit on the answer. I dropped a bowline over each one, led the line aft to the cockpit and winched it back until it groaned. It worked. The boat wasn't ripped in half despite being pulled at 2 knots above her hull speed, my friend woke up just in time to steer us into the magnificent harbour, and I'd learned a critical lesson about towing.

Sooner or later, from one end or the other, we all become involved in a tow. There's more to it than just passing a line and securing it at each end. In open water, the job demands good seamanship. In harbour, what may seem daunting can be made safe

157

and easy by adhering to one or two basic principles. There can be few organisations with more experience of towing yachtsmen than the lifeboats, so we asked one crew to show us how the professionals go about it.

One big message that came across from the lifeboat we took a tow from was that every tow is different, from the way the line is attached, to whether a drogue is advisable or if a lifeboat crew member should be on board. Much like a man-overboard recovery, we can offer general recommendations but, in the end, we all must think like seamen and make decisions based on what is happening at the time.

It might be a fisherman helping you off the mud, a clubmate towing you in on a calm evening when you've run out of fuel, or maybe you've got things badly wrong and the first craft on the scene to help you off a deadly lee shore is a big motorboat. In any of these cases, the principles spelled out here will stand you in good stead. Sometimes there might be a lifeboat involved and the coxswain Howard Lester was at pains to remind us that the lifeboats are not a maritime pick-up service. They exists primarily to preserve life. If a boat can be saved sensibly into the bargain, that's a bonus, although towing is sometimes the safest option for the people too. If you feel you're getting into trouble and that

things may get worse before they're better, it's best to call the Coastguard in good time. They will decide whether to alert the lifeboat, the helicopter, both, or neither. Howard said quite bluntly that it's a lot easier and safer to take someone in tow in deep water with danger a mile to leeward than to wait an hour, then have to try and pull them off a breaking shingle bank in an onshore gale.

Being towed

Drogue

Yachts often need towing because they've lost their rudder or steering linkage. A rudderless vessel can be a nightmare to tow, because she will sheer from side to side like a drunk on Saturday night. The drag from a drogue over her stern will keep her more or less in line. Drogues are also used for long downwind tows in a big sea where a yacht may surf, causing snatching to the towline and major steering issues.

Passing the drogue

The drogue used by our lifeboat is a stout fabric funnel, open at both ends and secured to a long nylon line. The lifeboat approached our stern and passed us the bitter end of the drogue line, keeping the drogue itself on her own deck. We secured the line to a stern cleat rather than using a bowline, so we could slip it in an emergency. The loads on it were

going to be huge, we were advised, so we set things up accordingly. The lifeboat then moved off and her crew tossed the drogue over when the line was fully extended.

Boarding the casualty

Next, the lifeboat, very well fendered, came alongside and crewman Graham Benton hopped on board. He brought with him a hand-held VHF radio with which to commu-

As we keep dead ahead, the lifeboat approaches our stern and throws the drogue line, then reverses until the line is extended and the drogue can be set

A drogue towed by the casualty yacht will aid steering

Six steps to secure a towrope

1. Remove the anchor from the bow roller and store it in the anchor locker

2. The lifeboat will reverse up to your bow and throw over their towing line

3. Tie the tow line in a big bowline around both foredeck cleats

4. Set a leather chafe sleeve at chafe points. Secure the tow rope in the bow roller with a line

5. Untie the sheets from the headsail

6. Using bowlines, tie the sheets onto the tow line, near the cleats. Winch them taut from the cockpit

nicate with Howard, coxswain of the lifeboat. Graham took charge of our end of the operation. In a heavy sea, and if the coxswain judges the yacht's crew are capable, it can be safer not to attempt a crew transfer. If so, the yacht is thoroughly briefed via VHF, or by a loud pair of lungs.

Passing the tow

The lifeboat manoeuvred close to windward, to heave a line across to Graham on our foredeck. Using that line, we could now pull the heavy tow line on board from the lifeboat. This is nylon and has a leather chafe guard near the end. Most yachts don't carry a heavy towline, but any cruiser worthy of the name ships a decent kedge warp that can be brought into play when one yacht has to tow another. Whatever is used,

it should be as long as possible and, ideally, stretchy nylon.

Securing the tow

I was curious to see how Graham was going to set about this task. For best steerage, the rope should leave the yacht on the centreline, which usually means a bow roller. If there isn't one, it's an initiative test to achieve something like the same result. In our case, we had an extended roller with the anchor stowed in it, so our first job was to remove the anchor and stow it in the foredeck well, with the chain and windlass. That cleared the decks for action.

Rather than securing the towrope to one or other of the cleats, Graham passed a bight of it around them both and made a bowline forward of them. Thus, we had a loop on

our foredeck hooked over the after horns of both cleats. Next, he worked the leather chafing piece up to the bow roller and made it fast with a light line. This also served to secure the towrope into the roller so that it couldn't jump out and tear off the pulpit. The issue of chafe is a serious one. On the lifeboat, during a long tow, they veer a little extra rope every so often to 'freshen the nip' and reduce chafe on a single point. This is impractical on most yachts, so extreme care must be taken to prevent wear and tear.

Spreading the load

As I'd discovered off South America all those years ago, one of the biggest problems with towing is the forces involved. Bow cleats unassisted may be ripped out of the deck, so Graham

The full set-up, with lifeboat towing yacht towing drogue

Keep a close watch on the tow line at all potential chafe points

asked us to relieve them with lines led aft to the primary winches in the cockpit. We simply used the headsail sheets. Rather than hitching these to the cleats themselves, he tied them with bowlines around the towing loop close to the cleats, so that when we winched hard, they dragged the tow rope a tiny bit off the cleats and eased their loading.

Where to secure
This is the classic case of no two yachts being the same. A sensible, seamanlike response is required. If the cleats look good, start with these. If there's a suitable windlass that you're confident is well attached, try that. A wooden yacht's keel-mounted bitts or Samson post may serve. A keel-stepped mast may work, but using a deck-stepped spar is generally a bad idea.

If the bow is cluttered up and no fair lead can be achieved via a bow roller, it may be necessary to rig a bridle from the bow cleats and secure the towrope with a bowline

to this. And so on. Common sense, backed up by an assumption that nothing is as strong as it appears, will generally win the day.

Under tow
With all set up, Graham is now free to give the go-ahead to the lifeboat, by VHF radio or by making a recognised sign of crossed forearms. As the tow commences, the towed boat, if she has a rudder, steers towards the stern of the towing vessel. If the rudder has gone, keep weight as far aft as you sensibly can and watch for chafe as the boat inevitably veers about. Where a drogue is in operation, don't forget that the loads on it are as great as the action up front, so watch out for inquisitive fingers getting anywhere near the line. Communicate with the towing craft and give the tow itself as much rope as you have.

The sag alone in a 50m rope will create drag as it hits the water. This defuses any snatching and keeps the whole thing gentle. Howard said he never finds it necessary to damp a tow by deploying weights on the rope, however he has seen it done by tugs on occasion.

If you are towing and the rope is not really man enough and is snatching, you can hang something off it halfway along, between the two boats. Ideally, use a couple of old motor tyres. You may not happen to have a tyre on board, so try a fender

Ensure weight is aft in the towed yacht, keep a lookout for chafe issues and steer towards the stern of the yacht doing the towing

It may seem obvious, but it is vital to keep close contact between the two boats at all times. If you have no working VHF radio, the crossed forearms sign is useful for indicating 'ready to begin tow'

or three, a kedge anchor or anything else that serves.

Towing from your yacht
If you are the one towing another yacht, the primary requirement is to get the tow as near to the middle of your stern as you can, so that you can steer. I have towed many times from many yachts and have found that this is generally best achieved by rigging a bridle from either quarter and securing the towrope to this

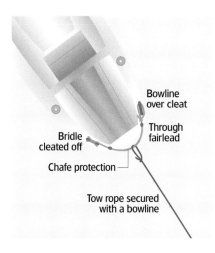

This is one method for setting up a towing bridle but you must find the best solution for your boat and circumstances

Above: This is how a lifeboat tows alongside, but for yacht-to-yacht alongside towing, the relationship between the two boats needs to be as shown below. The tow rope becomes a bow line

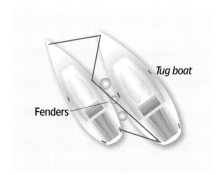

with a bowline.

The important thing to remember is that if one end of the bridle is cleated or secured to a winch, rather than both ends being on bowlines, you will be able to slip the tow under load in an emergency. This is a prime requirement.

Coming alongside

At the end of a tow, the casualty will need to be brought to a safe berth, often alongside. While it's possible to slip the tow at a suitable moment and let the casualty steer in with the last of her way – so long as she has a rudder – the technique is somewhat hit and miss, and is not favoured by our lifeboat.

Instead, Howard brings the yacht alongside when he's in calmer water just outside harbour and tows her in under full control. The lifeboat slows down and, as the yacht surges alongside, the towrope is shortened and used as a bow line. A stern line and two springs are now passed

across. If the towed vessel is smaller than the lifeboat, then the crew will make sure the yacht's stern hangs out beyond her own. The stern line is then brought aboard the lifeboat via the midships fairlead. If it were secured directly up to the quarter and the boat rolled, the yacht's cleats might suffer damage.

However, for yacht-to-yacht alongside towing, the technique is different. Here, the 'tug' will be far less powerful than a lifeboat, and the crew should ensure the tug's stern is at or abaft the stern of the towed vessel. This is to allow easier steering by the towing yacht. If her rudder is in line with the towed yacht's keel, the directional force of the tug's rudder will be diminished. Move the towed yacht's keel forward and the tug can push or pull the casualty around far more easily. Even with

the two vessels in this staggered position, it is important that both steer if they can.

It is best to notify the port control or harbourmaster that you are towing before you arrive. This will also let other nearby craft know of your restricted ability to manoeuvre.

Generally, most alongside tows are very similar, but for towing astern, you must decide what is right for the circumstances.

Above and right: The desired result. The casualty is safely delivered alongside, with no harm to either crew or boat

Man overboard!

It a skipper's worst nightmare – a crew member falling overboard. Whether it happens in heavy weather, at night or in calm conditions in daylight, it's important to have a strategy for how you're going to get back to them

Eyeball the MOB
Make sure that someone on the yacht is eyeballing the casualty at all times, so you don't lose sight of the MOB

Crash stop
When somebody falls overboard, the first reaction must be to crash-stop the yacht immediately:
> Helm hard over and tack, leaving the headsail pinned in

Get ready
As you begin your approach to the MOB:
> Make sure you have a heaving-line ready to throw

Missed first time?
If you fail to recover the MOB on your first pass:
> Toss the casualty a lifebuoy
> Deploy your danbuoy
> Reassure the swimmer that you're sailing away to manoeuvre but will soon be back alongside

Kit & clothing
> Without his inflated lifejacket and a buoyant immersion suit, our MOB would have floated lower in the water. It would have been much harder for the yacht's crew to keep sight of him
> It's impractical to wear an immersion suit at all times, but if you fall in wearing normal clothes, cold shock can kill

t's easy – even tempting – to become dogmatic about MOB recovery, but there is danger in this as well as comfort. The first MOB I experienced personally was long ago when I was skippering an open lugger with no inboard power in the Mediterranean. When one of my crew went overboard I had received no formal training and had given little thought to what I would do.

I was, however, a reasonably competent boat handler. In the Mistral that was blowing I realised we could easily lose sight of our man, so I detailed one hand to look out for him, then the rest of us somehow sailed the boat round and stopped her to windward of the casualty. As way came off we dumped our canvas and began to make leeway. Soon, he was alongside, to be bundled aboard by willing arms as we rolled our

gunwale down on the waves. I don't recall exactly how I brought the boat through the wind, but I must have tacked because we needed to deploy a sweep as we dipped the lug. Nothing in any training manual could have told me about that, so I think the point is that being assertive about the textbook way things should be done may lead us astray. Instinct plays a part. Boats vary, so do wind and sea conditions and the number and ability of crew.

The RYA is the UK's main source of seamanship training and I have worked alongside it for many years. I have also been involved with similar schemes in the USA. Back in the 1970s, it was unsafe to assume that a yacht's engine would start whenever it was asked, so my first lessons in MOB as a novice instructor were undertaken on that assumption. Interestingly, my boss

recommended gybing as part of the favoured system.

An engineless approach was still the first choice of the establishment when I became an examiner in 1978, although by then gybing was less favoured than tacking. Driving a Contessa 32 with a full crew, any decent skipper would choose canvas over power because these gutsy yachts sail much better than they motor. With minimal windage, good static lateral resistance from their long fins, superb balance and low freeboard for rolling a casualty aboard, they remain the prefect teaching tool. We regularly did our exercises outside the Needles in the dark under sail with a reasonable degree of success. I tried the job under power in the same circumstances, but unlike a high-revving engine of today, the old-fashioned Sabb diesel with its heavy flywheel

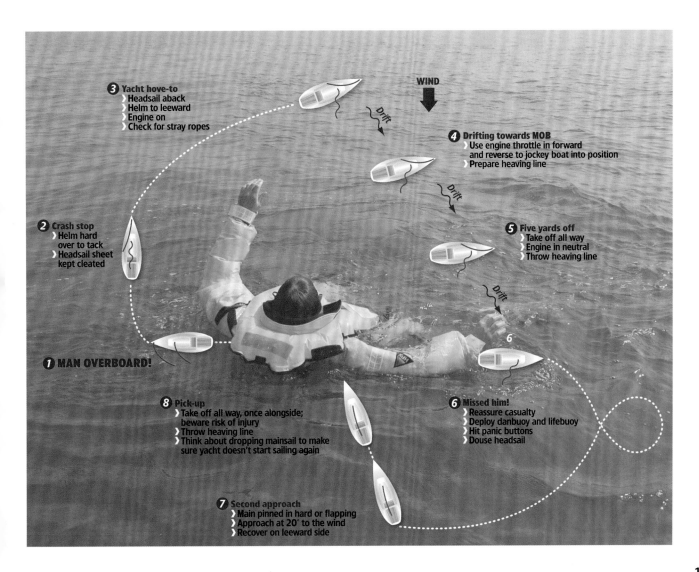

WIND

3 Yacht hove-to
› Headsail aback
› Helm to leeward
› Engine on
› Check for stray ropes

4 Drifting towards MOB
› Use engine throttle in forward and reverse to jockey boat into position
› Prepare heaving line

2 Crash stop
› Helm hard over to tack
› Headsail sheet kept cleated

5 Five yards off
› Take off all way
› Engine in neutral
› Throw heaving line

1 MAN OVERBOARD!

8 Pick-up
› Take off all way, once alongside; beware risk of injury
› Throw heaving line
› Think about dropping mainsail to make sure yacht doesn't start sailing again

6 Missed him!
› Reassure casualty
› Deploy danbuoy and lifebuoy
› Hit panic buttons
› Douse headsail

7 Second approach
› Main pinned in hard or flapping
› Approach at 20° to the wind
› Recover on leeward side

took several seconds to whip up any torque, making the results far less reliable. The techniques we worked out for picking up under sail alone were, incidentally, equally effective on a 72ft Robert Clark-designed ketch.

The contrast for the skipper of a beamy, high-freeboard cruiser with poor hull balance, massive windage and a short fin keel could not be more marked. Trying to sail such a yacht slowly, on the edge of a stall, in a big sea and half a gale is a nightmare, especially if she also has aft-swept spreaders which stop her main spilling wind properly. For her, the answer must be to have her engine turning over ready to assist, or even to use as her main propulsion unit.

The RYA's guidance would be unnecessary if we were all full-time sailors and knew our boats inside out. In real life, most of us so rarely practise handling yachts in broken water that some sort of 'one-size-fits-all' system is a sound idea. Contrary to popular imagining, the RYA's and the American sail training establishment's policy is not to have 'methods', but to educate broadly and advise. Nonetheless, the two national establishments have come up with similar MOB recovery systems. Most other authorities agree in principle, and so do I. You could, therefore, be forgiven for believing this to be the 'approved method'. I don't like that sort of talk myself, and here's why.

I recently heard about an incident

involving a chap called Ben Pester, who lost one of his crew overboard in heavy weather and open water. When the crew member went overboard, only two crew were left aboard his 36-footer, including Ben. One was below. It was blowing a full Force 6 and following the knock-down, it was several seconds before Ben realised he'd lost someone, and she was already well astern by the time he spotted her. He had to act promptly.

Ben's priorities were not to lose sight, and to get onto something like a reciprocal course. Sailing under furling genoa, with the mainsail stowed, he had to pass through the wind by either tacking or gybing. If he'd turned up to windward single-handed in that sea and without a mainsail, there was a fighting chance he'd miss stays.

However, he could gybe readily, with no danger, so he did, keeping an eye on his MOB through the relatively low-stress manoeuvre.

He then sailed back to the casualty, starting his engine to make sure. In the event he didn't need power, so he shut it down again to be certain not to foul either his prop or the casualty. He rolled away his genoa, lost way to leeward of the lady in the water, and his crew tossed her a line.

The two men, who could not be described as youngsters, then hove her in and managed to muscle her over the low-freeboard capping rail of the rolling yacht. Not long afterwards, the casualty herself was

wanting to get back to cooking the supper.

If anyone had a mind to criticise this manoeuvre on the basis of what most textbooks (including three I've written myself) recommend, he'd have no difficulty pulling it to pieces, but if I'd been there off the South Coast of Ireland with the wild Atlantic shouting at me, I'd have been delighted that my skipper was seaman enough to break the rules and do what was undoubtedly best under the circumstances.

This lesson should always be in the back of our minds as we practise any MOB recovery method. It's also vital we recall that most training takes place in calm, sheltered water with a full crew who are briefed, ready, and waiting for the call. Things may be very different in real life.

Manoeuvring to the casualty

The generally approved training manoeuvre for MOB assumes a yacht sailing under plain canvas, sloop-rigged and without any flying kites. Any departure from this will demand lateral thinking, but the classic set-piece is such a sound starting point that we'll go with the flow, discussing options as we sail.

There is simply not space here to consider all the permutations of what may or may not happen. Details of how to recover the person to the deck once secured are covered in the section below.

Should I press the panic buttons?

> Certainly use the red distress caller on a DSC radio if you don't recover the MOB on your first hove-to pass. If short-handed, don't bother with any of the usual rigmarole – just hold the button down until it beeps. The rescue services now know you're in real trouble. Regardless of what you

have or haven't said, if they're in radio range, they're on their way.

> The GPS MOB button can be a mixed blessing. With two knots of tide running, the guy in the drink has drifted almost a quarter of a mile from where the GPS says he is in seven minutes.

By all means hit that button, but, importantly, note the time as well. If the casualty is lost, the data only makes an accurate starting point for a search if you know when you pressed it.

MOB recovery under power

This technique is often the best bet for the skipper of a typical modern cruiser with a reliable engine

Crash stop, heave-to

> Beating, or on a two-sail reach, the instant reaction when someone goes overboard must be to crash-stop the yacht. No thinking time. Just bang the helm hard down (or wheel to windward) and stuff her through the wind. If you're on a broad reach, some yachts may baulk at this unless the mainsheet is hove in to help them round. It's vital to leave

Hove-to after a crash stop: headsail aback and helm to leeward, fore-reaching towards the casualty

the headsail sheet made up – don't let it go whatever you do. The headsail will then back after the 'tack', which is actually the standard method for heaving-to in a hurry.
> The final action on heaving-to is to steer to windward once way is lost, to counteract the backed headsail trying to shove your bow to leeward. The result, if you're lucky, will be a boat that is crabbing downwind. If you tacked quickly enough in the first place, with the ground you made to windward, you might well find the boat is slithering down towards the casualty.

Start the engine

> At this stage, it will usually make sense to get the engine going, but do not even think about operating that starter until you've checked all round for lines over the

side. Once it's running, don't engage gear until you've checked again. Stressed people become careless with ropes.
> With engine and backed sails, you may find you can manoeuvre close enough to heave a line to the swimmer. Assuming he or she is conscious and capable, this is what you are trying to achieve. The hope that you may be lucky from the outset is your number one option.
> Don't imagine that heaving-to will stop a modern yacht. In anything of a breeze, it won't, but it will slow her down enough to give you a chance, especially if assisted by reliable power not compromised by a halyard tail around the propeller.

If you miss first time

> There's a good chance you won't get lucky making physical contact with your casualty on the 'hove-to pass'. At least, however, the comparatively stable state gives an opportunity to deploy any MOB gear. Toss him the danbuoy and a lifebuoy (with light if appropriate) – and make sure it has a drogue, or you may as well not bother on a windy day.
> It's also important to reassure him that you are about to manoeuvre away

but will be right back to pick him up. He's getting cold and he'll appreciate the reassurance!

Panic buttons

> Now is also a good time to hit any 'panic buttons' that take your fancy (see box opposite).

Coming round again

> If you haven't got close enough while hove-to, the boat must be manoeuvred so as to approach the casualty from 10 or 20 degrees off an upwind heading. This means you must first move her downwind. To achieve this the following must be done, in no particular order.
> Douse the headsail. It gets in the way of deck workers, its flapping could throw another person overboard, and its uncontrolled windage with the boat very close to the breeze is worse than detrimental.
> The boat must somehow pass through the wind. Tacking under power is safer, but it will move her upwind. Gybing helps her arrive at a good place for the final pickup. It can be perfectly safe too, but only if you're confident you can manage it without drama.
> With the yacht positively downwind of the swimmer, she approaches a point five yards or so away, under

power, with the main either pinned in tight to steady her or flapping to spill wind. The ideal approach is around 20 degrees from the wind. This is because the last thing you want when you lose all way is to be dead head-to-wind. Once stalled 'in irons', you have no control over which side she will fall off. Whether you are picking up to windward or to leeward, the boat is going to fall away to beam-on, or even somewhat downwind of this, so it's vital to know whether she will swing to port or starboard.
> Arriving by the casualty, take off all way and heave a line. Be mindful at all times of the danger of injury from a turning propeller.
> Depending on your boat, you may consider dropping the mainsail at some stage. The danger of keeping it up is that, as the boat's head falls off when her way is lost, it may fill and start her moving again. This is particularly dangerous with aft-swept spreaders and a shallow forefoot, whereas an old-fashioned Nicholson 35 will sit forever beam-on, going nowhere, with jib rolled away and main flapping. Bear in mind that recovery may take some time, which gives a boat ample opportunity to misbehave.

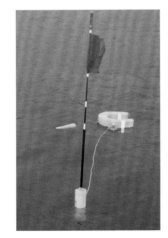

If you miss the MOB on the first pass, deploy your danbuoy and horseshoe lifebuoy immediately

Sweptback spreaders, such as these, make it harder to depower the mainsail and more likely that it will start the boat moving while you're busy hauling the casualty back on board

MOB recovery under sail

This is unlikely to be the main choice with today's reliable engines. The general lack of practice also makes it an unpopular selection, but we've already noted that in the kerfuffle that may accompany a MOB, it's not beyond possibility that the propeller may be disabled by a rope.

› Given the two-sail situation we are working with, the first action is again to crash stop, try to recover the victim by steering the boat in the semi-hove-to state and, if this fails, deploy the MOB gear and press the buttons. Now comes the interesting part. The boat must somehow get herself onto the other tack, then approach under full control. This is best achieved by sailing on a close reach (around 60 degrees from the wind), allowing the mainsail to be spilled or sheeted in as required. The yacht can then be kept right on the edge of a stall, but still driving up to the last minute. To approach on a close reach, she must be manoeuvred so as to place her on this heading with the casualty in front of her. How this is done is the key.

› It is vital to continue to watch the person in the water, because you are going to sail away from him now, perhaps for 50 yards or more.

› From a position close to the casualty, steer onto a beam reach relative to the apparent wind (as indicated by the masthead pointer, not any linked electronics). If you can read the true wind on the water, something a little below a true beam reach is perfect.

› Sail off until far enough away to give ample room for manoeuvring on the reach back. If the boat sails well under main only and you're going to douse your headsail, do it now. If she's masthead rigged with a tiny main, keep some jib unrolled for a bit longer. You may even have to keep it throughout.

› Tack or gybe. Tacking is often safer, but it has the disadvantage of putting the boat upwind. Losing way can be a problem thereafter because the main cannot be spilled with the wind on the beam, let alone abaft it. A gybe generally leaves the boat with a direct close reach up to the casualty. However, we all know the potential hazards of gybing, so a rational decision must be made in view of conditions, crew, etc. The generally accepted view is, 'if in doubt, tack.'

› Immediately after turning, steer directly for the casualty and let fly all sheets. Will the mainsail spill? If 'Yes', pull

the sail some of the way in and proceed to the pick-up, controlling way using the sheet as a throttle. If 'No', turn sharply downwind to get below the beam reach line, then try again until you've got it right. If you can't actually lay the man in the water because he's 'above close-hauled', you've misjudged badly. You're too far downwind and will have to tack back up before finding the close reach.

› Approach with just enough way on to keep steering. If the boat suddenly wants to turn downwind, she has developed lee helm, which means she's stalling. Heave in the main quickly to regain control. Aim for a point a short way to windward of the casualty and, as he comes alongside, luff off the last of your way, but don't allow the boat to come head to wind. As she stops, her bow will fall off just as it would under power. From here, the job is exactly the same, except that you may have more sail up to deal with.

As you leave the helm to assist the person in the water, lash the tiller to leeward, or secure a wheel hard to weather. If the helm wobbles to amidships, the boat will start sailing away on a broad reach, which nobody wants, least of all the casualty.

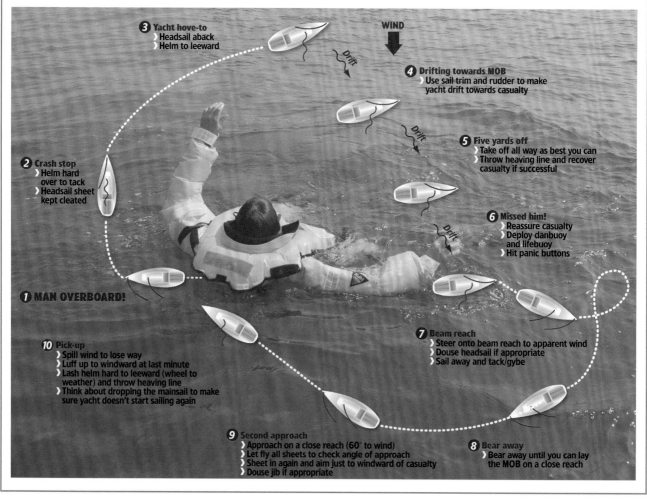

3 Yacht hove-to
› Headsail aback
› Helm to leeward

WIND

4 Drifting towards MOB
› Use sail trim and rudder to make yacht drift towards casualty

5 Five yards off
› Take off all way as best you can
› Throw heaving line and recover casualty if successful

2 Crash stop
› Helm hard over to tack
› Headsail sheet kept cleated

6 Missed him!
› Reassure casualty
› Deploy danbuoy and lifebuoy
› Hit panic buttons

1 MAN OVERBOARD!

10 Pick-up
› Spill wind to lose way
› Luff up to windward at last minute
› Lash helm hard to leeward (wheel to weather) and throw heaving line
› Think about dropping the mainsail to make sure yacht doesn't start sailing again

7 Beam reach
› Steer onto beam reach to apparent wind
› Douse headsail if appropriate
› Sail away and tack/gybe

9 Second approach
› Approach on a close reach (60° to wind)
› Let fly all sheets to check angle of approach
› Sheet in again and aim just to windward of casualty
› Douse jib if appropriate

8 Bear away
› Bear away until you can lay the MOB on a close reach

The final five yards

If the casualty is conscious, take off all way five yards off and throw them a heaving-line rather than motoring right up to them

Pick- up to windward or leeward?

A person in the water makes a lot less leeway than a shallow-bodied, fin-keeled yacht that has lost way. The generally accepted choice is to pick up on the boat's lee side. In fact, both sides have something to be said for them. So long as the pros and cons are understood in the context of the yacht and the conditions, a rational decision can be made on the day.

Recovery from the windward side

Plus points: So long as the yacht is stopped with the casualty on her windward side, she cannot be driven down onto him/her by a big wave, perhaps causing serious or fatal injuries.

The person on the helm can see the casualty easily all the time an approach is made. At no time does the yacht have to turn her bow across the casualty, which could increase the risk of injury if the boat's too close to the MOB, and certainly means that the helmsman temporarily loses sight of the person in the water.

Minus points: As a yacht loses way, particularly one with a fin keel rather than a more traditional form, her lateral resistance disappears and she is blown rapidly sideways. The danger is that she now drifts out of range and cannot reach her crew.

Recovery from the leeward side

Plus points: By sitting between the casualty and the weather, the yacht creates a lee in which to work.

As she loses way and begins to drift sideways, she is moving towards the casualty, not inexorably away from him.

If the casualty is to be rolled aboard over the rail, she is heeling the right way in a breeze, even with no canvas set.

Minus points: At some point on the pick-up run, the helm may lose sight of the casualty, who may be quite close under the bow.

There is a risk of being washed down onto the swimmer by a wave.

Making the risk assessment

When considering the pick-up, the most important question to be asked is whether the chance of losing touch with a casualty on the weather side outweighs the chance of the boat running them over to leeward.

For what it is worth – and no two experiences will be the same – it seems to me that in most non-extreme cases the boat and the swimmer tend to go up and down on the same wave, rather negating the natural fear of running over the casualty.

A boat stopped to leeward of the casualty can slide away at frightening speed if the first heave of the line misses. The risk assessment therefore boils down to this:
> Am I more likely to lose touch by making leeway than I am to cause injury by sliding down onto the casualty?

The remaining questions can now be considered, but there is no spare time for the scratching of chins. If in doubt, place a fin-keeled, high-freeboard yacht to windward of the casualty. In a worst-case scenario it may be better to recover someone injured by the drifting boat than to lose touch altogether.

The danger of getting too close

It's safer to let a conscious casualty swim towards the boat than to motor right up to them. You can pull gently on the heaving-line to help them

Before anyone can be lifted or otherwise helped back on board, they must first be secured alongside. It's convenient when practising in sheltered water to take off the last of your way right alongside the floating dummy. If it's a person, I can testify from experience that having a boat coming straight at you is no joke, and with good reason.

With a sea running, the last thing any skipper should do is try to stop alongside a conscious casualty. Only if the person in the water is disabled and cannot help themselves is it worth the risk of getting too close and hitting them. Lose way five yards or so off, then heave a line. It's far safer and not nearly so difficult to execute. It only works, of course, if there's a heaving-line handy to the cockpit. If using a normal rope, add a bowline or figure-of-eight to give them something to cling on to.

Conclusion

I've tried to approach this complex subject in a thoughtful manner, allowing for different points of view. The reason is that we never know how we'll be rigged or how rough it will be when the worst happens. We may be motor-sailing, we may be stomping downwind under genoa only, we could even be reaching gently in the sunshine. Understanding the forces and how different boats may react is the crux, as much as having a single method that works for most yachts most of the time.

Recovering a man overboard

Manoeuvring your boat back to the crew member you have just lost overboard is only half the battle. Getting them back on board may look easy, but it takes consideration and skill to actually do it

Heave a line
Every yacht should have a dedicated heaving-line stowed neatly in the cockpit, within easy reach of the helm. Ours didn't, so we had to use a spare sheet

Take off all way
Make the boat come to a complete stop five yards away from the MOB. In this case, it means easing all sheets and furling the genoa. You

Lash the helm
One of the worst things that can happen while you're trying to recover a casualty is that the yacht bears off onto a broad reach and starts sailing again. Lashing the tiller to leeward (or wheel to windward) makes it much less likely to happen

Be aware of the prop You don't have to turn the engine off before hauling the MOB alongside the yacht, but be aware that propellers can cause horrific injuries to crewmen in the water, or even kill them.

The second half of the man overboard operation typically receives little more mention than a few bright ideas about how the secured swimmer can be safely recovered on deck. The task is liable to be different every time, on every boat, but one or two general principles can form a useful starting point.

To test some of these, I borrowed a Bénéteau Océanis 343 and sailed her out to find some English Channel waves. We kitted up our MOB volunteer in a full survival suit and shoved him into the drink. For purposes of clarity, I am assuming here that the casualty is conscious and capable of some degree of self-help, as this is usually the case. If he is unconscious and not wearing a lifejacket, his chances are slim. Even if he is floating right way up and able to breathe, thanks to wearing an automatically inflated lifejacket (a piece of kit by no means guaranteed on many yachts), it is more than likely that on some of today's high-freeboard boats, another crew member will have to get in the water to secure and assist the MOB. The dangers are too obvious to spell out. If it comes to this, any attempt by me to offer set rules or even advice about how to proceed would be hazardous. In this worst-case scenario, success can only be reasonably assured by good seamanship and mature judgement of the individual circumstances.

It's a subject on which opinions are strongly held, and rightly so. Boats and situations are specific. Any test, like this one, has to generalise and is based on conditions on the day, plus personal experience augmented by documented events that have happened to others. It should be read in that light.

Safety first

Our MOB volunteer was dressed in a full-floatation drysuit and an auto-inflating lifejacket fitted with crotch straps. We also hired a RIB to act as backup if our attempts from the yacht failed.

It's arguable that those on deck assisting the casualty should have been clipped on. I was the most mobile of the crew, preferring to leave the winching to younger, more muscular characters. I'm comfortable moving around a boat and I assessed the risk of my falling over as less of a hazard than being tripped up or otherwise inconvenienced by a harness tether.

Had it been blowing hard and the boat lurching and staggering around, I would have opted for the harness. I mention this to make the point that we must think for ourselves rather than blindly obey some 'rule' set up by an outside authority that is not there on the day.

Four options for recovery

The formal MOB exercises so well executed by sailing schools inevitably involve some sort of dummy (often a bucket hitched to a fender). To recover this with the boathook, the yacht has to lose the last of her way alongside it.

In reality, this remains the case with an unconscious casualty but for the more common situation, where swimmers can help themselves, it is far, far safer not to attempt this. Instead, the yacht is stopped a few metres from him or her, a line is tossed, and they are hauled in. The helmsman's job is much easier and there is no chance of running down the MOB, which, as any instructor who has watched a few exercises will agree, is otherwise a risk.

'Different boats, different long splices' was the adage in the days when such eclectic skills were in popular use. Today, we could equally correctly say, 'different boats, different MOB recoveries'. The four most likely options available to a skipper recovering a conscious casualty are:

❯ Helping him climb up the transom-mounted bathing ladder,

if the yacht has one.
❯ Winching him back aboard, attached to a halyard.
❯ Parbuckling, either with a makeshift lash-up such as a storm jib tied to the rail, or with a dedicated safety device.
❯ Launching an inflatable dinghy or liferaft, to recover the casualty.

My own yacht has no stern platform and no bathing ladder, so the first choice of recovery, set out below, is a non-starter. I do have a sort of rope ladder affair that a fit swimmer can use to clamber out of the water, but I don't think it would help an overweight person much, especially if the boat was bouncing around in a seaway.

Many modern yachts – especially those with a Mediterranean ancestry – have a permanently rigged swim ladder and so, with certain caveats, this must be the first choice.

How my own life was saved at sea

When I fell overboard myself on the Grand Banks of Newfoundland a long time ago, with no radio and only my wife left on board to save my life, we tried another option –

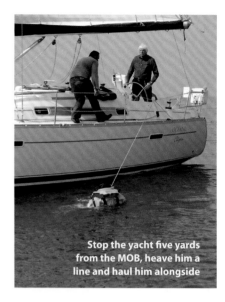

Stop the yacht five yards from the MOB, heave him a line and haul him alongside

the sheet bight.

My wife trailed a bight of the staysail sheet from the foredeck, over the side where I was floating and back up to a cockpit winch. I manage to get my feet into the bight and, as the boat rolled, she snatched up the slack on the winch.

After three rolls, I was standing, albeit precariously, high enough to grab the rail and scramble aboard with her help.

I tried this recently on a modern yacht with nothing to speak of below the water but the keel. It didn't work. The yacht where it succeeded so magnificently had a serious underbody.

1. The bathing ladder

Even in these gentle conditions, it was much easier to climb the bathing ladder when the boat was lying beam-on to the swell

As soon as we had manoeuvred back to our bold swimmer and had hauled him alongside, the blindingly obvious first choice was to bring him aft, drop the ladder and help him clamber up. A proviso soon made itself abundantly clear. Even in the modest sea prevailing, if we kept the boat head-up to it, her pitching subjected the ladder to a plunging motion that our man did not enjoy. In 4ft waves it could have been dangerous. However, by letting her follow her natural inclinations and fall beam-on, she rolled, but the up-and-down movement of the ladder was minimised.

We can therefore state categorically that living with the rolling is safer than trying to stop it happening. Fortunately, most sailing yachts end up in this sort of attitude when left to their own devices with the helm lashed so as to steer upwind. This allows the helmsman to leave his post to join the rescuers or deal with it himself if he's on his own.

2. Winching the MOB

On board our yacht, we had myself (a biggish sort of chap, not as fit as I was, but still useful), Graham Snook, a youthful photographer and Kieran Flatt, also young and moderately strong. It was immediately obvious that we weren't going to be able to manhandle our MOB anywhere other than at the stern platform, so we didn't even try. I have literally dragged folk from the water successfully in low-freeboard yachts, but on this Bénéteau – a typical modern cruising yacht, with high topsides – manhandling the casualty aboard was a non-starter.

The importance of good winches

Our casualty's lifejacket featured a stout lifting ring, so we handed him the spinnaker halyard, he clipped it on, we put our strongest man on the winch and cranked him up.

'How's it going?' I asked the winchman in mid-lift.

'Piece of cake,' he replied, not even panting. And so it turned out. This particular yacht had commendably powerful, self-tailing winches that could easily handle the straight lift. I took a heft at the handle and concluded with some surprise that a woman of moderate strength could, if properly motivated, have lifted a reasonable-sized man by the same technique. On a more typical yacht with tiny halyard winches, or none at all, this would not have worked.

Winch or windlass?

Without a direct lead to the sort of big halyard winches that we were enjoying, an alternative source of power has to be contrived. Here are two likely possibilities. You can often re-lead the spare halyard to the biggest sheet winch. If this is still too feeble, try the anchor windlass. If yours is power driven, it's the obvious candidate. I weigh in at the thick end of 16 stone, but my nine-stone wife can lift me out on our Simpson-Lawrence electric windlass (selected so as to have a warping drum – no windlass should be sold without one). We use a spare halyard that is kept long and heavy just for this purpose.

Block-and-tackle

If there isn't a winch on board that'll do the trick, the only other option is a tackle of some sort. This is best rigged from a spare halyard or the topping lift. In the past, various possibilities have been recommended, including removing and inverting a kicking strap tackle. All this is subject to numerous gremlins, so unless you've done it with a real person, you are likely to find the fall is too short, or the shackles seize, or that the parts twist terminally as soon as the load comes on. Using the boom as a crane seems horribly complicated, and besides, there is the issue of the sail. Keep it simple, is the watchword.

Practice makes perfect

Needless to say, it's vital to practise these and any further options in controlled conditions. Any special gear can then be organised and stowed before you need it, and any awkward leads can be tried. No amount of theoretical thinking can substitute for actually lifting your heaviest crew member on a calm day, imagining all the while how things would differ on a wild night.

The lifting

Not everyone who falls overboard is conveniently wearing a modern lifejacket, properly secured with a crotch strap and carrying a big, stainless steel ring to attach lifting gear. A boat therefore needs some sort of sling that can be lowered, passed under the armpits, and brought together ready for attaching a lifting device. This might be a basic helicopter strop or it may be part of a more complex rescue system. Strops are available that support the legs as well, but these will be more difficult to deploy in a rough sea and the general stress of the moment. Another option is to pass a bowline around the casualty's knees and secure it on a shortish length to the lifting ring so that he is raised in a more horizontal position. Whatever you choose, anything is better than a bowline under the arms. This will cut in and can exacerbate potentially fatal chest pressure .

1

Halyard attached to MOB's lifejacket, winching starts

2

Tom pushes off while the MOB grabs a shroud to steady himself

3

Casualty gets one leg over the rail and rolls aboard

Danger of lifting the casualty vertically by winch

Much has been said and written in recent years about the danger of lifting a casualty from the water in a vertical position, supported via some sort of device encircling the chest. Post-rescue trauma can set in after he or she is on deck, following unfair compression of the organs and the inevitable blood draining downwards in the body, especially if the casualty is by now very cold. Our man in the drink reported no discomfort or bad effects, but he was in good shape, youngish and was well padded by all the kit he was wearing. I wondered about this, so I took the opportunity on another yacht to attach a halyard to my lifejacket and be winched up a few feet. The compression on my chest was awful. After only a few seconds I was urgently asking to be let down. Imagining that this reflected the fact that I am not a 30-year-old who spends his leisure in the gym rather than the pub, I invited a young friend whose fitness is legendary to try it. She reported the same effects. The message is obvious. Lift vertically if it's life or death, but don't do it if there's any choice.

3. Parbuckling recovery method

Classical textbooks used to recommend lifting a casualty by attaching the foot of a storm jib to the rail, passing the bunt under the person who is floating horizontally, attaching a halyard to the head of the sail then heaving up on it. The swimmer was thus rolled up the side of the yacht until the deck was reached. This is the ancient technique called parbuckling,

employed in days gone by for lifting heavy barrels up ships' sides. It works in principle, and has a remarkable diminishing effect on the weight. Unfortunately, few people now have a handy storm jib in the locker, and in any case, rigging such a lash-up wasn't easy, if it were possible at all in a big wind.

Various products have been available over the years

to do this properly. I own a Tri-buckle and brought it along for our test. It rigged easily on the yacht's rail, we passed it without difficulty under our man, and winching him up was so easy a child could have managed it. He also came up horizontally, so we awarded the system a gold star.

At least one authority has suggested that using

one of these in a big sea doesn't work. I can't answer that, but you don't always take a tumble in Force 10. Sometimes it's a moment's inattention on a nice day that suddenly turns nasty. If you can lay hands on one of these devices, it's a good investment.

Tri-buckle in its bag, ready for action

Tying it to the rail

Towing the MOB to the Tri-buckle

Tom makes sure the MOB is properly positioned in the Tri-buckle before the winching starts

He then acts as a brace, preventing the device from crushing the casualty against the hull

Got him! Casualty back on deck after a comfortable lift. It would be easy to forget the heaving-line trailing over the side...

4. Deploy a dinghy or liferaft

A useful dinghy boarding ladder.

One final option to consider is launching the yacht's inflatable tender, if you have one, or – as a last resort – the liferaft. This could be appropriate if your yacht has very high topsides, or if there's a big sea running and you fear that bringing the MOB alongside may result in serious injury. Or if you judge the other techniques listed here are not appropriate for the circumstances.

If manhandling is the only realistic option, it's far easier to roll a casualty over the low, rounded topsides of a tender or liferaft than to heave them up the gunwale of a yacht. Liferafts have the added benefit of a specially designed boarding ladder to help the casualty clamber aboard. If the person in the water is weak, panicking or injured, you may have to send another crewman to help secure them, and it's often a much better idea to do this with a liferaft or dinghy than to send a second crewman for a swim without anything as a back-up.

ABOVE Using a dinghy to recover a man overboard.
BELOW Liferafts have low freeboard and boarding ladders

Can you cut the guardrails?

Guardrails stand about two and a half feet above the toerail of most yachts. For anyone trying to scrabble back aboard, they are a major obstacle. In a properly rigged yacht, the aft end is set up with lanyards. When you don't want them in a hurry, you can take a knife out of your pocket and cut them free.

The expensive – and arguably dangerous – alternative is to set them up with a bottlescrew. Many yachts are fitted with these, and some even have a locking screw or seizing wire to boot. Try getting rid of that lot in a trice and you'll see why most experienced skippers prefer to use a simple rope lashing instead.

It takes time to remove guardrails fixed with bottlescrews – not what you want in an emergency, with one of your shipmates in peril overboard

Push that red button!

If you have a DSC VHF radio – and many of us do – it may well be worth pressing (and holding down) the red emergency button, if the first attempt at MOB pick-up fails. In the past, the problem with calling for assistance was the basic truth that a skipper left short or single-handed could lose sight of the casualty while below at the radio. There was also the fact that sending a Mayday and responding might consume a minute or two of critical time, especially if the water is cold. This left skippers with a horrible dilemma. DSC has changed all that. If you are out of range of assistance, so be it, but there are recorded incidents of casualties in contact with the boat in home waters who have been lost through failure of their crewmates to recover them from the water. Lifting exhausted people safely from rough seas is what search-and-rescue crews do. If you've put out a Mayday earlier, then got on with your own rescue, as most of us would, you might be near despair after a couple of failed lifts when you hear the reassuring thrash of the helicopter overhead.

173

Air-sea rescue

A crew member needs airlifting to hospital, you've radioed
a Mayday and now there's a rescue helicopter buzzing
overhead. Most yachtsmen think it's a situation that won't
happen to them, but it pays to be prepared, just in case

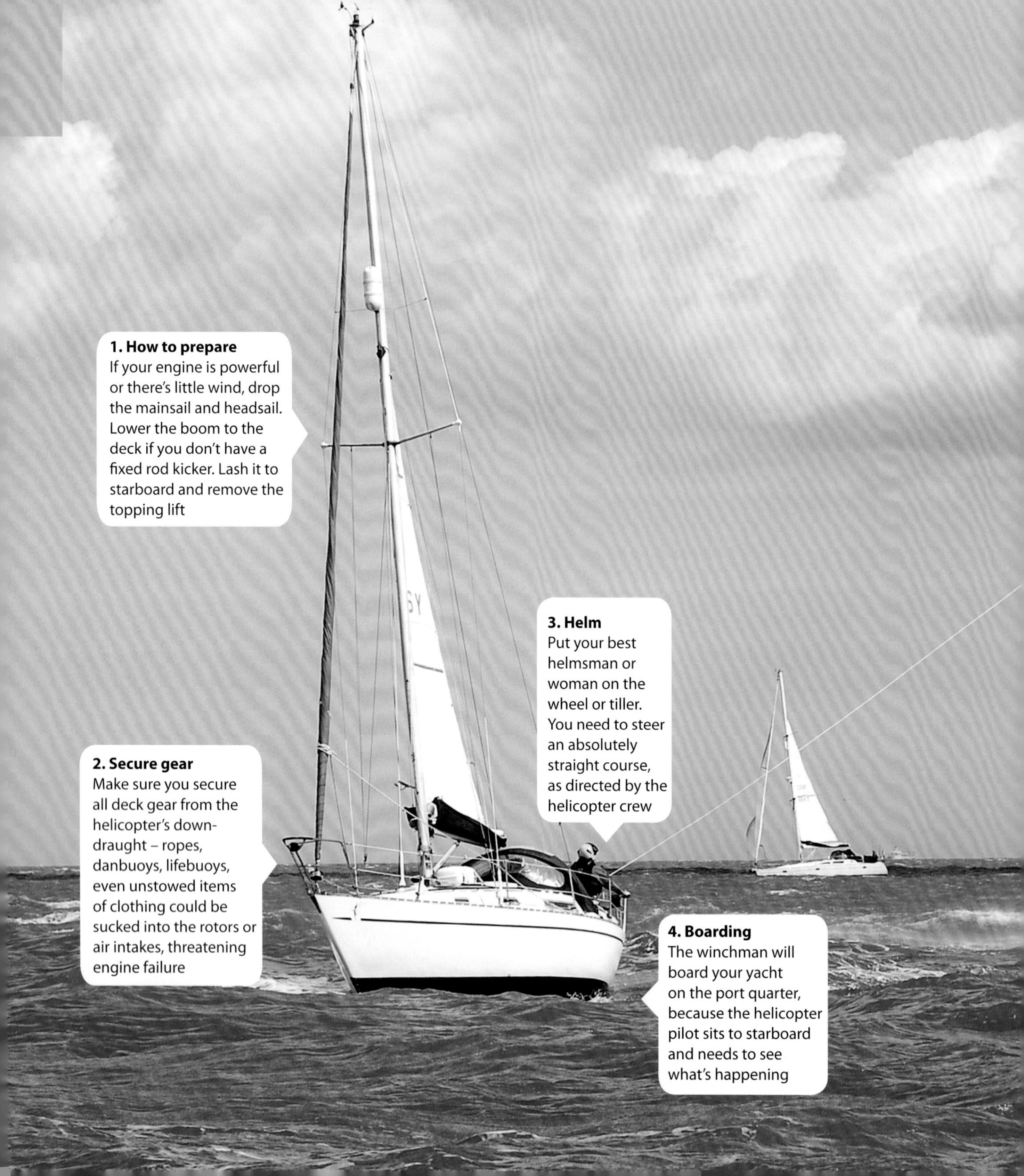

1. How to prepare
If your engine is powerful
or there's little wind, drop
the mainsail and headsail.
Lower the boom to the
deck if you don't have a
fixed rod kicker. Lash it to
starboard and remove the
topping lift

3. Helm
Put your best
helmsman or
woman on the
wheel or tiller.
You need to steer
an absolutely
straight course,
as directed by the
helicopter crew

2. Secure gear
Make sure you secure
all deck gear from the
helicopter's down-
draught – ropes,
danbuoys, lifebuoys,
even unstowed items
of clothing could be
sucked into the rotors or
air intakes, threatening
engine failure

4. Boarding
The winchman will
board your yacht
on the port quarter,
because the helicopter
pilot sits to starboard
and needs to see
what's happening

7. Pilot's worst scenario
'The yacht's helmsman needs to focus on the job. The worst problem is they tend to look up at the aircraft, which means the yacht wanders about or even tacks'

6. Flying time
The Agusta Westland 139 is developed from a successful executive helicopter and has a speed of 160 knots, a range of 200nm and a crew of four.

8. The winches
There are two winches, each with a 300ft steel cable. The winch operator's remote control can even control the helicopter in an autopilot hover mode

5. The hi-line When the hi-line is lowered, flake it on deck. Keep taking up or giving slack. Keep it away from the propeller. A winchman or rescue device will be lowered

Most of the boats featured in this book were chartered or borrowed for the purpose, but on this occasion our photographer, Graham Snook, offered us *Pixie*, his Sadler 32. The date, chosen weeks in advance, brought a gale. It's all very well photographing emergency procedures in flat calm. It's another matter altogether in 35 knots of breeze, with wind against tide. For this reason, the exercise was without doubt the most useful and dramatic hi-line demo I've ever been involved with, and I've seen a lot.

Pixie was almost literally standing on her ends as we scrabbled to grab the hi-line. While the winchman was trying to land on deck, Graham had a serious job working the slack in the hi-line and heaving him in. Meanwhile, I was trying to concentrate on keeping the yacht in a straight line. On the VHF, I overheard the mention of our stern 'going up and down three metres'. No wonder the poor SAR guy had a struggle, but he kept his cool, our crew managed to do what they'd been told, and he arrived without too many bruises. One of our crew on *Pixie* was duly hoisted skywards to be lowered into the lifeboat RIB, and we retrieved him later.

Rescue! We all hope we'll never need it, yet the possibility that one day we might tends to polarise sailors into two groups. One crowd shrink into a state of denial and expend no effort schooling themselves for the eventuality. The others can easily become 'safety bores', obsessive about how to shout for help and what to do when it arrives. They forget that good seamen concentrate on never having to bother the search and rescue (SAR) services without good cause.

My own natural inclination is to sign on with the first crew, but years of involvement with the training establishment has changed my thinking. If we sail for long enough, sooner or later we'll all be caught out by a mistake – through shoddy gear, lack of maintenance, or by circumstances genuinely beyond our control. The healthy approach, as in so many things, is to take a middle view, doing all we can to avoid pressing the red button on our DSC radios, but knowing the system by rote in case the time finally comes.

A hundred years ago, a sailor in distress fired a flare and prayed. With luck, a pulling lifeboat would put out through the surf and local seamen in real risk of their lives would row out to save him. The contrast today is extreme. We make our distress signal electronically, perhaps backing it up with flares. If we're anywhere near civilisation, we receive prompt attention. This may come via a lifeboat or, as is increasingly likely, a helicopter manned by highly trained professionals. Aircrew have a well-tried system for dealing with yachts but, for it to work as it should, those on board must do their share.

When it comes to educating ourselves, there's no proper substitute for the real thing, but sitting under the hammering blades of a six-ton Agusta Westland AW139 in a gale of wind isn't an experience open to everyone. RYA Yachtmaster Instructor courses often manage a session with the local SAR people, but not many private yachtsmen get the chance because, apart from difficulties of liaison, it costs a fortune to keep a helicopter in the air. On this occasion, the coastguard managed to slot us into their schedule on

The noise of the helicopter can make communications difficult

the understanding that the exercise would be called off if their life-and-death services were needed for real.

A classic 'hi-line transfer'

The theory
More helicopter rescues involve lifting a person from a yacht able to manoeuvre than a yacht disabled in some way. The technique is called a hi-line transfer. Landing the heli-

copter crewman, plus a stretcher, or lifting strop, in the cockpit of a pitching yacht is far from easy. The hi-line makes it possible.

Preparation
A helicopter has limited flying time. The rescue needs to be smartly executed, so the crew awaiting the SAR people should do all they can to prepare.
> Secure all loose gear on deck, or stow it below. Unsecured covers,

The hi-line, a light line with a weight attached, is lowered

Grab the line and flake it onto the deck or cockpit sole

Take up or give out slack before the winchman starts his descent

Take in the slack to heave him aboard. He'll earth the static

ropes, even unstowed bits of clothing, are easily lifted by the downdraught of the rotors. They can cause chaos on deck. They can even be sucked into the helicopter's air intakes and threaten engine failure.

› The winchman will board you on the port quarter because the pilot sits to starboard in the aircraft and he needs to see you. Their hatch is on that side too, so clear away everything movable from the critical area, including danbuoys, aerials and even the ensign staff.

› If your engine is powerful and reliable, or if there's very little wind, drop the mainsail and headsail. Now lower the boom to the deck if you don't have a fixed rod kicker. Lash it down to starboard and take the topping lift to the mast.

› If you don't trust your engine or are in any doubt about it, get ready to sail closehauled on the port tack.

› Put your best helmsman or woman on the job. Once things start happening, their task will be to steer absolutely straight in the direction the helicopter crew ask for. The helm must not be distracted, whatever happens.

What to do when the helicopter arrives

› If the area is crowded with other craft, you may well spot the helicopter before its crew identify you. Do anything you can to say: 'It's us!' An orange smoke flare is best by day. If you don't have one, wave the ensign or a hi-vis life jacket. Try VHF radio (Ch 67), then imagine yourself in the pilot's seat and advise along these lines: 'I am ahead of you and to your port side,' for example. At night or in bad visibility, use a red pinpoint flare, but never use a parachute flare.

› Helicopters are unbelievably noisy, and communicating by radio during the action can be a challenge, so don't feel embarrassed to ask the rescue crew to 'say again' any message.

› If there's been a breakdown in communication, the helicopter may well fly past showing a large sign

The winchman operates from the starboard side of the helicopter

with something like 'VHF 67' on it. Comply if you can. If your radio is down, make suitable gestures and be ready to receive a hi-line or a lifting strop.

› Stand by to receive instructions. You won't want to be down below, or doing the old 'jack-in-the-box' act up and down the hatch, so if you have a hand-held radio, use it. If you're short-handed, give it to the helm and let him/her relay instructions. The best line handler, or the strongest person in your crew, should be the one chosen to deal with the hi-line.

› The pilot will brief you. Listen carefully and don't be afraid to ask for a repeat.

› You'll probably be asked to motor as fast as you comfortably can upwind. If communication fails and it's breezy, steer straight to weather or closehauled on the port tack,

making your best speed. At night, the helicopter may survey you for some time with searchlights to locate obstructions. Be ready to turn any deck lights on or off as requested.

› Once briefed, get going. This is where you and the SAR guys will be glad you chose the best person to steer. It's so tempting to look up, but don't let it happen. Given half a chance, a modern yacht jumps off course like a bluebottle in a hot kitchen, which makes the helicopter pilot's job impossible.

› Don't be alarmed by the shocking racket of a helicopter overhead at low altitude, and don't worry about the downdraught. Unless there's no wind, the aircraft stays out on your quarter during the transfer and it's not a problem.

The big lift

If it's very calm or your yacht is very big, the helicopter may lower a lifting strop directly to you after a briefing about its use. Alternatively, and more likely, they will send a winchman straight down to direct operations. In most other circumstances, the crew will opt for this 'hi-line transfer' method.

The hi-line is a light line with a weight on its lower end, attached by a weak link to the helicopter's winch cable. Its purpose is to allow the yacht's crew to guide the main winch wire while the winchman, a stretcher, or a lifting strop is lowered and lifted away again. Here's how it happens:

› The helicopter hovers more or less overhead and lowers the hi-line to you.

› Your job is to grab this and take in the slack. Gloves are a good idea.

Left: The helicopter winchman is lowered with a lifting strop

Follow the winchman's instructions once he's aboard

Flake the hi-line light line , but never secure it

Flake it onto the deck or cockpit sole. Some people use a big bucket, but whatever you do, don't secure it. If it gets snagged, and a 'tug of war' results, the weak link snaps and they'll send you down another.

› The helicopter moves away over your quarter while the pilot gets his bearings. Keep taking up or giving slack so that the hi-line is clear for action and has no chance whatever of finding your propeller.

› Next, a winchman or a rescue device is lowered on the main winch cable. Take up the slack on the hi-line as it comes, then use it to heave him or the device to safety on board. This might need a hefty pull, so don't give the job to little Johnnie. Whatever is coming down, an earthing wire will be lowered into the water from the main wire before you grab it. You will not get a static

electric shock from the hi-line.

› If a winchman is lowered, he's in charge, so follow his instructions. These will be hard to hear because of the noise from above. Don't be shy of putting your ear right next to him. If only a strop comes down, secure evacuees as appropriate and signal to lift with 'thumbs up'. A lifting strop features a toggle to tighten it under the arms for security. If it's you on the wire, keep your arms by your sides.

› The yacht crew now ease out on the hi-line, keeping enough tension to stop the lift swinging wildly. Don't release it altogether if it might be required again.

› When no further lifts are needed and when you are instructed to do so, let go the end of the hi-line, keeping an eye on the weight so it doesn't swing and injure someone.

› The helicopter winch can easily lift

two or more people. If quick evacuation of more than one casualty is in order, two strops may come down.

› When conditions are so dire that even hi-lining is dangerous, the helicopter pilot may direct you to stream a casualty astern in a dinghy or even in a liferaft on a long painter. In the most extreme circumstances, such as abandoning ship, you might be instructed to get into the water. If so, make sure all crew are wearing lifejackets and don't jump until directed. You don't want to be in the water for any longer than necessary. Note also that helicopters carry special double strops for raising vulnerable people, such as hypothermia victims, who are at risk from the 'post-rescue collapse' caused by lifting in a vertical attitude.

Follow the winchman's instructions once he's aboard

Left: The helicopter winchman is lowered with a lifting strop

Flake the hi-line light line , but never secure it

Flake it onto the deck or cockpit sole. Some people use a big bucket, but whatever you do, don't secure it. If it gets snagged, and a 'tug of war' results, the weak link snaps and they'll send you down another.

❭ The helicopter moves away over your quarter while the pilot gets his bearings. Keep taking up or giving slack so that the hi-line is clear for action and has no chance whatever of finding your propeller.

❭ Next, a winchman or a rescue device is lowered on the main winch cable. Take up the slack on the hi-line as it comes, then use it to heave him or the device to safety on board. This might need a hefty pull, so don't give the job to little Johnnie. Whatever is coming down, an earthing wire will be lowered into the water from the main wire before you grab it. You will not get a static

electric shock from the hi-line.

❭ If a winchman is lowered, he's in charge, so follow his instructions. These will be hard to hear because of the noise from above. Don't be shy of putting your ear right next to him. If only a strop comes down, secure evacuees as appropriate and signal to lift with 'thumbs up'. A lifting strop features a toggle to tighten it under the arms for security. If it's you on the wire, keep your arms by your sides.

❭ The yacht crew now ease out on the hi-line, keeping enough tension to stop the lift swinging wildly. Don't release it altogether if it might be required again.

❭ When no further lifts are needed and when you are instructed to do so, let go the end of the hi-line, keeping an eye on the weight so it doesn't swing and injure someone.

❭ The helicopter winch can easily lift

two or more people. If quick evacuation of more than one casualty is in order, two strops may come down.

❭ When conditions are so dire that even hi-lining is dangerous, the helicopter pilot may direct you to stream a casualty astern in a dinghy or even in a liferaft on a long painter. In the most extreme circumstances, such as abandoning ship, you might be instructed to get into the water. If so, make sure all crew are wearing lifejackets and don't jump until directed. You don't want to be in the water for any longer than necessary. Note also that helicopters carry special double strops for raising vulnerable people, such as hypothermia victims, who are at risk from the 'post-rescue collapse' caused by lifting in a vertical attitude.